Table o

About the Author   vii

Acknowledgments   ix

Preface   xiii

Part I: My Journey

Chapter 1
Immigration   1

Chapter 2
University Years   13

Chapter 3
My Career takes Shape   35

Chapter 4
Memoirs of a Curious Traveller   45

Chapter 5
My Quest Ends   61

Part II: The Walrond Name

Chapter 6
Hunstman Waleran and the Domesday Book   67

Chapter 7
Westward Bound from the Mediterranean   81

Chapter 8
Slavery: Its Origins and its Nature   91

Chapter 9
Barbados   97

Chapter 10
The Slave Trade Expands and Dies   111

Chapter 11
A New World   127

Chapter 12
The Walronds of Trinidad and Guyana   143

Part III: My Father's Life

Chapter 13
The Memoirs of Randolph Osric Walrond   163

Chapter 14
My Father's Guide and Patron, Dr. McShine   189

Chapter 15
Princes Town and the Caledonia E.C. School   195

Chapter 16
Tying My Memories to My Father's Diary   215

Chapter 17
My Mother's Family A Bicultural Experience   225

Chapter 18
Land   239

Chapter 19
My Father's Books, Magazines, and Other Papers   249

Chapter 20
Saying Goodbye   261

Part IV: Appendixes

Appendix A: Pictures   273

Appendix B: The Legacy of Randolph Walrond   291

Appendix C: The Chronology
of Randolph Walrond   345

Appendix D: The Kings and Queens of England
from William the Conqueror to Charles I   349

Appendix E: The Lineage of Waleran Venator   351

Appendix F: The Lineage of the Martin, Chandler
and Walrond Families   353

Appendix G: Bibliography   359

About the Author

Lawrence Maxim Walrond was born in Couva on the Caribbean island of Trinidad. He received his elementary and primary education at the Couva Anglican School, where his father was the principal. In 1960, he graduated from Queen's Royal College in Port of Spain. After working as a junior civil servant for four years, he migrated to Canada and attended McGill University in Montreal. He graduated in 1968 with a bachelor's degree in French and Spanish Language and Literature. His minors were Latin, Geography, and Philosophy. He has maintained a steadfast interest in these subjects as well as in History.

He is also a graduate of British Columbia's Simon Fraser University teacher-training program. In September 1970, he began a 40-year-long career as a French and Spanish teacher in Nanaimo, on Vancouver Island. He still lives there with his wife Beth. Their two children and two grandchildren live in the Vancouver area.

Walrond has travelled extensively in Canada, the United States, Europe, South and Central America, and the Caribbean. He is an award-winning amateur photographer and belongs to the Nanaimo Arts Council, where he sometimes volunteers.

He has self-published two books on the history of his immediate family, who all greatly appreciated his efforts in this regard.

Writing this book has allowed him to explore the origin and expand the history of his family name, and it has given him the opportunity to know and understand his paternal and maternal ancestors in a way more profound and meaningful than he ever expected.

Acknowledgments

I am very grateful for the assistance I have received from three of my high school friends while I was planning and writing this book. In 1955, we were all young boys just beginning our high school career at Queen's Royal College. We have managed to keep in touch with each other over these many years.

To Ronald "Ramchy" Ramcharan, I owe thanks for the serendipitous help I got while he was driving me around Port of Spain during one of my all-too-infrequent visits to Trinidad in 2008. Somehow our conversation turned to the national holiday known as Indian Arrival Day. I had heard about it, but my knowledge was limited. I asked for more information, and he mentioned the *Fatel Razak*, the ship which transported the first indentured immigrants from India to Trinidad. I immediately got the idea of a parallel section in my book regarding the first ship to transport immigrants from China to Trinidad. My Chinese ancestor travelled on this ship, the *Clarendon*. The Internet helped me complete these two sections.

To Paul "Pablo" Alcala, I owe thanks for the section on the ballerina Dai Ailian and the one on the House at Isaac Junction. Without his timely e-mail, these two sections would most likely not have been written — at least the one on Dai Ailian certainly would not be there. Pablo was also instrumental in facilitating the contact with Errol Patrick.

To David "Darpy" Patrick, I owe thanks for the connection I made with Errol "Junior" Patrick. Errol is the grandson of Christopher Patrick, who was a mentor and advisor to my father, Randolph Walrond. Errol was also the youngest guest at the 1935 wedding ceremony of my parents. I contacted Errol at his home in Toronto, Canada, and after a delightful chat about "the old days," he graciously agreed to send me pictures of Christopher Patrick, of his step-grandmother, and of himself. The picture of Christopher filled a large void in my story. I am very grateful to Errol for his willingness to supply the pictures and for giving me his permission to use them in my book.

Ronald, David, Paul, and myself, "Charlie," Thank you, gentlemen!

Thanks to the help of my brother Kermitt, I was able to contact Arthur McShine. I am greatly indebted to him for granting me permission to use the iconic picture of his grandfather, Dr. Arthur Hutton McShine. Arthur McShine was also a student at Queen's Royal College. We had an enjoyable chat and reminded each other of great times, now long past.

I also acknowledge the help I received from Frank Sealey, who was able to search through his father's papers and find a picture of my father's friend Ben. He readily gave me permission to include this picture in my book. I will be forever grateful for this contribution.

Grateful appreciation is also extended to Marjorie Stewart for her thorough proofreading of my manuscript. I could not have found a better person for this task. I know I could not have done it myself.

I am also indebted to my wife Beth, who painstakingly read and reread my manuscripts looking for typos. Thank you, Beth!

I would not have been able to complete this book without the skill, journalistic talent and tactical advice of my editor Vivian Moreau. Her guidance through three rewrites have taught me so much about writing that I would not have known how to persevere to the point of readiness for publication. At several points, I felt like a lump of clay in the hands of a potter. Some of her hints were subtle, and others weren't hints at all: an emphatic "nope, nope, nope." How could I argue with that? All this accompanied with an encouraging "You can do it."

And so I did it.

Thank you, Viv!

Dedication

This Book is dedicated to My Parents
Randolph Walrond: 13 June 1899 - 27 July 1996
Floris Walrond: 10 October 1918 - 31 May 2015

Preface

In December of 1964, I was asked a very simple question: "What kind of a name is Walrond?"

Unfortunately, I could offer no answer other than it was most probably an English name. From that point on, I became very interested in finding out all I could about my family name. I was under the impression that most names actually meant something or said something about the person, or at least about the first person to carry that name. I intended to satisfy my curiosity in this regard.

Fifty years later, early in 2013, I found that I had amassed a lot of information about the name. In March of this year, I started writing this story with several objectives in mind. Of primary importance was my desire to record my efforts, along with all its successes and failures, with regard to finding out all I could about the name Walrond.

The second objective was to find the link that I felt must have existed between England and my family. I wondered what reasons and circumstances resulted in this link being forged in the first place. Once it was found, I hoped to explore it to its fullest extent.

Third, because I knew that my father's family had come from Barbados, I was curious as to what brought them to Trinidad and above all why they left Barbados. In other words, I wanted to find out about the sociology of my Barbadian connection.

Finally, I simply had to find a way to include as much as possible of the information left by my father — information he collected and kept for so many years. All these many bits of paper have become an important part of my memories of him. They were in fact a graphic depiction of the times in which he lived. It was a picture the likes of which is not likely to be found elsewhere. I also somehow had to include the stories that he told me about himself.

There can be no doubt that my personal history and its connection to what I would like to call the history of global events is what drove me to approach this story in the way in which I did. I firmly believe that sometimes disparate and almost insignificant facts are somehow related to each other. All that has to be done is to look for the connection, no matter how long the task takes. These connections can form an undeniable legacy to humanity in general and certainly to those who are closely associated with them.

In addition to all the connections I was able to make, I have to say that I learned a lot about the history of the world. I would also be negligent if I did not mention the fact that I had a lot of fun putting this information together. For through it all, there was I, living life as I wanted to and enjoying myself. Recalling long-forgotten memories and adventures, realigning my thoughts and making new connections — these are some of the serendipitous advantages I derived from this altogether enjoyable activity.

Part I: My Journey

Chapter 1
Immigration

I walked out onto the front porch on this cold December morning in Montreal, my coat buttoned up almost to my neck. I stood a moment, waiting for the spring-loaded door to close. When the click came, it seemed louder than usual due to the momentary lull in the normally heavy traffic, a pause caused no doubt by the traffic signals at the far end of the block.

The noise of the closing door startled a squirrel, which peeped out from the far side of the tree trunk on which he was climbing. There were no more leaves on the trees. The wind had piled them all around the base of its trunk. The squirrel stopped a moment and looked at me. Our eyes met, for the tree was quite close to the little porch. Suddenly I sneezed, and my furry friend jerked his head a bit higher, turned, scampered back behind the tree, and a moment later jumped across to another branch and disappeared among the twigs of a nearby tree.

I fastened the last button on my coat, for there was a slight breeze that seemed determined to find the warmth of my body. I went down the few steps, turned, and headed along Hutchison Street towards Milton Street, which led through the magnificent Milton Gates, directly onto the McGill campus where I was a student. Along the way, Christmas lights were visible through the windows of a few of the houses.

As I walked slowly — my class was a late one that morning — my thoughts went tumbling back to early September and the nine days I had spent in New York City en route to Montreal from my home in Trinidad.

The first time I walked through Central Park, I was intrigued by the large number of squirrels that were busy laying in their winter supplies. I had never seen such a display of apparently tame fauna before. In fact, everything in the city was pure novelty.

I had left Trinidad on 31 August 1964, which is the island's Independence Day. It became mine as well. I had flown on a Pan American Boeing 707, my favourite airplane at the time. I had always admired its sleek fuselage. After brief stops in Barbados and Antigua, the jet landed at the John F. Kennedy airport late at night. I still remember this flight, my first ever. I was able to identify some of the islands that we flew over. I had always enjoyed studying the geography of the West Indies.

The year 1964 was turning out to be one of many firsts for me. When I showed my father my letter of acceptance at McGill University earlier in the year, he had shown no surprise, but I knew from his brief smile and a slight nodding of his head that he was pleased. I also knew he was surprised, because I had told no one that I was applying to go off to university. My intention was to take courses in French and Spanish and eventually become a secondary high school language teacher.

The acceptance letter had outlined a list of official tasks to be done by my father and by myself in preparation for my leaving for Canada. The most important was to prepare an affidavit, signed by my father and forwarded to the university. In it, he had to promise to support me financially during the course of my studies. He was happy to do this. I had imagined he might have been reluctant to assist me, because I had five younger siblings who might also need financial help at some point.

I forwarded a medical report to the university and tendered my resignation to the government of Trinidad and Tobago. I was working as an accounts clerk at the Parliament Office in the Red House in Port of Spain. I also applied for a passport and later booked my passage to Montreal, via New York City.

Of a less formal nature, I visited Mr. McIvor, my father's tailor, and was measured for a going-away suit. This turned out to be a real going-away suit because I only ever wore it once. I gained too much weight in a very short space of time after moving to Canada. I also bought a large grey suitcase, or in Trinidadian parlance, a *grip*. These suitcases were usually so crammed and heavy that you really had to maintain a firm grasp on the handle. (In my early years in Canada, I did a lot of travelling, and my suitcase was always heavy, so much so that a bus driver once asked me if I was carrying around the crown jewels.) These preparatory activities were all very new and interesting. I smiled all the way home carrying that empty suitcase. I was so proud of what I was doing.

Most exciting, though, was the realization that I was going to enjoy a wonderful ten-day stopover in one of the largest cities on earth. They were going to be the halcyon days of my vanishing youth. After all, I would turn 22 in October. I was due to register at the university on September 9. Till then, New York was My Apple, and I was going to enjoy it — within the limits of my budget, of course.

Leaving home for the first time is always alarming. I always said afterwards that I did not just leave my home and my family; I also left the country. Indeed, if Trinidad were a mere 10 degrees farther south, I would have left the hemisphere altogether. If I had, though, I would not have been the first, for as I was to find out later, one of my ancestors had done something similar many years before. The difference was that he went from east to west, while I was going from south to north.

I was the third of my eight siblings to leave home in search of a higher education. My two elder brothers had preceded me by some five or six years. One went to England, and the other went to British Columbia in Canada. Many young Trinidadians at the time were travelling abroad, all of them bent on bettering their opportunities. Tertiary education has always been an important aspect of Caribbean life.

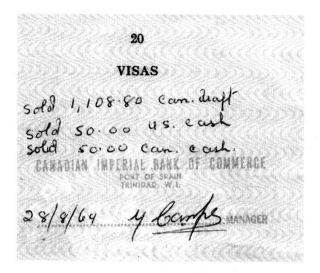

The very last page of my first Trinidad passport shows my
financial assets at the start of my life in Canada.

My arrival in New York was an exciting learning experience. My first
night in this large city was not without its moments of strange, novel, and
unforeseen situations. There is no doubt that my tolerance for novelties was
stretched to the limit, but not in a negative way.

The events of my first evening in the Big Apple are forever etched in my
memory. I was fortunate enough to have been able to make arrangements to
spend the nine nights at the home of a friend of a friend. Acquaintances such
as these, though few and far between, are always very much appreciated. I
was met at the airport and rode with him to his apartment.

I left my suitcase in the car and went in to meet his family. Once in the
apartment, I was faced with a strange spectacle. Boxes, cartons, suitcases, and
other household articles were stacked or lying on the floor in the corridors.
The bedroom doors were open, and there was a similar scene in each room.
Quite a few people were sitting around in the kitchen, drinking beer, tea,
coffee, and who knows what else. In other words, there was a party going on
amid the chaos on the floors.

By this time, it was about 11:00 or so at night, and I was tired. Very, very
tired. I may even have been hungry, but I was too exhausted to tell the difference. I finally summoned up the courage to ask someone what was going on.

"They're moving to a new apartment," was the answer.

"When?"

"Tonight, sometime."

"But why are they not moving?"

"It's too hot."

"Well, when are they going to move?"

"When it cools down."

I figured I had asked enough questions. I had not really noticed that it was hot. I imagine that was because I had left Trinidad only a few hours earlier, and it seemed no hotter here than there.

It was well after midnight when the actual move began. After the van, trailers, and other vehicles were packed with as much as they were going to hold, there still remained a few items. Everything had been brought down to the sidewalk, because the new tenants were expected soon. They too had been waiting for the temperature to drop.

Among the items left on the sidewalk was my suitcase. There was an obvious problem: All manpower was needed to offload the vehicles at the other end. I volunteered to sit and wait with the items on the sidewalk. It was the least I could do. My offer was accepted. They all thought it was a good idea.

You can imagine me then, dressed in my tight-fitting going-away suit, sitting atop my new suitcase on a deserted New York City sidewalk, surrounded by a pile of household impedimenta. I had absolutely no idea where I was, how long the moving party would be gone, when next I was going to have a meal, or even exactly where I was going to spend the night. In fact, I had no idea about anything. However, I do remember repeatedly asking myself, "What the hell am I doing here?" I had no answer.

Time went by and my host returned. The rest of the move was completed without further delay. It was not till the wee hours of the morning that I eventually got to sleep. I awoke later that morning to brilliant sunshine streaming through undraped windows into a bedroom of my new friends' apartment. It was located on the top floor of a brownstone building, located at the corner of Rogers Avenue and Lincoln Place in Brooklyn. The large suite of rooms commanded a view of the corner.

The good weather lasted throughout my visit. There was a subway station nearby, and I very quickly learned to use the trains. I bought a good map of the lines and a large folding one of the streets of New York. With a subway pass in my pocket and my trusty Ricoh Twin-Lens Reflex camera swinging around my neck, I set off to make the best of my nine-day adventure in the city of New York. My meals consisted of assorted fast foods, bought and eaten on the run.

It has always been my belief that travelling is a most effective means of education. My holiday in New York was my way of learning firsthand about many of the places I had only read about. In this way, history and geography are combined and together leave a more lasting impression on the mind.

Almost everything I had planned to do necessitated my going into Manhattan. All the sights, all the buildings, all the events that interested me were connected via the subway system. Brooklyn was my launch pad, but Manhattan was my main destination.

My first landing was outside the 1931 Empire State Building. I stood on the sidewalk for a while, in awe of its architecture. Then I went in. The lobby was just as beautiful. I was astounded by the size and splendour of the wall that faced the main entry. Three storeys high, it featured a two-dimensional engraved art deco aluminum sculpture of the building. From the top of this etched replica emanated rays of sunlight. The effect was one of a shrine dedicated to the Empire State Building. After a short while, I left. Riding the elevator to the observation deck on one of the upper floors was not an option for me. It was too costly. Back outside. I crossed the street and almost wrenched my neck trying to see the top of this celebrated building.

Another planned stop was at Carnegie Hall. I had heard so much about this venue that I simply had to at least see it from the outside. Given my lack of funds, there was no question of my going to an event there. When I got to this beautiful building, I stood admiring the large doors that led no doubt to an enormous lobby. Suddenly, one of the doors opened, and a uniformed Negro gentleman came out. He obviously worked there. I wished him good morning and asked him if there was a chance I could see what the hall looked like on the inside. He surprised me with a broad smile and immediately answered, "Sure thing. Go on in."

I thanked him and went through the doors and into the lobby. It was as magnificent as I thought it would be. I crossed the vestibule and entered the concert hall. I sat down in one of the very plush seats at the back. I had not dared walk down the aisle. My knees were shaking too much. The house lights were on but not fully so. It was a humbling experience to sit in Carnegie Hall. Though the chamber was empty and silent, my imagination went to work. Once again I heard Harry Belafonte singing "Jamaica Farewell." Nat King Cole and Frank Sinatra came magically to life and sang imaginary numbers on the stage that seemed so far away. I got up and walked slowly through the doors and said thank you to the gentleman, who was still there.

Next on my list was the Bronx Zoo. It was a long subway ride out there, through Harlem. In the fall of 1964, going to or through Harlem was considered risky to all non locals. Memories of the Harlem Riot of July that year were still fresh in the minds of many people. My nervousness was somewhat soothed by the fact that I was on a subway train and not on the streets above.

Back in Trinidad, I used to spend some of my lunch hour in the vicinity of the Emperor Valley Zoo in Port of Spain. It was a short walk from my high school. The zoo in Trinidad could have lost itself in the entrance area of the Bronx Zoo. This New York facility is huge. I am sure I did not see all that there was to see, but my visit was informative though somewhat tiring. I enjoyed looking at the animals, reptiles, and birds. In spite of this, the awful smell that pervaded the site was overpowering. It occurred to me that considering the zoo's importance, fame, glory, and educational value, the administration there should do something to reduce the stench, especially at the primates' cages.

I will always remember the Museum of Natural History, the Guggenheim Museum, and Central Park as some of the places that I enjoyed visiting. Not least of such places was the 1964 World's Fair held at Flushing Meadows Park. Everything I saw at this huge exposition was new and interesting. I was especially entranced by the Ford Motor Company's exhibit and in particular one item in it: the brand-new 1964 Ford Mustang. I fell in love with it and made a silent promise to myself that one day I would buy one. I also managed a visit and tour of the United Nations building. In those days, I had vague visions of being a simultaneous translator with this agency.

My overall impression of being in New York could be summed up in a short conversation I had with a rider on the subway. "Excuse me, sir," I said. "Could you tell me how to get to . . .?"

"No, I can't help you. I have only been living here for ten years."

The days flew by, and soon it was time to continue on to Montreal. Thanks to the squirrel outside my apartment building on Hutchison Street, I had enjoyed a short mental revisit of my time in New York as I made my way to the university that cold December morning.

My walk seemed to have taken longer than usual. My reminiscing had buoyed my spirits though, and I entered the classroom a bit happier than usual. There was still about ten minutes before the lecture was due to begin, so I sat down next to the only other student in the room. This was a Canadian girl to whom I had nodded before. She smiled when I sat down, and I opened with a risky, "Merry Christmas!" — risky because there were many Jewish people at the university, and I did not want to upset a fellow student.

"Merry Christmas," she answered with a pleasant smile. "Where are you from?"

"Trinidad," I replied. "It's an island in the Caribbean, near South America."

"How do you say 'Merry Christmas' in Trinidad?"

"Merry Christmas," I answered.

"Thank you, but how do you say 'Merry Christmas' in Trinidad?"

"Merry Christmas," I repeated.

"Yes but . . ." she started. Then she got it and laughed.

"What's your name?" I asked.

She told me and asked what mine was. I answered, adding my family name. She was a firm believer in the art of conversation, and she kept this one going by asking another question: "What kind of name is Walrond?"

For this, I had no immediate answer. "It's an English name, I believe," I answered hesitantly. "Somewhere I read about an English 'Lord Walrond.'" I could add nothing more. Besides, other students had entered and the room was filling up, so our conversation came to an end.

The class started, but I was more than a little concerned that I did not know more about my family name. For the next hour, my mind wandered, and all sorts of thoughts vied for attention with what was being presented that day.

I had always been interested in names. Christian names mostly, or what are now known as first names. Most of us know where and how surnames like Butcher, Carpenter, Mason, Palmer and so on originated. But what of Walrond? In June of 1964, two months before I left Trinidad, I had sat down with my parents and had them give me whatever information they could about their parents and siblings; this information was later incorporated into a photographic history of my family. But I have to confess that my family name represented an enigma to which I had no solution.

After that day in class, I made up my mind to try to solve it.

* * *

That evening, on my way home, passing the building in which my land-lady lived, I recalled my first day in Montreal. I had arrived quite late at the Dorval airport and was met by a friend of another friend. After a night at his house, he drove me to the university and nearby area, where he said I would be sure to find an apartment. I thanked him and started walking around.

There were several "À *Louer* — *For Rent*" signs pinned to doors in the neighbourhood. All the while, I was mindful of the fact that I would have to walk to school. Soon I found myself on Hutchison Street. I selected one of the signs and knocked on the door. A rather short elderly woman answered, and I stated my wishes. Yes, she had some apartments for rent. She spoke with a decidedly Germanic accent. We walked down a few doors, and with a jangling flourish of a ring of keys, she selected one. We climbed a short flight of steps onto a porch, and she opened a door. We entered a small vestibule. There was an apartment to the left. She led me past this to the rear of the building. She opened a door and showed me in.

The room was small but not too much so. There was a desk and chair on the right side of the room. Along the wall to the left of the door was a counter with a hotplate for cooking and a small sink for washing dishes. Below the counter was a fridge and some cupboards. The back of the room was taken up by a window that looked out onto a cluttered back yard and a fence, behind which was an alley. The floor of the room was carpeted in dark grey. What looked like a metal frame of some kind took up part of the wall to the left. She walked up to it and pulled deftly on a short cord. Down came the frame, which evolved into a bed and mattress. She told me it was a Murphy bed. "It makes cleaning the room easier," she explained. I silently thanked Mr. Murphy for his contribution to good housekeeping.

The rent was $52 a month, and she would supply linen. Not one to quibble, I agreed, and we walked back to her apartment to sign some papers. We chatted amiably while she filled out the forms. I was busy looking around the room. Along three walls, there were several cabinets and cupboards with glass doors in which a varied and colourful collection of glass, porcelain, and metal *objets d'art* were displayed. The room looked like a small private museum.

When all the signing was complete, she opened the glass door of one of the cabinets and took out a bottle of sherry and two small glasses. No questions were asked, and no comments were made. She poured a little into each glass and offered me one. What could I do? I accepted.

She kept up a lively monologue while she was entertaining me. She welcomed me to *Montreal* and advised me to be careful when the weather turned cold and it began to snow. For example, she warned me to walk slowly and not slip on the "'hice" outside the "'ouse" in the wintertime. As I sipped, I wondered if an invitation to supper would follow.

Such was not the case, however, and my visit ended when she handed me my copies of the agreements and two keys. I walked over to Park Avenue and took a bus to the address of my newfound friend. His wife was at home, as he said she would be. I claimed my bags and gave her my heartfelt and ever-lasting thanks. I hailed a taxi back to my new home and began to settle in.

At that point, I took a closer look at the entrance vestibule. In addition to the first apartment on the left, there was a communal bathroom on the right. The door to this facility was directly opposite my door. I had no problem with that. To the right of my door was another door, which represented a bit of a puzzle. It was designated 1C. I was in room 1B. The apartment nearest the front door was 1A.

So far, so good. What puzzled me was the fact that above the door 1C was an exit sign. But there was also a sturdy keyed lock on the door. There was no doorknob or handle. A puzzle, to be sure, for a long while — especially when one considered that the space behind that door was occupied. There was no doubt about that. Muffled sounds were to be heard on occasion.

The little old lady in the front apartment was never heard. She was seldom seen, and this only because she shared the bathroom with the rest of the tenants. She always seemed nervous.

The inhabitant of 1C was almost as quiet and at first was quite invisible. One day, I caught him opening his door. We said "hi" and introduced ourselves. Mr. Harnan was well-dressed and carried a briefcase, like I did, so I thought him harmless. He was from India and was pursuing a Ph.D. degree at McGill. After our first little conversation, we reverted to our very individual schedules, and I continued not to see much of him.

Mr. Harnan did have one friend who came to visit him, though. One Friday evening, the friend arrived and knocked. When there was no response after about 15 minutes, he went away. He returned on Saturday morning and repeated his performance. Again there was no answer, so he left. On Saturday evening, he returned for an encore performance. On each occasion I remained in my room, not wanting to get involved. That Saturday evening, however, the friend could stand it no more. He knocked on my door. I opened, and he fairly accused me, albeit in an interrogatory manner, of having seen his friend.

He had a hard time accepting that I had not seen Mr. Harnan. He wondered what he should do. What if his friend were dead inside? He skipped the possibility of his friend being away. I suggested that he go see the landlady, who lived a few doors down. I gave him the address, and off he went. I returned to the peace and quiet of my room.

This proved to be short-lived, however, as the friend and the landlady soon returned. With the customary jingle of her key ring, and amid repeated avowals that she did not like going into tenants' rooms uninvited, she dismissed his suggestions that Mr. Harnan might be dead on the inside. She selected a key and opened the door.

My curiosity about what was behind the exit door 1C was about to be satisfied. I jumped up and went out. I peeked into the room. It was not a room. It was, in effect, a corridor. A bed, a table, a chair, and I believe a counter and sink lined one side of this passage, which terminated in a rear door. It really was the fire-exit passageway converted into an apartment. The puzzle was solved. So, too, was the mystery of Mr. Harnan. He simply was not there.

Late on Sunday evening, I heard someone out in the hallway. I went out. It was my long-lost neighbor. I told him of his friend's concern and of the events of the weekend. He explained that he had been called away to a conference and had to leave in a hurry. "Not to worry about my friend," he said comfortingly. "He gets like that all the time."

As the weeks went by, in order to relieve the boredom and monotony of my student's life during the fall of my first year, I enjoyed walking around the streets of my neighborhood. On one occasion while walking along Pine Avenue, I discovered a flight of steps that went up the side of Mount Royal, the English translation of Montreal. It was a long, steep ascent. It took me at least ten minutes to get to the top. But it was worth it. The steps ended at a trail, which I followed. Several signs indicated a pavilion along the way.

As I walked, the odd *calèche* — a horse-drawn carriage — would roll by, filled with laughing tourists, for the season had not yet quite ended. As I went along, I would nod or say "hi" to strangers whose eyes I caught.

Now and again, during the rest of that first year at university, I would pause and think about my family name. I still wanted to get more information about it, and I began to wonder how to do this. No easy answer came to me.

Chapter 2
University Years

Just before the school year at McGill University ended in 1965, I began to think of jobs. I needed to earn money for my second year. My efforts in this regard were fruitful. I managed to find a position at the *Montreal Gazette*. I was given a small kiosk to work from, a list of names and phone numbers, and a script to follow.

Say hello to telemarketing!

My first call went like this: "Hello. I am phoning from the *Montreal Gazette*. Do you currently have this newspaper delivered to your home?"

"None of your damn business!" Click.

That was also my last call.

Say goodbye to telemarketing.

Soon after that episode, with the assistance of my brother Wilbur, who lived in Richmond, just south of Vancouver, I got the promise of a job with the British Columbia Forest Service if I went out to British Columbia. I accepted the offer, and at the end of the semester, I packed my books and things I would not need there, left them at a friend's apartment, and arranged passage to Vancouver.

My plane ticket from Trinidad to Montreal also included a flight between that city and Toronto. I used it and then boarded the *Canadian*, a train belonging to the Canadian Pacific Railway (CPR), at the Toronto Union Station.

It was the late spring of 1965, and I was bound for Vancouver, British Columbia.

* * *

I have always loved trains. In the mid-1950s, I lived in the small town of Couva, located near the west coast of central Trinidad. It was named after the Rio de Cuba, which flowed near to the original village. I used to enjoy going to the railway station on Friday evenings, supposedly to meet my brothers who were coming home for the weekend. They went to school in Port of Spain. In reality, I wanted to see and hear the mighty steam locomotive pull into the station, hissing and puffing. What power! On occasion, a green diesel-electric locomotive would come squealing in. This one was more sedate and less noisy — definitely not as dramatic as the steam locomotive — but I enjoyed watching it pull into the station anyway.

During the last three years of high school in Trinidad, I rode the 6:57 train from St. Joseph into Port of Spain. Every afternoon, I took either the 3:45 or the 4:10 back home. Those were pleasant times. The steam locomotives used were built in Montreal. If you were lucky and put your head out of the carriage window at the right time, a lusty puff of smoke and soot would fill your eyes and nose. What fun! Over the windows of the carriages, the designation "Canadian Pacific Railway" had been painted over but was still visible. I had no idea at the time that one day I would be riding in carriages operated by that company. I guess my guardian angel was sending me hints of what was to happen. Sadly, exactly one year after I left Trinidad, the government decided to stop using the railway system, and overnight it was scrapped. The event is celebrated, Trinidad style, in a popular calypso entitled "Last Train to San Fernando."

It is difficult for me to say when my interest in trains began. In 1945, I was 3 years old, and we lived on La Croix Street in Couva. This street runs parallel to the town's main street. Looking down two blocks from our house, one could see the railway station. On occasion, in the evening, I would accompany my father to his weekly chess game with Mr. D'Arnaud, the station master.

The daily passenger train from Port of Spain left around 5:00 p.m. Its arrival in Couva coincided with the setting of the sun. Just before it was due, the station master would leave his chess game and go to a small outbuilding. Shortly after, there would be a loud outburst, and a puff of smoke would come out of a low-set exhaust pipe. He had started up the small gas-powered electric generator. Almost immediately, a series of bulbs would spring to life, and the station would be bathed in a yellow glow. Only then would the chess game continue.

At its appointed time, the train would rumble into the station. There would be a hustle and a bustle for a few minutes as passengers alighted and luggage and goods were taken off or put on, and then the train would depart, in a huff and a puff, to end its run in San Fernando, the second largest town in Trinidad. In less than a minute, it would cross a bridge over the nearby Couva River, round a bend, and be out of sight.

My latest foray by train was in 2010 when my wife and I travelled by the American Amtrak system from Vancouver, BC, to San Francisco and then to Los Angeles, California. Quite possibly the excursions to the station in Couva were the start of my delight in seeing trains arrive and depart and explain why I so enjoy travelling by them, even to this day.

* * *

When I boarded the train in Toronto in the spring of 1965, it was like being back in Trinidad. The only thing missing was the jovial companion-ship of my schoolmates and other friends. Of course, the seats were much more comfortable, and the journey was going to last considerably more than the 25 minutes I was used to. This trip was scheduled to take three days and three nights. I had taken a day-coach seat, for I was determined to sit up and see as much of the Canadian countryside as I could.

As the train slipped out of the station, I began to look around at my fellow passengers. I also made sure to keep an eye on the ever-changing view outside my window. From a car or bus window, one sees the facades of a city's buildings. From a train window, one sees the back yards of buildings. Piles of garbage, dilapidated staircases, clothes lines, and other sometimes unattractive scenes greet the eyes. This view is more revealing of a town's character, I believe.

Across the aisle there was a young girl. She looked about 20 or so, but she could have been younger. What attracted my attention was her constantly changing facial expressions. It was unmistakable, the alternating pictures she presented. One moment she looked at peace with herself, almost happy. At other times she looked as though she had been crying into her hands as she sat rubbing her eyes.

I observed her for a while and finally went over and started talking to her. It turned out that she was leaving home, at the express wishes of her father. She had fallen in love with a boy not of her faith. She was Jewish, he was not. She was sad that her father had thrown her out but happy that she was going to be with her love. She got off the train in Winnipeg, and I wished her well.

Later on, I spoke with an older woman on the train. She was also Jewish and had spent some time in a concentration camp in Poland. She was eager to tell me of her experiences and was more than happy to raise her sleeve and show me the number tattooed on her arm. I believe she found it quite therapeutic to talk of her trials and escapes in Europe, and she was especially excited to talk about the different but more pleasant life she was enjoying in Canada. She smiled broadly as she spoke with me.

As I wrote about these two instances, I was reminded of an incident that took place during my first summer working in British Columbia. I mention it to people who ask me what, if any, were my experiences in Canada with regards to racial discrimination.

My job required me to drive into the Vancouver Island town of Campbell River two or three times per week from the Forestry Camp at which I was stationed. One of my duties was to hand in a list to a grocery store manager as soon as I got into town and later to park the panel truck out front for it to be loaded up with the supplies that the cook had ordered.

One day I parked the vehicle, checked in with the grocery store manager, and set off along the mall to a coffee shop. A man noticed me, and our eyes met. I could tell from his summer attire that he was probably an American tourist. He smiled as he approached me and stuck out his right hand. In a soft but clear voice, he whispered, "Sir, I have always wanted to shake the hand of a black man. Do you mind?"

"Not at all," I answered, smiling and offering my hand. I suddenly remembered the gentleman who had let me into Carnegie Hall in New York. The tourist and I shook hands, and with his left hand, he wiped a tear from his eyes.

* * *

The *Canadian* pulled into the CPR station in Vancouver just before midnight of the third day. With a firm grip on my suitcase, I found my way to the lobby and the telephone booths. I had to phone my brother to come to meet me. As I fumbled in my pockets for a dime, an old lady hobbled up to me and held out a dime. "Here's one, if you need it."

Just then my fingers closed in on a coin in the palm of my hand. "Oh! Thanks, I've got one."

We both smiled. I had been told that Vancouverites were characteristically friendlier than Montrealers, and in my first few minutes here I found this to be true.

A few days later I travelled to Victoria on Vancouver Island, and I checked in at the office of the British Columbia Forest Service, popularly known as the BCFS. I was soon on my way to their station at Mesachie Lake in the Cowichan Valley, located a one-hour drive north of Victoria. I had to attend an introductory course in BCFS policy, procedures, and expectations. There were other university students present as well. They came mostly from British Columbia, but there was at least one student from Ontario.

Two weeks after this preliminary session, I went back to Vancouver and took the Pacific Great Eastern Railway to Lillooet, a small town in the Fraser River Canyon, 240 kilometres north of Vancouver. That was a memorable trip. The scenery changed constantly from steep cliffs bedecked with fast-flowing waterfalls to wide valleys, where picturesque villages were surrounded by plains dotted with grazing cattle and horses. It was as though I had at my disposal a large picture atlas of this part of Canada.

After another short stay at this BCFS camp at Lillooet where I was an odd-job man, I was transferred back to Campbell River on Vancouver Island and spent the rest of the summer at another camp some miles out of this town. My travels in Canada had begun.

At first I kept track of the number of miles I travelled, as my knowledge of this vast country grew rapidly. I stopped when the total reached 25,000, the length of the equator. This took me about two or three years.

I have to mention that throughout my travels I was never without a camera. Different ones over the many years, of course. I have always been a passionate photographer, firmly believing in the old adage that a picture is worth a thousand words. I bought my first camera in 1959, the year before I graduated from high school. This was a simple Kodak Brownie. I bought my first adjustable camera, the Ricoh, the year after I graduated. I used it quite a lot during this first exciting summer in this westernmost province of Canada. However, that summer quickly drew to an end.

In late August 1965, I returned to Montreal. As I crossed Canada, again by train, the spring colours of shades of green were turning to ones of yellow, red, purple, and orange. Fall was on the way. On the prairies, the fields, too, were of a different colour than in the spring — more russet and brown. Some had been harvested and even ploughed. Once, as we raced along across the flat prairie landscape, I used the mile posts and my watch to time the train at a bit over 100 miles an hour. Travelling west in the spring, the train had been late arriving in Winnipeg but was on time in Medicine Hat. Between these two cities, the terrain was flat, and the train tracks had barely a curve.

One night, as the train sped westward, I noticed a faint but definite glow in the far northern sky. It glimmered and shivered as if not sure what to do. I was looking at a display of the Northern Lights. It was not a spectacular display, but I enjoyed it.

* * *

During my second year at McGill, I roomed with two other students from Trinidad. Our apartment was the entire second floor of an old brick building on Édouard-Charles Avenue, on the other side of Mount Royal Park from the university, just off Park Avenue. I took a bus to Milton Street and then walked to school. The bus fare was offset by being able to pay a lower rent. However, as the saying goes, three's a crowd.

Later that year, at Christmas time, the brother of one of my roommates drove up from Alabama for a visit. There was a third brother who lived in Montreal as well, and they all liked to get together for the season.

Just before he left to return to Alabama, Guy, my roommate, asked me if I wanted to drive with his brother to Toronto. I agreed. He drove an older Porsche. I just could not resist. We left Montreal, and for a while all went well. However, like their cousins the Volkswagens, Porsches at the time were not noted for an efficient heating system. For most of the trip, we were cold.

Driving the 401 Highway between Montreal and Toronto is never fun. In the middle of winter, it is even less so. For one thing, it is a very long drive. That winter, just before the sun went down, we stopped and took a few pictures. After sunset, it got colder, and snow began to fall. Soon a blizzard was raging. That evening, I saw hefty cars being blown halfway across the highway lane.

We got to Toronto and spent the night at a friend's home. Next morning, Guy's brother left for Alabama. I did not envy him. Supposedly, though, as he went south, the weather would get better.

I said goodbye to my new friends and took a bus to Niagara Falls. I had always wanted to see these falls. See them I did. They were all frozen over except for a small, persistent stream of water that roared noisily over the frigid rocks. The entire area over the falls was covered with a cold blanket of almost stationary mist and spray. A dense fog spread itself along the course of the river in both directions for a short distance.

It was too cold to walk around, so I took a taxi tour. Part of the driver's routine was to stop at the base of a viewing tower and allow his passengers to take a ride to the top. I was too poor to afford the cost, so the driver went in and spoke to the person in charge. I was allowed to go up to the top of the tower for free. What a thrill!

I saw a barge that, as the guide explained, had broken its moorings upstream many years before and had started drifting downstream towards the falls. The story was told that there were three men on board that dark night, and there was no way to stop the barge. Not far from the falls, the barge got stuck on those exposed rocks. Next morning, a helicopter was able to take the men off and to safety. During the night, the hair on the head of one of the men went from black to white. The barge is still stuck on those rocks, these many years later.

I returned to Montreal by bus, and life went on. Living with two roommates seemed to have taken its toll on my studies. My marks dropped a bit, and I decided that the next year I would go back to living alone. It had been a very busy year, and I'd had no time to continue researching my family name. My resolve was in no way diminished, though. It was just that I had no time.

In the spring of 1966, I returned to BC. My summer job with the BCFS was mine for as long as I wanted it. This time I used the Canadian National Railway. It took a more northerly route across the prairies between Winnipeg and Jasper and a different route south through most of BC. I wanted to see as much of the country as I could. This route was not as scenic as the CPR, so I resolved never to use it again.

I spent that summer at a remote BCFS Camp about 225 miles north of the city of Prince George, the geographical center of British Columbia. At the camp I worked primarily with maps. I had taken a course in cartography at McGill the previous year, which qualified me for this job. The journey from Prince George to the campsite took about four hours.

I mention these details only because this area was the site of one of the largest development projects in the history of BC. The British Columbia Hydro Authority was building a huge hydroelectric dam on the Peace River, downstream from Finlay Forks. The BCFS was clearing several areas at the 2,200-foot contour line. This was the intended elevation of the top of the dam. These cleared areas were to be beach accesses to the lake that would be formed when the dam was finished and the area was flooded.

To this end, the BCFS was using, among other machinery, two massive instruments of destruction called *tree crushers*. I had never before seen such huge machines. These diesel-electric behemoths rolled along on gigantic cylindrical metal wheels fitted with diagonal steel flanges. The edges of these blade-like attachments were supposed to chop or at least break the trees into small bits as the heavy machines rolled over them, after the trees had been pushed over by a huge frontal beam.

When the weather was dry and the terrain reasonably flat, these machines worked. However, these two elements were not always in favour. The larger of the two behemoths spent a lot of time either mired in mud or broken down. Parts had to be shipped from Texas and always took a while to arrive. The smaller one, though a bit more successful, also had its moments of dysfunction. It was left abandoned on a hilltop when the project ended. The larger one was broken into six huge parts, transported by flatbed trucks to a new town called Mackenzie, and reassembled, minus the engines and motors, as a tourist attraction billed as "The World's Largest Tree Crusher." I felt lucky to be able to witness some aspects of this giant Western Canadian project, but in late August 1966, I returned to Montreal.

I immediately found new lodgings on Hutchison Street. The beautiful houses on this historic street date from 1899. My former landlady remembered me, and there were no problems. I lived alone on the second floor of an older building where there were two apartments — one to the front of the building and mine to the rear, overlooking the back alley.

I had two rooms, separated by a wide archway. This was my introduction to the "open concept" of living. One room I used as a study/bedroom. The other was basically the kitchen. It contained an ancient cylindrical hot water tank about 5 feet tall and 12 inches in diameter. This tank rested on a steel pedestal and stood about 15 inches away from the wall. On the exterior of the bottom of the cylinder was a metal cage that housed a gas burner, over which was set a copper coil. In the morning, I would light the burner and heat the coil and the water, which then flowed into the tank. It was very efficient, taking only about 15 to 20 minutes to heat enough water for my needs. I would then turn off the burner until I next needed hot water. This room also gave access to my bathroom.

To the right of the water tank was another relic: an old oil stove, with burners on the top. This I used for heating the apartment. It, too, was quite efficient. I lit it only when the weather got cold enough, usually by the middle of September. Once it was lit, I had to turn the flame down to almost "off" during the day when I was away at school and raise the temperature again when I came home in the evenings. From the top of this appliance, an asbestos-wrapped chimney disappeared into the attic of the building. I used an electric hotplate for cooking.

One morning I left for classes, hoping to be gone for about two hours. After my class, I went to the library and decided to remain there for longer than I had intended. I returned home later that afternoon to the smell of heat. I had left the hot water tank burner on for over four hours.

I immediately shut off the gas and went into the bathroom and opened the window at the back of this room. Then I opened the hot water tap in the bathtub and quickly left the room, shutting the door. The pipes took over ten minutes, loudly hissing and spitting, to clear themselves of the steam, which then filled the bathroom and escaped through the window. From the kitchen window, the operation looked like a steam locomotive that had the vague shape of a house.

A few weeks later, I did the same thing again — only this time I was gone for about eight hours. The results were even more catastrophic. It took much longer to clear the system of steam. The heat had spread itself along most of the copper pipes in the building. The tenant from downstairs came up to complain. A water pipe had burst over her closet and soaked her clothes. I opened my closet and, sure enough, the heat had melted a joint in the copper tubing. This joint was a good 20 feet away from the tank. I turned off the water at the tank and placed a bucket under the burst pipe, which continued to leak. It took about 15 minutes to fill the bucket, which I emptied and replaced.

At 8:00 the next morning, I phoned a plumber for help. I can't remember how I achieved this, because I did not have a telephone. I may have asked my neighbor to use his. Fifteen minutes after the plumber arrived and $80 later, I finally went to sleep. I was not too pleased with myself over this incident, considering that my monthly rental was about the cost of the repairs.

Not long after this second escapade with the hot water tank, I came home about 9:00 at night to an even more intense heat and an even stranger smell. I opened the door and went in. The smoke was as intense as the heat. Through the haze, I could see a tall red streak that rose from the top of the oil stove and disappeared with a pulsing, shimmering glow into the attic. It was the chimney. I had left the stove burning at too high of a setting. I turned off the oil supply and went next door. I hammered on my sleeping neighbour's door until he answered. I babbled something about *fire, telephone, fire station* . . . He understood immediately what I had tried so desperately to say.

Shortly after, I heard the sirens wailing. The fire station was only about six blocks away. However, it was separated from the street on which I lived by one of the most complicated systems of over- and underpasses, ramps, and roadways I have ever seen — not the most complicated but a close second. I think it took the fire trucks at least ten minutes to arrive. It may have been less, but panic had overcome me, and I had lost all sense of time.

By the time the officers arrived, the glow of the chimney had disappeared, the smoke had almost completely dissipated, and only the overpowering stench remained. If not for that, I am sure I would have been arrested for wasting the valuable time of the Montreal Fire Department.

The chief officer took out his pen and notebook. "Who owns this building?" he asked.

"Concordia," I replied, this being the name of the real estate company connected with the building.

"Concordia!" he repeated, nodding his head in recognition. He closed his notebook and put it and his pencil back into his pocket. He turned, stomped down the stairs, and was gone. Apparently, the Montreal Fire Department was already on speaking terms with the company. Concordia either owned and rented or looked after over 70 percent of the buildings in the student ghetto, as the area around the university was called. My landlady was actually an agent of this company.

Just before the Christmas break, there was a knock on the door. I opened to see a uniformed man. He had come to read my electric meter. I pleaded ignorance of any such equipment. He insisted that it was just above the door, and if he could just come in, he would show me. I looked, and sure enough, there it was, its silver disc spinning around as merrily as ever. I let the meter-reader in, and he did his job. He was a friendly sort and engaged me in some idle conversation. Perhaps he was overly friendly. I say this only because within two minutes, his talk became unpleasant. I politely but firmly hustled him out the door. He left, but not before turning back to ask me not to tell his boss. A stern glare was all I could muster, but it worked. He left, and I never saw him again.

With all the problems I was having with the utilities of this apartment — gas, water, oil, and electricity — it was surprising that I did not move out. But soon winter turned into spring, and the new year arrived.

* * *

1967 was Canada's 100th anniversary. The then Prime Minister Trudeau urged everyone to have a Centennial project. Mine was to drive from Montreal to Vancouver. These two cities are 3,052 miles (4,912 kilometres) apart. It was possible at the time to shuttle a car to Vancouver for delivery to a dealership that specialized in used vehicles. All that was necessary was that the driver supply gas and oil.

I quickly arranged the adventure through Sandra, a fellow student and an interesting girl to say the least. She also wanted to make the trip with two of her friends. Sandra once told me she had come to class stoned out of her mind and sat and stared at the professor for one hour. I was walking down the street with her one day. We came up to a car that had a parking ticket stuck under one of its windshield wipers. She removed the ticket, tore it to bits, and said, "He doesn't need that."

After the arrangements for our trip were made, I waited patiently for the end of the semester. It came soon enough. Sometime close to the end of April, four of us — John, Sandra, another girl whose name I have forgotten, and I — left Montreal in a 1964 Thunderbird convertible. John and I drove, changing posts every time we stopped for gas. The girls literally came along for the ride.

This bird really flew. I remember driving at over 100 miles per hour, approaching Regina. Across the highway I noticed a police car heading east. In my rear-view mirror, I spotted the cloud of dust as he braked and spun around and started after me. I stopped, and the officer came up. Remember, this car was in transit to a dealership in Vancouver. It had no license plates, just a sheet of paper stuck to the windscreen.

"Where are you headed?" asked the officer.

"Regina," I answered politely.

"Why are you driving so fast?"

"I want to get to Regina before it gets too late."

"Well, you still have a couple of hours driving. Slow down."

"Thank you, officer."

We spent the night in a motel. Showers and a hot breakfast were in order. As we got ready to leave Regina the next morning, we decided to put the top down. When we finally achieved our objective — we had to take all the bags out of the trunk and rearrange them on the back seat — we roared off.

It was John's turn at the wheel as we came barrelling through the Rockies. He was racing a couple of guys in a little sports car. Turning, twisting, uphill and down. It was fun. In Hope, we gassed up and I took over. It started to rain, but I was fairly familiar with the road. We pulled up at my brother's house in Richmond, tired but happy.

Driving from Montreal had given me time to reflect on a trip I had done a few weeks before I left Trinidad. I borrowed my father's car and left on a drive around Trinidad with a friend. I calculated we would be gone all day. Our trip took us east through Sangre Grande and included a short stop at Manzanilla Beach, where we had a swim in the ocean. We drove down the eastern coast and through Rio Claro and Princes Town to San Fernando. This was a very tricky town to navigate because of the hills. We left and headed north to St. Joseph. We were back home by 4:00 in the afternoon. This was much sooner than expected. Still, it was an exciting "goodbye, Trinidad" trip. In contrast, the trip to Vancouver from Montreal had taken almost four days at considerably faster speeds.

The next morning, I drove us all to the used-car dealership on Kingsway in Vancouver. The agent came out, and we handed over the keys. He walked around the vehicle, no doubt looking for dents and scratches. There were none. He stopped at the rear left tire. "Looks like we have to replace this one," he said. John and I looked at it. A lot of canvas and numerous threads were showing through the rubber on the side of the tire. We shook our heads as we remembered driving across the prairies and through the Rockies at top speed. Sometimes having fun can be dangerous.

Later that day, John and the two girls flew to San Francisco. Haight-Ashbury was beckoning them, and the summer of 1967 was the best time for members of the hippy generation to be there. It was the summer of love and other things. Years later, I visited this area of San Francisco and found it still attractive.

I spent the summer of 1967 at Finlay Forks, BC. I again worked in the office with maps. My second stay at this remote Forestry Camp was highlighted by three aerial tours I was able to make. The first was a helicopter trip up the Finlay River to an outpost called Fort Ware. This aboriginal community was first called Kwadacha. It is located in the Rocky Mountain Trench and is now referred to as Ware. The settlement was named after William Ware, from Manchester, England, who headed the trading post that was established there by the Hudson's Bay Company.

My second flight was by fixed-wing aircraft down the Peace River to the site of the W.A.C. Bennett Dam that was being built near the town of Hudson's Hope. The Peace River Canyon is a remarkable sight from the air. The muddy water, swirling through steep rocky walls, belies the name Peace.

The river is a rapidly flowing and dangerous body of tremendously power-ful water. I remember looking down on it from the cliffs at Finlay Forks and staring at the turbulent waters of the Peace River. It was by no means a peaceful river.

The construction site itself was extensive. Looking down from above, I had to remind myself that I was seeing the bottom of what was going to be a huge dam and lake. An impressive conveyor belt transported the fill mate-rial from a nearby glacial moraine. It was in operation 24 hours a day. This project was massive, and people have written volumes about it. Many years after it was finished, on a driving tour through BC, I had the opportunity to visit the dam and was taken underground to the vast turbine room. It was a pleasure to behold the ten generators as they spun with just a soft whirring sound. I could feel the power of the water as it fell through the channels.

My third flight was by helicopter, again to the Hudson's Hope area. On this occasion, we landed. The engineer had some business to conduct at the BC Hydro camp located there. We had dinner and boarded the helicopter for the return flight to Finlay Forks. The helicopter rose into the air and was pivoted around to face our destination. The engine was revved, but the aircraft went nowhere. The engine was revved even higher, but the craft remained hovering over the pad. The pilot landed the machine and announced that the wind was whistling down the canyon at precisely the maximum speed of the helicopter. There was no way the helicopter could combat such a force. We had to spend the night at the camp, and we returned to our location the next morning.

Still, it was quite boring to be living so far from civilization. In an attempt to relieve my ennui, I asked a colleague to buy me some balsa wood, glue, and other materials. I spent the rest of the summer designing and building an 18-inch model of a cabin cruiser. I still have this boat.

Later in 1967, when the W.A.C. Bennett Dam was opened with great fanfare, I was already back in Montreal.

* * *

My last year at McGill started in September. These were exciting times for Montreal and for me. This was the year of Expo '67, the Montreal World's Fair. It had opened in the spring while I was en route to Vancouver and was due to close soon after I returned to Montreal. With memories of the 1964 New York World's Fair in my head, I did manage to get in a few visits.

I was also impressed with the new subway system that had been inaugurated that spring. I had followed its construction with great interest and was eager to try it out. I was not disappointed. The Montreal Metro system is a beautiful and efficient one.

I was looking forward to continuing my search for information on my family name. I had never forgotten my desire to find out all I could about the name Walrond. I found the time to do some searching at the McGill library, but I found nothing. To complicate matters, this was a heavy year for me, academically speaking. Spare time was a rarity.

For my final year, I got together with a student from Sir George Williams University and rented an apartment on Sainte-Famille Street. He was from Trinidad as well. Everything went well. We shared the shopping, cooking, and cleaning. He introduced me to the St. Lawrence Market, where many West Indians did their shopping. It was an excellent source of Caribbean foods. The year went by quickly.

The winter of 1967 to 1968 was a memorable one on another front. The weather conditions broke all the records that were kept by the university as well as those that radio and television stations had on file. Snowfall and wind-chill factors were both way over normal, and minimum temperatures were much lower than ever before. One morning, it was 40 degrees below zero with a very strong wind gusting along the streets. I usually took about ten minutes to walk to the university, but during the coldest part of this weather abnormality, I was able to shorten the time to about six minutes.

I was thankful that this was to be my last winter in Montreal. When spring came, it was none too soon for many people, including myself.

* * *

My parents were invited to come to my graduation, and they gladly accepted. Convocation was slated for Friday, 31 May 1968. They arrived shortly before that. This was their first trip abroad.

Many years before, while still a young boy, my father had aspired to become a doctor. He was working towards this goal when his father died. He was 14 years old, and his plans and hopes had to be altered. Instead, he had to finish his high school education and remain in Trinidad in order to care for his mother and 2-year-old brother. There were other siblings to consider as well. That was when he decided to become a teacher. Now, 53 years later, here he was with my mother in Montreal. I am sure that he was elated at finally being able to travel abroad, and that he was going to witness the graduation of one of his children from a highly recognised university.

My parents enjoyed four wonderful days there. I had found a room for them in a house opposite the one in which I lived. An elderly lady from Trinidad ran what would be called in this day and age a bed and breakfast.

The first day I walked with my parents through the McGill campus. We entered at the Milton Gates and went up the walk towards Dawson Hall, part of the main Arts Building. Some workmen were repairing the winter damage to the steps that led up to the paved area in front of this historic building. My father stopped and looked intently at the men, a somewhat puzzled look on his face. I thought for a moment he was interested in what they were doing. I asked him what was the matter. He looked at me and whispered, "They are all white." It was the first time he'd seen a group of white workmen.

He also stood in amazement at his first sight of Canadian "hippies" as they strolled through the campus. I believe he would have loved to sit them down, one by one, give them a haircut, and lecture them on the necessity of always being presentable. He, of course, was dressed in a jacket and tie.

I felt honoured to escort my parents to some of the popular tourist sites. The Montreal Basilica was high on the list. A ride on the subway delighted them. St. Joseph's Oratory was a must-see, which they thoroughly enjoyed. A walk on Mount Royal was a pleasant outing.

Graduation day was rainy, cold, and windy. Because of this, the ceremony was held in the university's Molson Stadium. This did not make it any warmer, but at least we were dry.

My parents hosted a small after-graduation and farewell celebration with myself and my colleagues: Herbert Webb, who was my roommate for my last year and who came from San Fernando; Desmond and Roosevelt Williams, two brothers who had lived in Couva and had attended the school at which my father was principal; and Junior Payne, who used to live two blocks away from our house in Champs Fleurs. His sisters were some of my train-mates while we were in high school. It was a small but jovial party.

Soon it was time for us to leave Montreal. I packed my books and other belongings and left them with some friends, and on 1 June, I flew with my parents to Vancouver. My brother Wilbur met us and took us to his home.

* * *

I did not want to sit around and do nothing all summer, so I began checking the local newspapers for jobs. The outlook was bleak. Then, just as I was losing hope, a very good friend of mine, Brian Logan, asked me to come work for him in the Queen Charlotte Islands, where he was a forestry technician for a large logging company. These islands are the home of the Haida Nation of aboriginals and are now called Haida Gwaii.

I had met Brian the year before at Finlay Forks and had worked with him as well. When I later married in 1972, he was my best man. His offer was immediately accepted, and on Sunday, 9 June, I flew up to meet him.

A short drive from the Sandspit Airport took us to a muddy logging camp and office operated by the Rayonier Logging Company. This company was a subsidiary of the International Telephone and Telegraph Corporation of America. The driver checked in, and a few minutes later we set off along a very bumpy and even muddier logging road across the island to Moresby Camp at the head of Cumshewa Inlet.

I met Brian there, and within an hour or so we left together in a small boat, about 15 feet long, outfitted with an outboard motor. This hour-long coast-hugging trip took us down Cumshewa Inlet and on to our destination campsite. We went through Carmichael Passage and then Louise Narrows, which was no more than 30 feet wide at high tide and about 5 feet deep at some points at low tide. We finally headed up Sewell Inlet to our base camp for the summer.

The camp was at the very end of this inlet. My friend and I spent the first few nights in a small cabin perched up a short but fairly steep incline. My arrival at this site verged on the catastrophic. We pulled up beside a long dock. Brian got out and tied up the boat. I tried to get out and promptly fell into the water, right up to my neck. He hauled me out unceremoniously, then reached into the boat and got out my suitcase. This I hauled up to the cabin, and after changing into some dry clothes, I went back down to the boat to help unload the rest of the supplies. I got back into the boat, placed some items on the dock, and then got out of the boat and fell into the water a second time. If my first bath was funny, the second was hilarious — at least to Brian. Myself, I was getting slightly peeved.

My friend finally stopped laughing and gave me a short but sensible lesson in climbing out of a small boat: "You are either in the boat or on the dock," he explained. "You can't have one foot on the dock and one foot on the boat. This isn't a train or a bus." That was all he said. It all made sense, so I tried it and it worked. I have never since fallen out of a boat.

I mention this because a few days later, I had to return — alone — to Moresby Camp to pick up some supplies, including a new propeller for another 20-foot cabin cruiser that was stationed at the Sewell Inlet Camp. I did not want to go, but Brian, my boss, insisted. So, wearing one life jacket and supplied with at least two more for emergency support, I set off. I was not and am still not a swimmer. He gave me simple instructions: "Just cut across Sewell Inlet, hug the coast, and you will be okay."

Off I went, following his suggestions. I remained in sight of the coast but not within sound of it — underwater scraping sounds, that is. The reason the cabin cruiser needed a new propeller was precisely because it had been in contact with unseen rocks. I got through the narrow passage, and as I went along, I kept a keen lookout for floating debris and kelp. I also paid close attention to how far I was from the coastline. Time did nothing to ease my troubled mind, because the return trip would be equally as long and just as frightening to me, a landlubber who had never before piloted a boat of any kind or size.

About 15 minutes after I went through Louise Narrows and was in Carmichael Passage, I looked over to my right — the coastline was on my left — and there, about 15 feet away from the boat, just coming out of the water, was a huge head. Just the top of the head, mind you. Enough to reveal a single large eye, looking straight at me. It stared at me long enough for us to see each other and assure each other that we were both there. It looked very much like a whale of some kind. There was nothing but the large head and the eye. It was too large to be a dolphin. The creature swam alongside the boat, at the same speed, for about 30 seconds or more, and then sank slowly and silently beneath the water, leaving only a few gentle ripples which were soon left far behind. The moment left me speechless, not that I had anyone to talk to.

The amazing thing about this experience was that afterwards, I no longer felt afraid. I completed the outward trip, picked up the new prop and other supplies, and returned to Sewell Inlet with a composure that would suggest that I had done the trip many times before. I was happy that I did not have to repeat the solo journey, but I learned one important fact: Guardian angels are not always of the flying variety. Some can swim.

When the new prop was installed, Brian and I used the boat to check on other logging operations in the many bays and inlets close to our home base. In addition to these official functions, we also used the cruiser for water skiing. I did the piloting, Brian did the skiing. Sometimes, on the way home from the official expeditions, we would fish for cod. On occasion, Brian would don his wetsuit and weight belts and dive for abalone. Harvesting this delicacy has since been banned. Brian did once convince me to put on his wetsuit, but he had to push me into the water. I was not going in on my own accord.

About a week after our initial arrival at the head of Sewell Inlet, a large floating complex was towed up the inlet and tied up to the dock. It was made up of three units: a cook house with dining room and chef's bedroom, sleeping accommodations for a small crew, and a toilet and laundry room. There was also one small room separated from the toilet and laundry by a narrow passage. This room housed a diesel-powered electric generator.

Along with this floating complex came a cook, fallers, machine operators, and other workers. Our main reason for being here was to clear a site for a new camp. One of my jobs was, at the end of the day, to grease and oil the long boom on a large excavator. I learned a lot about these large machines that summer.

Among the fallers were two brothers, one of whom brought his wife and little daughter up for a short holiday sometime during the few weeks I spent there. One day after work, we all sat talking in the dining room area, which also doubled as a lounge, complete with a sofa and some comfortable chairs. The little girl came up to me, and we began chatting. At one point she held my hands in hers, turned them over, and said, "You better go and wash your hands before dinner."

"I already did," I replied, holding my hands out to her.

"Well," she commented self-assuredly, "they are dirty again."

I had to explain that that was their natural colour. She seemed satisfied with my explanation.

I spent a wonderful nine weeks on Moresby Island. The weather there was beautiful when it was sunny. When it was not, the clouds hung persistently low on the mountainsides, and the wind blew horizontally along the ground. Any accompanying rain hit your face with a stinging pain. Then the winds would blow the clouds away, and the sun would appear and make amends. All was beautiful again till the next outburst.

Many, many years later, when I lived in Nanaimo, I ran into a young aboriginal lady who worked as a cashier at the grocery store I frequented. She looked Haida, so I asked her where she was from. She answered that she was born at the Sewell Logging Camp on the Queen Charlotte Islands. She was a student at the local college. I was proud to tell her that I had had a small hand in preparing the area for the campsite in 1968. She was both surprised and impressed. She said that she never thought she would ever meet anyone in Nanaimo who would know anything about her homeland, not to mention someone who had help prepare her home camp.

Soon the day came when I had to leave the Queen Charlotte Islands. I promised myself that someday I would return and spend more time enjoying myself rather than working. Forty years later, in 2008, I did return with my wife, and together we spent a wonderful three weeks exploring the islands.

* * *

While I was away working, my parents were entertained by my brother and his family. My parents met several old friends from Trinidad and visited the Musqueam First Nations Reserve, Stanley Park, and Queen Elizabeth Park, among many other places of interest.

I had introduced my parents to Brian's mom and dad, Elspeth and John. My father and John were both Freemasons and had a lot to talk about. Mr. Logan also took my father to several Lodge meetings, where he made many friends. These friendships lasted for the rest of their respective lives.

While in Vancouver, my father, always the teacher, embraced the opportunity to visit several elementary schools. He was very impressed with the way the Canadian schools operated and how lessons were presented. Time spent shopping and sitting quietly at home filled up most of the days.

Late in August 1968, I flew with my parents to Toronto and saw them safely aboard a plane back to Trinidad. I went on to Montreal, collected my belongings, and shipped them out to Vancouver. I then got on a train for my final journey by rail across to the West Coast. I was finished with Montreal, as far as living and studying there was concerned. I had had a wonderful four years, had met some quite interesting people, and had accomplished most of my goals.

To be sure, I would visit this exciting city again. But I still had one thing left to do: Find out more about my family name. Over the years, I had spent some time — not much, I must admit — in the McGill library, looking at the table of contents of some books on English history. I had nothing specific in mind; I was just looking. I found nothing that I thought would be relevant, but I just kept on looking. Perhaps I would have better luck in Vancouver.

The more I searched and found nothing, the more convinced I became that there was something out there to be discovered.

Chapter 3
My Career takes Shape

Once I was firmly established in Vancouver, people began asking me the inevitable question: "What next?" I would explain that I wanted to teach high school French. One day, in response to this answer, someone — I think it was Brian's father, Mr. Logan — asked me, "Do you have any teacher training?"

"No, I don't have any formal training as teacher," I answered.

"Then you'd better get some," came his authoritative advice.

It turned out that Mr. Logan had once worked as a school bus driver and knew a lot about children and perhaps even more about teachers than I had suspected.

As a result of this conversation, I applied to Simon Fraser University for enrollment in their teacher-training course. Called the Professional Development Program, it was reputed to be better than the one offered by the University of British Columbia. I was immediately accepted, "on transfer from McGill," as it was put. However, the next year-long session was not due to begin until January of 1969.

I now had four months at my disposal with no definite income-earning plans in mind. I had to remedy this situation. August turned into September. I tried my hand at selling copies of *Encyclopaedia Britannica.* In one week, I sold three sets and earned $90 per set. I was elated.

When I discovered what was going on, I began to have doubts about the morality of the job. The company supplied me with lists of names and addresses of people who had filled out entry forms at the Pacific National Exhibition that summer — these lucky people had won a prize. I believe it was a cruise to the Caribbean or a trip to some other exotic place — Mexico, perhaps. But the winners had to pay for something. I think it was the hotel accommodations. The residents were all expecting me to call at the appointed time.

I was there simply to deliver the prize, but they had to listen to my presentation. It said so on the contest form. I soon found out that almost everyone who had entered the contest had won. The company believed that because the winners had to contribute to the so-called prize, very few or perhaps even none of them would actually be going on any trip. The company benefitted in that they had won entry into countless homes, and they counted on people like me to make the sales presentations. They were sure some sales would result. I proved them right in that assumption.

As I said, I sold three sets in one week. I thought I was doing well. Then one evening, I arrived at a home where, of course, I was expected. The door was opened by a lady who was extremely happy because she had never won anything before in her life. She kept repeating this fact. It was not long before I realized that her happiness, though it was doubtlessly precipitated by her winnings, had also obviously been encouraged by something out of a bottle. Her spirits were assuredly high. My presentation was a lost cause, my will to sell encyclopaedias to wishful dupes disappeared, and my desire to continue in this line of misadventure evaporated. I turned in my kit and surrendered my fate to the winds of chance.

Not long after, I got a phone call from Brian, whom I thought I had left on Haida Gwaii. He had quit his job and was in Vancouver. He had enrolled in the University of British Columbia's forestry program and planned to become a Registered Professional Forester.

We struck a deal. He and I would share an apartment on which he would pay the rent. After finishing my teacher-training course, I would get a job and would pay the rent until all was square. He also got me a job with another forestry consulting firm located in the Marine Building on Burrard Street in Vancouver.

In late October 1968, I was sent with an engineer into the Callaghan Lake area south of Whistler, BC, to complete a road layout job. This area was later to become the venue for the 2010 Winter Olympics Nordic Games sports events. Once we left the main road, we had to walk through waist-high snow to the lake. Remember, there was no road as yet. As a matter of fact, we were working on laying out part of the yet-to-be-built road. We carried all we needed for a two-week stay, including a tent and food.

I was employed as the engineer's assistant. This involved blazing trees by stripping a small piece of the outer bark so that other workers could see the route of the future road at a distance. I also held the end of the tape measure, or *chain* as it is called in road construction, so correct distances could be recorded.

The weather made this the toughest job I ever had. Working, sleeping, eating, and even going to the bathroom in cold, snowy conditions was not my idea of a job. I did not enjoy myself, and I guess it showed on my face. The engineer told me I was the surliest guy he ever worked with. Of course, he did not know that I had been told that he had a snarky disposition. I had taken the job anyway and was determined to show him I could be every bit as nasty as he was reputed to be. (Shortly after the job was completed, I heard he had left British Columbia to work in the Far East. I guess he did not like the cold weather, either.)

Once the road layout was finished, we packed up and started out. It was going to be a long trek, longer even than the walk in. This was because we had managed to get a helicopter ride part of the way in. A truck would be parked at the end of our hike to the main road. The engineer had a set of keys.

Somewhere along the way, while I was trying to negotiate a fallen tree, the bark gave way and my heavy backpack threw me to the ground. I twisted my left knee and heard something snap. I raised myself and trudged on. Within a few minutes, I could feel my knee swelling up. Only my jeans seemed to be holding my leg together. We finished the walk out and the drive into Vancouver. It was late October. Halloween was upon us. So, too, was my 26th birthday.

We dropped our gear off at the office, and I caught a bus to my apartment in South Burnaby. I had spent two weeks in a smoky tent, so my clothes reeked. There was a definite abundance of seats around me that night. Fortunately, it was very late, and the bus was not crowded.

It was almost midnight by the time I got home and managed to peel my jeans off. I threw my clothes out on the balcony, had a shower, found something to eat, and crawled into bed. A tremendous pain in my left leg woke me the next morning. I phoned a doctor, a family friend from Trinidad, and had no problem getting in to see him. His office was next to the Royal Columbian Hospital in New Westminster.

After a quick but thorough examination of my knee, the worst was confirmed: The meniscus had broken, and a small piece was on the loose. It had to come out. A date had to be set for surgery. However, my classes were due to begin early in January. After a week of orientation, my first assignment would be to spend five weeks teaching in a school. I could not miss that part of the course, so surgery was set for late February.

* * *

I was assigned to the Port Coquitlam Junior Secondary School as part of a team of three student teachers. By some strange coincidence, one of the other students was a Trinidadian who had attended the same high school as I had and at the same time as well. I had not seen him in many years. He was a graduate of the University of Manitoba. The other student, whose name I have forgotten, was originally from Hungary.

The three of us were teamed up with three French teachers at the school. The five weeks were a jumble of six adults and about 30 students in the one classroom, literally falling over each other. The main purpose of these first five weeks was to allow us student teachers to get a taste of what teaching would be like and to decide whether this was really the profession we wanted to get into.

To say the least, it was a revealing experience for me. This was my first time in a Canadian high school, and seeing such a large number of students in one classroom was rather intimidating. Just observing the teenage culture in action was perhaps the best learning experience afforded by this part of the course.

Planning lessons and executing them before the associate teachers and then having them evaluated was all part of the process. Getting to meet the student council and hearing about its role in the function of the school was all new to me. Even learning to cope with snowfalls and snowballs on a school ground was pure novelty. The time went by quickly, and I learned a lot.

This first teaching session came to a close on 19 February 1969. This date is unforgettable. When the last class ended, the associate and student teachers left, headed for the staff room. Our last evaluation meeting would take place there. I lingered behind and watched the students file out of the room.

As the last student was leaving, she made an abrupt turn and approached me. She stuck out her hand, and I did the same. She deposited a folded sheet of paper in the palm of my hand. I looked at it and saw that it was a note. By the time I had raised my head, she had exited the door and was lost forever in the moving throng of students.

Much later in the day, when all the meetings and discussions were over and goodbyes were said, I returned to the university. It was only then that I had the time and opportunity to look at the note. It was signed by Sandi B. of Division 33, and it turned out to be the best teacher evaluation I have ever received.

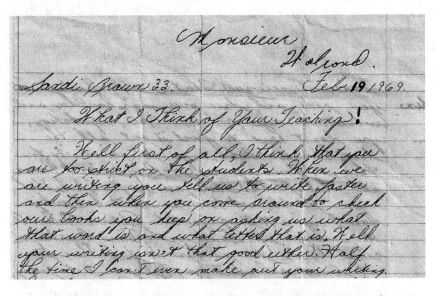

It was entitled "What I think of your teaching!" and it came from the heart of a grade eight student. Her handwriting was quite legible, and spelling errors were few. The note was critical but analytical at the same time. She informed me that I was too strict on the students and should relax a bit. My pacing the floor of the classroom and looking over their shoulders while they worked made the students nervous. I should not be too critical of the students' handwriting, because mine was not perfect either.

On she went. I should be mindful of the fact that in the class, some students had taken French before, some of it measured in terms of years. I should therefore be careful of not boring some students in the name of teaching others. She realized that putting her name at the top of the note might have resulted in her being victimized by me, but at the same time she wanted to be direct and straightforward, and she hoped that I would see it that way. She advised me to be watchful of cheaters and to be strong enough to ask students not to disrupt the learning process. She ended by suggesting that cutting out the undesirable things she mentioned would help my future teaching.

I still have this note, and throughout my 40 years of teaching, I have read it several times. I am sure that Sandi B. wrote the note, but I am not sure that she actually gave it to me herself. It was folded multiple times, and on the back of it are the words "Mr. Walrond. Could you please give it to him." I think she may have given it to someone else to give to me. At least, that seems to have been the plan. Of course, she may have changed her mind at the last moment and given it to me personally.

In any event, I don't remember what Sandi looked like. However, there is no doubt in my mind that this evaluation was the most helpful of all that I have ever received. Over the many years of my teaching career, I came to remember Sandi as yet another incarnation of my guardian angel.

* * *

Shortly after my first teaching session ended, I underwent my knee surgery. For a few weeks afterwards, I hobbled along on crutches as I went about my courses at the university. My social life here was a lot more relaxed than at McGill. In the student dining hall, there was a group of tables that came to be designated the International Corner. I soon became a member of the group of West Indian and African students who frequented this spot along with our Canadian friends. It was a very busy section of the dining hall as students came and went throughout the day.

One morning as I sat with friends, a young lady came and sat down. She was introduced, and the conversation went on. When I heard her name, my ears perked up. It was a French name, the first I had heard since I left Montreal. I instantly decided that I would like get to know her better. Her rosy cheeks and smiling face indicated an inner beauty that I wanted to know. But very soon after she arrived, she jumped up, saying she had to get to class, and was off.

I too, jumped up and hobbled after her as fast as my one leg and pair of crutches would allow. I called after her, and she stopped and turned around. I caught up to her and held out my right hand, introducing myself. She held out her hand, and I took it in mine and shook it. But then, turning her palm face down, I raised it, bent down, and kissed the back of her hand. She quickly let go of my hand, giggled in embarrassment, and was off like a shot.

I think I made an impression on Beth Moreau. She had certainly made an impression on me.

* * *

My on-campus courses lasted from February to August that year. I was able to spend some time in the Simon Fraser Library doing research on my family name. I found a few books on Trinidad and on the Caribbean area. There was nothing on my name, though. I kept up the process, however, always hoping to find something of interest.

Because my injury had occurred while I was on a job, it was classified as a Workers' Compensation Board case. In early May of 1969, I received a financial offer from the WCB: a lifetime pension of some cents a month or a lump sum cheque of a few thousand dollars. I accepted the latter.

A few weeks later, Brian and I moved into a basement suite in the Marpole area of South Vancouver, between Granville and Oak Streets. South Burnaby was proving too far for Brian to travel on a daily commute to the UBC campus.

In time, a cheque arrived in the mail and was deposited in my bank. One morning in early June, I got on a bus and rode up Granville Street to 41st Avenue. I entered the Brown Brothers Ford dealership and began looking around. I was totally ignored by the salesmen, who stood chatting a few feet away. In disgust, I exited the building, got on another bus, and rode up to Dominion Ford Motors on Seymour Street.

I entered the dealership and began to look around. I was immediately approached by a salesman. One hour later, I drove out in a brand-new 1969 Ford Mustang. It was the Fastback model in Acapulco blue and soon became my pride and delight. My thoughts wandered back to the Ford pavilion at the 1964 New York World's Fair and the newly introduced Ford Mustang. I also remembered the promise I had made to myself during that visit. On my way back to my apartment, as I drove through the intersection of Granville Street and 41st Avenue, I looked over and stuck my tongue out at the Brown Brothers building.

* * *

The rest of the year went by quickly, and all went well. In September, I started a three-month stint of classroom teaching at Lord Byng High School in Vancouver and thoroughly enjoyed myself. My sponsor was a wonderful and very knowledgeable French teacher from Edmonton. I finished off in mid-December with a good mark and by 1 January 1970 was ready to join the teaching profession.

I had finally achieved the first of my objectives of coming to Canada. My tertiary education was successfully concluded. I had previously changed my status from being a student to being a landed immigrant. I received my teaching certificate in the mail and began working as a substitute teacher in the Vancouver School District. One of my first assignments was to fill in for my sponsor teacher from Lord Byng. She was scheduled to have some major surgery and needed a lengthy convalescence, and she had specifically asked for me to take over her classes.

All that spring, I kept watch in the local newspapers for job opportunities. Nothing was listed in the field of languages, although there were certainly a lot of rumours of vacancies in Vancouver and the other surrounding school districts.

Sometime late in May, I found a notice about a vacancy for a teacher of Junior French in Nanaimo. I remembered Nanaimo as being a small, friendly town on Vancouver Island. It was one of the termini of the BC ferry system. I had been through the city several times during my first summer in BC. I also remembered that I had liked the town. I sent in an application and waited. It was my only application.

By the middle of June, it looked as though I was headed for a second stint as a substitute teacher for the Vancouver School Board. One morning, as I lay in the living room of our basement suite, I was startled by a loud noise outside my window. I jumped up and looked out. The culprit was an ancient looking motorcycle. Its rider had dismounted. He was dressed in a military style uniform, complete with a cap with side flaps over his ears and goggles raised over his forehead. As a matter of fact, he reminded me of the dispatch riders featured in the sitcom *Hogan's Heroes*.

The driver made his way to my front door and rang the bell. I answered, and he handed me a small envelope. It was a telegram. He left. I opened envelope. I read the letter. I read it again. I rubbed my eyes and read it a third time. It was a response to the application I had sent to Nanaimo. I was offered the job and was given 48 hours to reply.

It took me less than a minute to phone the number listed and accept the job. I spoke to the principal, and he asked me to come over and see him. Two days later, I took a ferry and arrived at Woodlands Secondary School at lunch time. I met the principal and vice principal and had a short tour of the school, where later that year I began my career as a full-time teacher of French as a second language. I found a two-bedroom apartment and moved my belongings over in August of 1970.

I thoroughly enjoyed my new job, and a deep-seated feeling of satisfaction and achievement overwhelmed me. My students loved me, and I, them. I had no discipline problems and was the envy of most teachers. Before long, though, thoughts of going places began to haunt my soul. It did not help me much when, during my second year as a teacher, I was asked to teach a junior course centered on Tropical Geography. The principal thought that my coming from Trinidad was enough of a qualification.

He was right. I enjoyed myself and even managed to organise a field trip to the McMillan Bloedel Arboretum in Vancouver, which specialised in tropical flora and fauna. The students were amazed and, of course, learned a lot. As for me, the sight of so many tropical plants and birds reminded me in no small way of my childhood and of the various school excursions I went on while a student in the primary classes.

Chapter 4
Memoirs of a Curious Traveller

I was born in Couva, a small town in central Trinidad. One of the most striking aspects of life there was the presence of a large number of what I will call itinerant businesspeople who travelled around on foot or on bicycle, offering their services or products. They were not unlike the modern-day ice-cream vendor who roams the streets of small towns, announcing his arrival with an annoying bell.

Some of these peripatetic salespeople had very individual cries designed to attract the attention of any householder along their chosen routes. One woman sold produce from her garden. These provisions she carried aloft on a tray delicately balanced on her head. Her cry, which could be heard at least two houses away, was a strident "Coming to pass . . . Paaaass-ing! Coming to pass . . . Paaaass-ing!"

Another man rode a bicycle with a large box attached behind his saddle. This was his mobile workshop. His profession was that of a tinker. His cry, intermingled with the tinkling of his bicycle bell, was "Sharpening knives and scissooors! Sharpening knives and scissooors!" He also carried a small blowtorch, which he used to solder metals or mend holes in kitchen utensils. He was my favourite.

The man from whom my mother bought fish and other seafood was named Samundra. He used to buy his stock from the fishermen at Carli Bay, just west of Couva. He would pedal his bicycle to his regular customers. His fish were always very fresh. On one occasion, my mother bought a grouper from him. It was the only one that could feed 11 people, so it was fairly large. I remember this one because it was still alive and flipping, flapping, and flopping around while my mother tried to remove its scales. It was a powerful fish and just would not settle down. Finally, to get the upper hand, she made an incision where she thought the heart would be and took that organ out. All was calm after that.

And then there was the occasional travelling mendicant or professional beggar. My mother always had at least a thick slice of homemade bread and some butter or jam to hand out. Many blessings were showered on her in gratitude.

But the person who most impressed me was the old lady who appeared one day and offered to reveal my mother's fortune — for a price, of course. My mother was not interested, but the lady was persistent. Finally, as I stood around watching and listening, my mother relented and agreed to have the lady reveal my fortune instead of hers.

I was a child of about 6 or 7. The fortune-teller did not have a crystal ball, but she asked my mother to bring her a glass of water and an egg. The fortune-teller cracked the egg and allowed the white to fall into the glass of water. As it settled to the bottom, it spread and formed a milky pattern, which she studied carefully for a minute or two. Then she looked at me and said to my mother, "He will be a traveller."

She was right.

* * *

As a young child, I had two favourite books. One was called *Homes Far Away*. The stories and pictures in it heightened my interest in people and life around the world. The other was my geography book. The first sentence in this volume simply said, "Geography teaches us about the world in which we live." These two books greatly influenced my education and my zeal for travelling the world.

As stated earlier, I began to teach in September 1970. Beth Moreau graduated from Simon Fraser University in June of 1972, and on 29 July, she and I were married. She moved to Nanaimo, where we have lived ever since. Our wedding day was so sunny that even our eyelashes cast shadows on our face.

By the end of my second year of teaching, a certain amount of boredom had settled over my life. Marriage had brought with it a certain amount of impending routine. No wonder then, that in the spring of 1973, on a whim, I got together with the two other French teachers at my school and organised a trip to Paris for a group of 45 students. The travel bug had bitten me again. Beth came along with us as a chaperone. The trip was a lot of fun, and we all learned a lot.

This was the first of seven expeditions that I made with students to England, France, Spain, and Ottawa over the course of my teaching career, the last of which was made in 2001. My conviction that travel and learning can supplement each other had not diminished over the years.

These trips brought together many subjects I had studied in high school: Latin, English, French, Spanish, Geography, and History. For example, my first visit to Paris reminded me that the name of this large city was derived from the *Parisii,* a tribe of locals whom Julius Caesar had encountered on the little island set in the river Seine. That island, called Île de la Cité, is now the very centre of this amazing and dynamic city. Furthermore, I recognized French, the language that I had studied and now spoke, as a derivative of the Latin that I had also studied and which Caesar and his men spoke. In short, my secondary education was instrumental in allowing me to thoroughly enjoy my travels.

I am happy to say that throughout these journeys, some of the major attractions to me were the different manifestations of Roman influence in many of the towns and regions that I visited throughout France and Spain and England. Also as important as this were the legacies in Britain of the Norman invasion by William the Conqueror.

* * *

My visits to England afforded me a plethora of historical glimpses. It was exciting to stroll around the park at Runnymede and look closely at the display marking where King John had signed the Magna Carta. At Old Sarum, I was able to walk around the mound and ditch that mark the exact site of this old Bronze Age village. The sight of Salisbury Cathedral in the distance was so much more vivid than the picture by John Constable in

Lesson 31 of my fifth standard elementary school reader. It was an education in itself.

My trip to Stonehenge was markedly different from today's visits. In 1974, tourists were allowed to roam all over the site. The very mass of this ancient and mystical location is daunting. I sat on one of the smaller stones to have my picture taken. Tourists are no longer allowed to do this.

Warwick Castle and Windsor Castle have both evolved from forts built by William the Conqueror. The maze in the garden at Hampton Court intrigued us all. These three sites opened my eyes to, among other things, the glory of royalty. I remember taking a most beautiful picture of Windsor Castle from the window of my plane as it turned and banked on its way to London's Heathrow Airport.

At Stratford-upon-Avon, Shakespeare came alive. Once again I saw myself sitting in my classroom reading *Twelfth Night* and *A Midsummer Night's Dream*. My English teacher at Queen's Royal College, Mr. Laltoo, always made Shakespeare and Dickens very interesting. He had an uncanny knack of putting a Trinidadian twist to some of Dickens' descriptions. One instance in particular has remained with me. In Dickens' *A Tale of Two Cities,* the author describes the awakening of the marquis in the town and spends some time describing the little machine that the servant used to mill and froth the morning cup of hot chocolate for the aristocrat. Mr. Laltoo read the little passage just as Dickens would have wanted it read. Then he said, in a most Trinidadian tone, "Ah, a swizzle stick."

On a tour of the Bard's house, I learned of the origin of the expression "sleep tight." In early beds, mattresses were supported on a system of slim ropes strung lengthways and sideways from wooden frames. Pegs were used to keep these ropes in place. However, these ropes would stretch during the night, so every evening, the pegs were turned and the ropes were tightened in order to afford a more comfortable night's rest. (However, there was no explanation of the accompanying expression "Don't let the bedbugs bite." None was needed.)

One of my most memorable adventures took place on the last morning of one of our trips to London. Our bus was due to leave the hotel for the airport just after noon. I told the students that they had one last free morning. They could sleep in, go shopping, or just walk around the neighbourhood. Our hotel was in the Kensington Palace area, so there was a lot to see and do.

I awoke early, had a hurried breakfast, and took the underground to the station nearest to St. Paul's Cathedral. We had visited it earlier in the week, and I was totally attracted to its grandeur, its beauty, and its history. The Whispering Gallery quite amazed me. I simply had to have one last visit to this masterpiece of religious architecture.

My fascination with this building went back to 1954 and perhaps even earlier. Throughout this first visit, I could not help repeating to myself a sentence that we had had to analyse as part of the elementary school English Grammar program. The sentence was something to the effect that "St. Paul's Cathedral, designed and built by Sir Christopher Wren, was partially destroyed by bombs." As an innocent child, I could not help wondering why someone named Bombs would want to destroy a cathedral. It was only many years later that the full story of the Second World War revealed the rest of the cathedral's history.

I got to the cathedral that crisp morning and went in. I made my way up to the Whispering Gallery and walked around it a few times. There were very few visitors at this early hour, so my view of the lower level was magnificent. Having satisfied my curiosity, I was heading for the staircase and eventually the crypt, when, for the first time, I noticed a small door that was open.

I looked around. I was still alone. I slipped through the door and found myself in a narrow, curving passageway. I walked silently but quickly and soon came to a flight of wooden stairs. Up I went, noiselessly. The stairs curved around the wall. At the top of the staircase was another open door through which I passed. Another curving passage led to another flight of stairs, which I climbed.

At this point, I realised that I was climbing up between the inner walls of the great dome, which I had admired from the Whispering Gallery, and the outer shell of the dome that was visible from the streets below. My excitement at this point knew no limits. I continued upwards and around to one more door. Through this door was a very narrow circular veranda protected by a low balcony on my right. Looking upwards, on my left I instantly recognised the lantern that sits atop St. Paul's Cathedral. I was at the very top of this magnificent church, 279 feet above the streets below. There was no further "up" for me to go.

I turned my attention to the balcony and looked out and over. There, before my eyes, was a large section of London. Laid out before me, as if on a gigantic map, were the streets and parks, the grounds and rooftops of palaces and other large buildings. The smaller buildings seemed to merge into one. It was a dizzying and magnificent view. And it was a quiet one. The early morning sounds of the streets so far beneath me did not, could not, reach my ears. Perhaps later in the day when London was more awake, the situation would be different.

I was not to know, because all the while I was bothered by the prospect that some guard on duty so far below me would discover the first open door I had entered and close it. I took one last look at the city before me and literally raced down the several flights and corridors that separated me from safety. Not till I was once again in the Whispering Gallery did I take a deep breath.

I went slowly down to the main floor. There, under the dome, lies the tomb of Sir Christopher Wren. On it is inscribed this epitaph:

Si monumentum requiris, circumspice. [If you are looking for his monument, look around you.]

Terse and precise, it was eloquent in its simplicity.

* * *

I have always been intrigued by the activities of the Romans. Reading the works of Horace, Caesar, Virgil, Livy, and Ovid has enlightened me, establishing and sustaining my interest in things Mediterranean, especially Roman.

I have had the good fortune to visit, with students, several of the countries of the northern shore of the Mediterranean Sea. On one occasion, after walking the cold and rain-soaked streets of Madrid for a few days, I found respite in enjoying two sun-filled days in Toledo, a walled city founded by Bronze Age inhabitants but rebuilt by the Romans, who called the city Toletum. On my return trip to Madrid, as the train rolled over the plains of La Mancha, I could not help thinking of the poor, unfortunate Don Quixote.

On this visit to Europe, we spent a few days in Barcelona. This is another city on the Mediterranean founded over 2,000 years ago by the Romans. On my first morning there, the sun had come up amid a blaze of gold and yellow, and its rays had crept in between the folds of the drapes that hung loosely over the windows of my hotel room. The brightness roused me, and I got up intending to close the curtains so I could steal a few more moments of sleep. Instead, I opened the drapes and gazed in wonder at the deep blue Mediterranean as it shimmered in the brilliant morning light. I stood for a few minutes, enjoying the scene before me. Although it was not my first glimpse of the Mediterranean, it was the most beautiful.

Later that morning, as I toured the city, I was awestruck by the art and architecture of Antoni Gaudí. Evidence of his talent was everywhere. Construction of his basilica, the Sagrada Família, was begun in 1882, and at the time of my visit in 2002, still under construction. It looked like an enormous prop from a science-fiction movie. Its beauty and symbolism are second to none in the modern world.

I have visited Carcassonne several times. The Visigoths developed this walled city in the south of France over a fortification established by the Romans. The turrets, walls, and drawbridge of this medieval city transported me to another age. After lunch one day, I sat on the green grass just inside the walls across the drawbridge. I fell asleep and dreamt of ancient times. On another visit, our guide took us down to an underground chamber that used to be part of a Roman house. The tiled floors and painted frescoes in this ancient room were a treasure to behold. Not many visitors to Carcassonne get to see this. I felt very privileged indeed.

A visit to Avignon and the Palace of the Popes made me recall the rift in the Catholic Church. The building is now a museum set in a beautiful hillside garden. A gentle climb up the hill behind the Palace allows visitors to look over a low wall and see the fabled Pont d'Avignon. I walked to the end of this bridge and was amazed at the power of the Rhône as its waters sped by. The strength of the current accounts for the erosion of more than half of this bridge. Almost overcome by vertigo — the bridge had no rails — I hurried back to safer ground.

On another occasion, as my train crawled through the city of Marseilles, I caught a glimpse of the remains of the Château d'If lying alone and sombre in the bay, both made famous in Dumas' novel *The Count of Monte Cristo*. The sight of the Château made me shiver. Marseilles had already been an ancient city by the time the Romans came along.

In Nîmes, I walked the arena, built 2,000 years ago by the Romans. It is now used for concerts and is still the venue for the odd bullfight. My visions of bloodstained Romans being butchered by animals made me glad to leave. It was intriguing to note, though, that the exit was justly labeled "VOMITORIUM." Romans sure had a way with words.

At Arles, I had a scary visit to the darkened underground passages formed by the stone supports of an enormous public building. These were also of Roman origins. The arena in this city was smaller and less impressive than the one at Nîmes. Nonetheless, it excited my imagination.

I was able to use the ancient water channel to walk across what is now called the Pont du Gard. It was built by the Romans early in the first century to supply water to the nearby city. At its inception, it was not really a bridge but part of an elaborate and lengthy siphon.

I enjoyed walking along the Promenade des Anglais in Nice, that charming and expensive city where I enjoyed my very first view of the Mediterranean. Looking over the parapet to see if there were any *nudistes* enjoying the sun was an interesting activity in futility. The weather was far too chilly. I was pleasantly surprised, though, while visiting another part of the city, to come upon the Russian Orthodox Cathedral at the end of a long driveway, almost hidden from the street by numerous palm trees and a high hedge of flowering shrubs. The cathedral looked almost out of place, but it is of great historical importance. It was closed to the public, so I did not get to see the inside.

At the hilltop town of Eze, I was amused at the welcoming poster that bade visitors, "Mettez-vous à Eze" (Put yourself at Eze). On a second visit there, I decided to visit the Jardin Exotique. This garden was even higher up the hill than the town, and it was filled with cacti and many other beautiful plants and flowers that thrived in the hot, dry climate of the hilltop. Walking around, I suddenly came upon the ruins of a 12th-century castle that was ordered destroyed by Louis XIV in 1706.

On a visit to Saint-Paul de Vence, another hilltop city, I had a chance to peek into the garden of the world-famous restaurant La Colombe d'Or. It was in this establishment that well-known but impoverished artists paid for their meals by hanging paintings on the walls. These works of art are still there, now worth considerably more than the meals they originally covered.

On one of several trips to Monaco, I was able to visit the Palace of Prince Rainier and watch the changing of the guards. I also visited the cathedral and was warned not to walk on the crypt where Princess Grace is buried. This city is also famous for the huge aquarium, managed for a time by Jacques Cousteau.

Walking into the Casino de Monte-Carlo with a couple of friends was an embarrassing experience. They were told to leave immediately — their runners had too many colours. I was allowed to go into the first room and no further — my shoes were all black leather. Once outside again, we all three walked into the Hôtel de Paris across the boulevard. This had even stranger results. No sooner had we entered than we were approached by a young employee who instructed us to turn around and leave. His voice did not permit any discussion, so we just obeyed.

Out on the street, I said to my friends, "I didn't mind being thrown out of there, you know."

"What do you mean?"

"Well," I answered, "I'm not a snob."

One trip across the border into Italy was rather different. We visited an outdoor market in the seaside town of San Remo. It was a crowded, cacophonous affair that, I was told, would be gone the next day. I was gone by evening. The beach, though covered in parts with boats of many colours, was more relaxing and pleasant.

Back in France, at Cannes, I once sat on the promenade and looked at the beautiful yachts and sailboats moored in the marinas. These moorage basins, found throughout the Mediterranean, are large and numerous.

Standing on the promenade at Cannes, I turned inland to study the architecture of this historically rich city. My eyes were immediately drawn to a tower that rose against the skyline like a small, square Cleopatra's Needle. I decided to find it. I set out, keeping my eyes on it but following the twists and turns of a city whose streets I did not know. Soon I began to climb. The terrain got steeper and steeper. After what I thought was a long while, I came to a small park. How far above sea level I was I did not know. I was glad to enjoy the shade of its trees and the beauty of the flowers.

Through the park was a paved pathway that zigzagged its way upwards. I, too, went onwards and upwards. Finally, I came to a level area that looked much like a large parking lot, although there was only one vehicle in it. Across this paved area was a wall with a massive iron gates set into it. The gates were open, and a plaque on the wall indicated that behind it was the

Castre Museum. I walked through the opening, and there in the compound was the now very tall and massive square tower I had spied from the waterfront. It was part of the museum. Thinking of benches and washrooms, I paid the price and entered.

I was asked to remove my knapsack, for fear I would bump into items. I saw displays of countless bits of pieces of ancient pottery, prehistoric mostly. Images of similar displays at the Louvre and at the British Museum in London flooded my mind. I was just getting bored with it all when I passed through a set of narrow doors into a long, fairly narrow room. I stood in amazement. Along each wall, hanging in a somewhat haphazard fashion, were ancient musical instruments. They looked as though they had been made up by amateur musicians.

I believe these instruments were used by musicians who travelled the Silk Roads of China. On such a long journey, if an instrument got broken or somehow needed mending, repairmen, called *luthiers*, were available along the way. If an instrument was too far damaged, the repairman would keep it in exchange for another. It was kept and later repaired as parts became available, or it was used as a source of parts to repair other instruments. Nothing was thrown away. Sometimes a completely new instrument would eventually evolve. I was reasonably sure that what I was looking at in this museum were examples of the result of such ingenuity and skill.

* * *

I am sure that over the years, these visits to Europe and those to many other parts of the world have done a lot to sustain my interest in the history of places, architecture, people, and above all, names, especially my own.

These trips were all designed to be learning experiences for my students. On the long journey back to Vancouver, I got into the habit of asking them to quietly write in my log book a personal retrospective of their experiences. In their writings, all the students remarked on how much they learned and how much fun they had. I felt that I had achieved my objectives.

The effects of these trips were far-reaching and in many cases totally unexpected. For example, one parent met me after our return and said, "Mr. Walrond, I don't know what you did, but thank you. I have been after

Tracy to clean up her room for years. She just ignored me. Two days after she returned from the trip, she cleaned up her room. Thank you."

Another girl quietly took in all she could on our trip. It was her first experience as a traveller. She was well-behaved and curious about a lot of things. A year or two after she graduated from senior high school, she opened her own travel agency, which she operated successfully for many years.

Yet another student, whom I considered a bit of a lost soul, had a different outcome. Previously, he had travelled to Denmark with his parents. Yet throughout our visit, I found I had to constantly rein him in and ask him to stay with the group. He had a tendency to try to wander off on his own. A few years after our return, I met his father and was told that his son had signed up with the Danish Merchant Marine Union and had been put on a waiting list. One day, he received a call for active duty, and he was off like a bullet. He ended up becoming a radio officer aboard ship and had a really interesting life. It turned out he had just wanted to get away from his domineering parents, and his trip with me was a personal trial to see whether he could survive being on his own. The last thing I heard, he was living the life of a businessman in San Francisco.

* * *

One of the most revealing trips I have ever undertaken was during the summer of 1974, two years after Beth and I were married. This year marked the tenth anniversary of my leaving for Canada. Beth and I landed in Trinidad on the first of July. It was her first visit to my homeland, and it was my first visit since 1964.

We spent a wonderful five weeks there, visiting family and friends enjoying the now almost-unfamiliar sights of this wonderful island. Of course, a trip to Tobago was also included. It was my first visit to this sister island and one that we both thoroughly enjoyed.

Early in August, we left Trinidad for a three-week trip through the top of South America and through Central America. I had long wanted to make such a journey. An early-morning departure landed us unexpectedly on the island of Curaçao. After a long, unexplained wait there, we went on to Caracas, Venezuela, for a short visit.

I had always wanted to visit Caracas, but I never expected it to be such a sprawling city. Set in the bottom of a huge bowl, Caracas spread out in all directions, up the sides of the mountains that encircled it. The beautiful and well-maintained parks were surrounded by tall skyscrapers. Caracas impressed both of us because it was the first city we had visited where every street corner was protected by at least two soldiers armed with machine guns. No wonder it was such a peaceful city. We were also both impressed by the beauty of the people there. Sadly, after four days, we had to move on.

Our next stop was Panama City. The big attraction there was, of course, the canal. We travelled by train to Colón. The rail line was built to service the construction of the canal. From our carriage window, we had many wonderful views of the waterway. Being able to catch glimpses of huge oceangoing freighters through lush, tropical vegetation was at first very strange. We returned to Panama City by bus. We visited the Mira Flores Locks and watch in amazement as small electric tractors pulled large boats through the locks to be floated up or down the different levels of the canal.

Two days later we arrived in Managua, Nicaragua. This city had been decimated by a massive earthquake two years earlier, and I was curious to see how it was recovering and rebuilding. Although much of the debris had been cleared away, reconstruction had not yet begun. The city looked almost deserted. Although many of the more modern skyscrapers were still standing, they were badly damaged and not in use. Amazingly enough, the old cathedral was still standing, almost intact. One hotel, built in the form of a pyramid, had suffered no damage at all. Perhaps the local aboriginals did have a better idea of how to erect buildings that would last.

Guatemala was our next stop. I had always wanted to see things Mayan, and we were not disappointed. We visited the market town of Chichicastenango, where ancient Mayan religious customs had melded with Catholic rites to create a unique blend of spiritual and religious ceremonies. Nowhere was this union more striking than in the Spanish-built church that overlooked the square where the vendors displayed their wares.

Inside the church, all but a few of the pews had been removed. Those that were left were used by the elders and tourists like ourselves. The other locals sat cross-legged in family circles on the floor, as was their custom. They burnt candles and incense as they prayed. The smoke and the scent lifted their prayers to their God on high. This custom was so old that the entire inner walls and ceiling of the church were blackened by the omnipresent soot and smoke. Whatever icons and statues that hung on the walls or stood on tables suffered the same fate. It was the most amazing image of religious tolerance I have ever seen.

On the way to Chichicastenango, I had noticed many Mayans walking to the market. They were all laden with whatever goods they hoped to sell. What struck me was the fact that most of these travellers had strung one or both of their shoes around their necks. While some walked barefoot, others wore both shoes. I questioned the guide, and he explained as follows:

> When they start off, they wear both shoes. When their feet start to hurt, they take one shoe off. That foot hurts a bit more than the other, or put another way, one foot hurts less than the other. But they keep going, for they have a long way to go. After a while, they change shoes and keep going. Or they may take both shoes off, then some distance further on put them both on again. Soon they reach their destination, where they can sit and rest. All pain is forgotten. It all has to do with the transfer of pain.

Our visit to Lake Atitlan was exciting. This mountain lake, surrounded by three dormant volcanoes, was a pristine body of water. Our guide spoke in glowing terms of its purity. The lake, which occupies a caldera formed over 84,000 years ago, has been called the most beautiful lake in the world.

Our final stop on this three-week odyssey was Mexico City. We spent a wonderful nine days there. Our most informative visit was to the ancient Nahuatl city of San Juan Teotihuacán, which means "Place of the Gods." We climbed to the top of the larger Pyramid of the Sun and were able to see the ruins of the entire city. The Pyramid of the Moon lay some distance off.

In Mexico City, we took in a performance of the Ballet Folklórico de México at the Palacio de Bellas Artes. We walked the Zócalo, reputed to be the largest public square in all of Latin America. And we enjoyed a visit to Chapultepec Park with its castle, a miniature version of Versailles in France. The Latin-American Tower was intriguing. Because Mexico City is situated on the dried-up bed of a huge lake, the ground isn't stable. This tall tower is built on huge waterproof caissons located deep below ground level. This allows the tower to sway in the event of an earthquake. I would not like to experience this.

Beth and I had a wonderful two months of travel and learning. My most enduring realization was that throughout all these countries, the aboriginals whom we saw or spoke to were all descendants of people who had streamed out of Asia across the Bering Land Bridge thousands of years ago. They had walked down the Rocky Mountain Trench and fanned out over the vast North American plains and prairies. They funnelled themselves through the Isthmus of Panama and down into Mexico and South America.

Whether they are known today as Caribs, Arawaks, Kunas, Mayans, Aztecs, Toltecs, Olmecs, Incas, or any of the many other names they bear, they are all descendants of people who migrated in search of something better. This search is and has always been a strong motivating force for people to move about the surface of the earth. We sometimes tend to forget this. This concept of movement for self-improvement is still prevalent today, and it is a feeling that I have always espoused and practiced.

* * *

With the exception of three more trips to Europe in the late 1980s, all of these journeys took place between 1972 and 1979. My wife and I also travelled to Hawaii and across Canada during this time.

Our son André was born on 24 October 1979, and we all visited Trinidad and New Orleans in 1980. Our daughter Larissa was born in September 1981. After Larissa's birth, our travelling days were over for a while. Our next overseas trip was in 1987 when we all went to Trinidad to celebrate my parents' 50th wedding anniversary.

As our children grew up and we began to travel together, I made sure to let them know that the world is an interesting place and that they should strive to see as much of it as they could. So far, André has visited Germany and Egypt. Larissa has spent time in Belgium as an exchange student, and she once had an exciting holiday in London.

Larissa also lived in Nova Scotia for a few years, and when she graduated with a bachelor of fine arts degree from NSCAD (Nova Scotia College of Art and Design) University in Halifax in 2005, we all were there to help her celebrate. Beth and I flew back to Vancouver, but Larissa and André drove her car from Halifax to Nanaimo. They spent ten days learning firsthand about Canada. Our friends were amazed that they did not fight with each other. It was a most engaging way for them both to end their university education.

Chapter 5
My Quest Ends

By early 1971, I was able to find the time to renew my search for information about my family name. With regard to my research, I had previously decided that the first thing that I had to do was find the link between the English Walronds and the Trinidadian Walronds. I had already realised that the name was English. I also knew that the transatlantic African slave trade, which had started around 1500 and lasted for 300 years, would certainly have a lot to do with the history of my name.

At first, my method of research was simple, almost primitive. But it was all that I had at my disposal. I would go into the history section of a library, select what seemed a likely title, and turn to the index at the back of the book. There I would seek the word "Walrond." If the name was not there, I would select another book and repeat the process.

Sometimes, before replacing the book, I would scan the chapter headings for any other perhaps relevant links. I had used this process at the McGill University library and at the Simon Fraser University library. At the former, I had found nothing. At the latter, I managed to find one book on the general history of Trinidad.

Now, I began this process at the Nanaimo library. It was housed in a rather small building, and not surprisingly, I had no success. Then I found out that there was a new branch on the north end of the town. This was an even smaller building. Undaunted, I went in and began looking around.

The books at these two libraries were rotated with books from other branches of the Vancouver Island Regional Library system. The region included other towns up and down Vancouver Island. With this in mind, I never gave up. Different titles would show up from time to time.

When I was beginning to lose heart, I expanded the limits of my research. It was now late 1974, or perhaps early 1975. I began to look at books dealing with history in general and Caribbean history in particular rather than just the history of Trinidad. In one of these more general books, I finally found the name Walrond. The name of the book was *History of the British West Indies* by Sir Alan Burns. The index referred me to page 234. I found it and read, "Such a man was Colonel Humphrey Walrond, a fanatical Royalist who gained considerable political influence in Barbados within a few years."

I could hardly contain my elation. The information that had eluded me for ten years was suddenly revealed to me in the most unsuspected place: a small branch of a regional library in the smallest Canadian town I had lived in. The moments of hopelessness that I had experienced now melted into insignificance.

In an instant, my mind went back to when, as a toddler, I had lived for a short time with my parents and my older siblings at my grandmother's house in the Curepe area of Trinidad. As I sat down at a table in a corner of the library in Nanaimo, I could almost hear my grandmother speaking with her strong *Barbadian* accent. Then I remembered that my father had told me in 1964, before I left Trinidad, that his parents and an uncle had in fact moved to Trinidad from Barbados. I checked the book out, for I needed to make some notes.

I knew then and there that I was on the right track. I simply had to double my efforts and find other libraries to visit. I even began to search through unlikely volumes. One day, in the same small library, I almost absentmindedly opened a book entitled *The Domesday Book: England's Heritage Then and Now*, edited by Thomas Hinde.

To this day, I cannot say what moved me to select this volume. Perhaps it was because although I had heard of the Domesday Book, I had only a vague idea of what it was all about. I suppose my motivation was more idle curiosity than a thirst for knowledge.

I turned, out of habit, to the index, looking for "Walrond." I did not really expect to find it. Imagine my surprise, however, when I did see the name Waleran and a reference to page 18. There I read the rather enigmatic commentary to the effect that "Waleran the Forester had substantial estates in Southern England." The name Waleran was too close to my family name to be ignored. My name had on occasion been spelt *Walerond,* so this reference definitely warranted further investigation.

Years went by. Years in which I added the Victoria Public Library to my list of possible sources of information. I eventually added the Vancouver Public Library after it was moved to Georgia Street. There I found several books that contained information about Colonel Humphrey Walrond and the history of Barbados. I photocopied pages and listed books and Dewey decimal code numbers, and I came home quite content.

My pile of information was growing. I now had two points of departure: One was the name Waleran in the Domesday Book, and the other was Humphrey Walrond who arrived in Barbados in 1649. Several questions occurred to me, especially with regard to Humphrey. I very much wanted to know, for example, what the term *Royalist* signified, why he was fanatical about being one, and above all how this fanaticism manifested itself. (I have to mention that in secondary school, my study of English history covered only the period of 1688 to 1815 — or as we called it, from William of Orange to Waterloo. This explains why I was so interested in the information I was slowly uncovering; it was all new to me.

In the early 1980s, my chances of success were suddenly and greatly enhanced by technology. The personal computer was introduced, and along with it came the Internet. The entire world was now at my fingertips. Henceforth I could move ahead at incredible speed.

Further investigation of the Domesday Book and the name Waleran led me to William the Conqueror. The more I read, the more interested I became. I soon came to understand that historical events of which I knew little or nothing had impacted the life of Humphrey Walrond.

I set myself the task of finding out all I could, and I discovered a lot of incidents, events, people, and places that at first seemed unconnected but in reality were closely linked and deeply impacted the lives of several people named Walrond. My curiosity, although satisfied in some respects, grew greater in others.

Once my pages of information had increased to the point where I could start writing this book, it was difficult to decide what to include and what to leave out. I was ever mindful of the fact that some readers would be more informed than others, especially myself. In the end, I included only those facts that lent themselves to my telling a cohesive and interesting story that helped fulfill my objective.

Considering the fact that my fellow student at McGill had asked me about my family name in 1964 and that it was now 1975, I had to conclude that ten years was indeed a long time to hold onto a dream. I now looked forward to having cogent answers to a lot of questions. For example, my knowledge of William the Conqueror was limited to what I had learned: that he came from Normandy in France, invaded England, killed King Harold at the Battle of Hastings in 1066, and founded the Norman dynasty. I simply had a lot more to learn.

Part II: The Walrond Name

Chapter 6
Hunstman Waleran and
the Domesday Book

In my research, I soon realised that William, Duke of Normandy, had played a pivotal part in the establishment in England of the name Walrond. Without him and his activities in England, there would be no story to tell. Besides, the story of his invasion of England was intriguing in itself.

William was the illegitimate son of Robert, Duke of Normandy, and Herleva of Falaise (a commune of Normandy, France). He was born in 1027 at the castle Château de Falaise. His mother eventually married Merlin of Conteville and had two more sons, Odo of Bayeux and Robert of Mortain. These two half-brothers were destined to play an important role in the life of William.

Duke Robert realised that William's illegitimacy would pose some problems in his acceptance as successor when the duke died. In 1035, Robert gathered his lords together and forced them to swear fealty to William. Later that same year, Robert died, and William inherited his father's title under the guardianship of some of the most faithful Normans. However, much as Robert had suspected, many barons, despite their sworn oath, still refused to accept a bastard as their leader, and several attempts were made on the young duke's life. In fact, during these attempts, his three most faithful guardians were murdered in quick succession.

William survived and eventually assumed his role as ruler of Normandy in 1045. Still, he faced constant opposition. In 1047, for example, he had to crush a rebellion at Val-ès-Dunes. But this was only the first of many such uprisings that he had to suppress. At Alençon, he had the limbs of some townsfolk amputated because they had insulted him by hanging some hides over a wall (his mother was the daughter of a tanner).

Slowly but surely, William gained control of his dukedom. In 1051, William was secure enough to visit his cousin King Edward of England. William claimed that during that visit, he was offered the throne of England.

In 1053, William married Matilda of Flanders, daughter of Count Baldwin V of Flanders. Though tumultuous at the beginning, this union was fruitful, and they had nine children over the next 16 years.

In 1064, Harold of Wessex, son of King Edward, was aboard a ship that was wrecked off the coast of Ponthieu in France. Harold was captured by Count Guy and placed in prison. William had Harold released into his care, and they both went to Rouen, France, where they engaged in battle against Conan II, Duke of Brittany. After the battle, William knighted Harold. During the ceremony, Harold swore that he would help William to become king when his father Edward died.

This event was timely. Edward died on 5 January 1065. However, Harold claimed that on his deathbed, Edward had promised him the throne. The next day, the Witan, made up of about 60 lords and bishops, decided that Harold was to be crowned the next king of England. When William objected and reminded Harold of his promise, Harold responded that he felt duty-bound to follow the wishes of the Witan, whose job, after all, was to determine who should rule England.

William's reaction was to prepare to invade England and claim by force what had been promised him. He also sought and eventually obtained blessings from Pope Alexander II. While William was organising and building his invasion fleet of ships, supplies, and men, Harold's brother Tostig was making plans of his own to seize the crown of England. He tried at first to team up with William but was not successful. Tostig then went to Norway and plotted with King Hardrada to invade England and seize the throne in an alliance.

In September 1066, Tostig and Hardrada landed in England. After burning the city of Scarborough, they sailed up the Humber and captured York. Harold heard of the invasion by the Norwegians and immediately marched north to do battle. He surprised the two invaders at Stamford Bridge, where they were resting with their soldiers.

Harold's army made short work of the invaders. Both Tostig and Hardrada were killed, and the Norwegians fled back home. Only 25 of the original fleet of 300 ships returned to Norway.

While Harold was busy in the north of England, William completed his preparations for invasion. His plans included engaging many barons and knights to accompany him. This was easily accomplished with promises of English land as rewards. He also prebuilt and then dismantled several forts and loaded them aboard some of his ships. The remaining vessels carried horses, food, and other necessities of war.

About 700 ships were ready to sail, but William had to wait for favourable winds before he could cross the channel. Finally, he was able to depart on the evening of 27 August. Early the next morning, he landed at Pevensey Bay and built a fortified camp at nearby Hastings. He next spent some time raiding the countryside.

When Harold heard about William's landing, he quickly marched his forces south from Stamford Bridge. In fact, he moved so rapidly that some of his men could not keep up with him. He arrived in London on 5 October and waited for the rest of his soldiers to arrive.

When the soldiers still had not arrived, Harold left London and took up a position at the top of Senlac Hill near Hastings. William and his army occupied the bottom of the slope. Both sides were heavily armed and ready for action. The battle was not long in starting. At 9:00 in the morning of 14 October, the Norman archers walked up Senlac Hill and fired their first volley at the English.

If it were not sad that men and horses were being killed, this battle could be described as a comedy of errors. But war was as serious then as it is now. When the Normans fired their first arrows, the English simply raised their shields and protected themselves. The Normans were forced to retreat down the hill.

The elated English charged down the hill behind the retreating Normans. William ordered his men to turn and fight. This strategy was very effective. The English suffered severe losses as they ran back up the hill. There was then a pause in the fighting while the opposing sides removed the dead and wounded — men and horses — from the field.

At about 1:00 in the afternoon, the battle resumed. At this point, William ordered his archers to aim their arrows high into the air. This tactic surprised the English, especially since it was followed by an uphill cavalry charge by the Normans. Both sides again suffered many casualties, including Harold's two brothers, Gyrth and Leofwine. The English line held fast, though, and the Normans again decided to retreat down the hill.

Once more the English broke ranks and chased them down the hill. William again ordered his men to turn and attack the English. For a second time, this tactic worked. The English suffered severe casualties, and a rest was called.

When the fight resumed, William changed tactics once more. Because many of his horses had been killed, he ordered his men to dismount and engage the enemy on foot. By this time, the original English line had also been severely diminished. Firing their arrows, the Normans charged up the hill and managed to breach the reduced English formation. By 4:00 in the afternoon, another charge had completely finished the English. Harold and most of his men were killed. Many of the soldiers who survived fled the scene. The Norman invasion of England and the subsequent Battle of Hastings were both successfully concluded.

I was thoroughly impressed by the way in which William planned and executed his mission. He seemed to me a man destined to win and overcome all struggles. His resourcefulness led me to believe that he was a great leader. This character trait proved to be necessary, because his troubles were not yet over.

He next moved to Dover, where he and his men rested for a week. They then went north through Canterbury and on to London. He met resistance wherever he went, in Southwark and even in London. He decided to leave London for a while. He marched through Surrey, Hampshire, and Berkshire, ravaging the countryside.

He then returned to London, where the people, now in the middle of a devastated landscape, were ready to submit to him. This plan of striking fear into the dissidents worked, as he knew it would. He had previously used this technique in 1053 while asserting his power in Maine, a section of Normandy.

On 25 December 1066, William was crowned King of England at Westminster Abbey by Aldred, Archbishop of York. Norman rule of England had started. It lasted till 1154. Although his mission was accomplished, his work as sovereign was just beginning.

* * *

In 1067, William left London and began travelling through England. He had several objectives in mind. As he went along, he built castles where he thought them necessary. He also spent time putting down rebellions and establishing law and order.

Armed resistance to William continued until 1071, when he defeated Hereward the Wake and his men on the Isle of Ely. To effect this triumph, William had to construct a pontoon bridge that enabled him and his Normans to reach the island refuge and overcome the rebels. The defeat of Hereward marked the end of both the Norman Invasion of England and of resistance to the new king.

Another objective of William's travels through England was to fulfill his promise of distributing land to those barons who had helped him defeat Harold at Hastings. To effectively accomplish this, William introduced a version of the French feudal system into England. One of the big differences, however, was that he did not grant one large piece of land to each of his barons. Instead, he gave each one several pieces of land in different and very often distant parts of England. The forward-thinking William did this in order to remove even the remotest possibility of any one baron secretly raising an army in opposition to William.

The new king started by distributing the lands and estates of the Saxon lords who had fought and died at the battle of Hastings. Of course, this caused some resentment and resistance among the remaining Saxons, who had hoped to inherit the land of the dead lords. This resistance led to more confiscations, and a cycle of appropriation and redistribution was established.

This distribution of land took about six years to complete. It was so effective that from 1072 until 1204, King William and his successors were for the most part absentee rulers, preferring to spend more time in Normandy. Obviously, the new Norman barons were happy with the system of land distribution used by King William.

In 1067, William returned to Normandy, leaving his half-brother Odo of Bayeux and William Fitz Osbern as co-rulers of England. William returned to England only to help put down rebellions and build castles, notably in Exeter, Durham, and other key cities. The famous Tower of London was one of his earliest English castles. Windsor Castle and Warwick Castle in their early incarnations were also of his creation.

After the Battle of Hastings, the social face of England changed forever. The transfer of land ownership was only one facet of this alteration. Another was the disappearance of the Old English language, which had been spoken for many years. It was replaced by what has been called Anglo-Norman. This was a dialect of Old French, which in turn had its base in Latin. Needless to say, for a while there must have been a certain amount of bilingualism as the two cultures gradually evolved through intermingling and intermarriage. Even the Church of England was reorganised. By the end of 1070, only two English bishops were left in place.

The Norman invasion was without a doubt the most important event to change the nature of English life. The significance of this event has been recorded for posterity on what is now known as the Bayeux Tapestry. This artifact is an embroidered work of art. Measuring over 230 feet in length, it is only 20 inches from top to bottom. Artisans used coloured wool on linen fabric to create more than 50 scenes recounting the events leading up to and including the Battle of Hastings and the death of Harold, Earl of Wessex. These scenes were then stitched together to make up the length of the "tapestry." It was made in England in the late 1700s and was re-discovered in the Bayeux Cathedral in 1729. Some historians call it the first comic strip ever made.

The Bayeux Tapestry is not the only tangible and important evidence of the coming of the Normans to England. The other is the Domesday Book. In 1085, 19 years to the month after his coronation as king, a very worried William held his Christmas court in Gloucester. After 19 years of settlement, redistribution of lands, and construction of castles, things were still not as he would have liked them to be. One of his major concerns was the opposition that he still faced. This was evident in the fact that Cnut of Denmark was contemplating an invasion of England.

To add to his problems, William's treasury was almost depleted. He wanted to know what financial support and loyalty he could count on in the event of a war with the Danes. He had granted extensive lands to only a relatively small number of barons, friends, companions, and other followers.

But these supporters controlled a large number of vassals, who in turn owed allegiance to their lords. The lands that were held in trust to William were scattered all over England. William wanted to know exactly what he owned as king and what the value was of all these possessions.

William carefully considered these points and ordered that a written survey be made of the lands in the counties, or shires, of England. To accomplish this, he sent men all over England to each shire. They were charged with finding out the size and value of each piece of property as well as the size and value of all livestock.

The survey resulted in what became known as the Domesday Book. This name, "The Day of Judgment Book," was applied because in the event of an appeal to it (in a court of law, for example), its content was to be considered to be set in stone. Any decision based on the book was irrevocable. Its information could neither be ignored nor challenged. Written in abbreviated Latin — a sort of shorthand — it has become a source of legal precedence and has been consulted within the reign of Queen Elizabeth II.

The survey was completed in seven months. In August 1086, the two volumes of the Domesday Book were presented to William. It is generally accepted that this extensive survey was commissioned so that William would know where he should look if and when he needed to raise funds. Once William knew who his main landowners were and how much they controlled, he called them together in Salisbury. There he made them swear a new oath of allegiance to him.

The information contained in the Domesday Book is still considered sacrosanct. It was collected by men of high rank, usually bishops or even dukes. The clerks who copied the data were invariably monks. All information was presented to the commissioners by sheriffs, reeves, or priests from the different areas being surveyed.

More than 13,000 names and places are listed in the Domesday Book. Waleran and his holdings are prominent among them.

In 1087, soon after William returned to Normandy, he heard that he had been insulted by King Philip of France. It was reported that Philip had described William, who had put on a lot of weight, as looking pregnant. William wasted no time. In a fit of anger, he attacked Mantes, a city in Philip's territory. He captured the town and burnt it.

After the battle, William was riding triumphantly through the smouldering ruins of the city and was thrown from his horse. Apparently, the horse did not much like walking through burning rubble. William suffered severe internal injuries and was taken to the convent of St. Gervais in Rouen, the Norman capital. There he bequeathed England to his son Rufus, who became King William II. William the Conqueror died on 9 September and was buried in St. Stephen's Monastery at Caen, Normandy.

* * *

The story of William the Conqueror and his creation of the Domesday Book was the background against which I was able to piece together the story of Waleran Venator. His name occurs several times in the venerable volume. The name is Latin for "Waleran the Huntsman," or "Huntsman Waleran."

Waleran now has many accepted variations of spelling. These include Waldram, Waldren, Waldron, and Walrond. Before the invention of the printing press, sound was all that mattered. Correct spelling was not yet an accepted prerequisite for communication, which was all oral.

The surname Waleran originated in the 7th century. It is believed to be derived from the Old German name Wala-hram. The literal translation of this name is "wall raven." Some historians believe that a likely interpretation of the name would be "strong bird," because walls are associated with strength, and the raven, as an icon of heraldry, is noted for its wisdom and mental agility. Some call this attribute "trickery." (I find it mildly amusing that a 7th-century German name that was inspired by a black bird, albeit a cunning one , should one day become associated with men and women who originated in Africa, known for many years as the Dark Continent.)

Waleran Venator is said to have been born in Wurzburg, Germany, in about 1039. Although the name Waleran may have been introduced into Saxon Britain as early the 8th century, the first recorded spellings are not found there until after the 1066 Norman invasion. This brings me back to the Domesday Book and some of the references to Waleran Venator.

The most interesting reference, to my mind, is the one that lists him as holding the small village of Steeple Langford in the county of Wiltshire. This hamlet contains thatched cottages, several manmade lakes, and a church. Some historians claim that the prefix "Steeple" refers to this church's steeple.

Although its font is Norman, parts of the church are made of stonework and sculptures that pre-date the Norman Conquest.

In 1857, when the chancel of this church was being demolished, a slab of marble was found. Measuring about 14 by 26 inches, it bears an etching of a man wearing a long robe. His hands are upraised, holding something that looks like a shield or receptacle of some sort. Over his left shoulder, he wears a strap from which hangs a horn. This man was at first identified as Waleran Venator, who held land in the parish in the 11th century. Unfortunately this is not a positive identification, yet it still gave me a vision of what Waleran the Huntsman might have looked like.

Here are some of the many references to him in the Domesday Book:

- Richard Jefferies, in his book *A Memoir of the Goddards of North Wilts*, states that Waleran Venator is recorded in the Domesday Book as holding lands at Coteford (Codford); Anestige (Ansty); Butremare (Buttermare); Stanniges (Antsy); Chenete (Kennet); Stanlege; Langeford (Langford). He also held lands at Bereford (Barford); Witford; Gremstede; Watedene; Alwarberie (Alderbury); Duene (Dene); and Herdicote.

- The Codford Parish Council also lists several references to the Domesday Book. Of major interest to my story is the second reference. Here it is, in part only:

- The second Coteford entry is for land held from the King by Waleran Venatoris in 1086, and that Erlebald had held it prior to the Norman Conquest when it had paid tax, usually an equal number of pence to each hide of land. (120 acres). This landholding probably refers to Codford St. Mary, held as East Codford by Oliver de Ingham, a descendant of Waleran.

- According to John Hitchins, the Dorset historian, "of the four ancient manors in Maiden Newton, one was held by Waleran Venator at the time of the Domesday, and by his successors, followed by St. Martin, Lovel, Popham and Rogers families."

Many of the huntsmen recorded in the Domesday Book were of limited responsibility, mostly in charge of local hunting facilities. Hawking and hunting were the principal peacetime pursuits of most kings and their nobles, both before and after the Conquest. Falconers, foresters, and huntsmen were therefore an essential part of the regal entourages and households. Dozens are recorded in the Domesday Book. The Bayeux Tapestry has vivid illustrations of Harold accompanied by his hawks and dogs on his fateful journey to Normandy.

However, a few huntsmen were significant landholders, especially in the royal heartlands of Dorset, Hampshire, Somerset, and Wiltshire. One quotation in *Huntsman* states that "a couple of them — Croc and Waleran — numbered among the few hundred wealthiest men in the kingdom."

West Tytherley is a small village near Romsey in Hampshire. In his book *The King's England*, Arthur Mee describes it as "lying lonely and lovely among the trees [. . .] with the plain 19th century church watching over it from the hill." This town appears in *The Domesday Book* under the name of Teduleg. The lord of the manor is listed as Waleran the Huntsman. That manor house remained in the hands of the Waleran family until the 16th century.

Sutton Waldron is a village in the Blackmore Valley of North Dorset. The Saxon name *Sutton* means "south farm" and refers to a village's position as being south of some well-known place. The addition of "Waldron," a derivative of Waleran, is the name of the huntsman who held the estate at the time of the Domesday Book, 1086.

In *The Domesday Book: England's Heritage Then and Now*, edited by Thomas Hinde, I found no less than 27 references to properties held in trust for the king by Waleran Venator. Another report states that he held 51 manors. There is no doubt in my mind that Waleran was indeed an important and influential follower and companion to William the Conqueror. These lands and domains were his legacy to his descendants.

I was able to find 22 male direct descendants of Waleran Venator within the period of 1066 to 1627. These descendants all inherited some portion of Waleran's domains. The line continues and still exists today; however, I decided to end my research with Colonel Humphrey Walrond. He was born about 1600 and inherited his father's estates in 1621. He was the Walrond who left England for Barbados in 1649. In other words, he was the link I had been looking for.

* * *

In tabulating the list of Waleran Venator's descendants, I noticed that historians invariably listed some of them as living during the reign of the relevant monarch. This indicated to me that the bond between the Walronds and their respective sovereigns remained strong.

I decided therefore to make a list of the sovereigns who ruled England during the same period of time (you can see my results in Appendix D). I started with William I, Duke of Normandy, and ended with Charles I, who ruled until his death in 1649. The coincidence of this year being both the one in which Colonel Walrond left for Barbados and the one in which King Charles I died was too curious to be ignored. I wondered if there was a cause-and-effect connection. A thorough investigation seemed to be in order.

William I died in 1087. His Norman dynasty ended in 1154 with the death of Stephen I. The Plantagenet dynasty followed the Norman and ended with the death of Richard II in 1399. The Houses of Lancaster and York formed the next dynasty of English rule. When Richard III died in 1485, the Tudor dynasty began with Henry VII and ended in 1603 when Elizabeth I died. The Tudors were followed by the Stuarts.

James I was the first Stuart king. He also held the title of James VI of Scotland. He ruled from 1603 to 1626. Charles, the second son of King James I of England and Anne of Denmark, was born in Fife on 19 November 1600. When his older brother, Henry, died in 1612, Charles became heir to England, Scotland, and Ireland. Four years later, on his 16th birthday, he became Prince of Wales.

King James I was a firm believer in the divine right of kings and passed on his beliefs to Charles, who became king on James's death in 1626. From its inception, Charles's reign was one of a constant and continuing conflict between forces loyal to the king and others led by officers who sided with Parliament. Several battles were waged between these opposing armies. Charles's desire to increase royal revenue in order to appease his spending habits was one source of strife. His marriage to a French Catholic was also a cause for concern, as it was seen as a major threat to English Catholicism as instituted by Henry VIII.

Charles became worried by the increasing power of the Puritans in Parliament; these men sought to eliminate the position of bishops within the church. This Puritan desire was another source of discontent. In an attempt to reduce this conflict, Charles dissolved and recalled Parliament several times during his reign. When Parliament was in session, the king was not above using deception and duplicity, intrigues and broken promises in his dealings with the members.

Finally, the king was arrested by Parliament, brought before the High Court of Justice, and charged with high treason against the people of England. He refused to recognise the authority of the court and to answer the charges. Nevertheless, he was found guilty and beheaded outside the Banqueting House at Whitehall on 30 January 1649.

Out of the smoke and mayhem of the battles and skirmishes between King Charles and Parliament, there arose two important figures. The first was Lord Thomas Fairfax of Cameron. In 1639, he commanded a troop of Yorkshire dragoons that marched with King Charles against the Scots in what was called the First Bishops' War. King Charles won this battle. In the Second Bishops' War, in 1640, Fairfax and the Royalist army were routed at the Battle of Newburn. In spite of this defeat, the following year, Thomas Fairfax was knighted by King Charles.

In 1641, the newly knighted Sir Thomas changed sides and joined the Parliamentarians. When the Civil War officially broke out in 1642, Sir Thomas was made lieutenant-general of horse and joined forces with the second figure to emerge from the struggles, Oliver Cromwell. On 2 July 1644, at the decisive battle of Marston Moor, Sir Thomas Fairfax and Oliver Cromwell won the engagement. The Royalists fled the battleground and the City of York. It was not long before almost all of the North of England had submitted to the Parliamentarians.

After the execution of Charles I in 1649, there followed 11 years of national control by Parliament. This rule was called the Commonwealth. During its struggle with Charles I, Parliament had raised its own army, known as *Roundheads*, to help it to achieve its military aims and objectives. These Roundheads were supported by the Puritans. The king's army were called Cavaliers.

As the struggles waged on, Parliament appointed Oliver Cromwell — the hero at the Battle of Marston Moor — to head its army. When he took over control of the army, and therefore the country, he decided that he should be called "Lord Protector" rather than king.

The Civil Wars in England spanned the period from 1642 to 1652. There were victories on both sides of the conflict. In 1642, the Parliamentary regiments that had been fighting all the battles against King Charles were disbanded and replaced by the New Model Army, led by Thomas Fairfax as lord general and by Cromwell as his lieutenant-general and cavalry commander.

It was not long before this new army demonstrated its worth. Lord Fairfax proved his ability and capacity at the decisive victory of Naseby on 14 June 1645. After battles at Leicester, Taunton, Bridgewater, and Bristol, the entire West of England was under the control of Parliament. Of these battles, the one at Naseby is of special importance to my story.

One of the hostages seized by Lord Fairfax after this battle was Humphrey Walrond, who was born about 1600. He succeeded to the family estates and title on 17 February 1621 on the death of his father and became Humphrey Walrond of Sea. When the Civil War broke out in 1642, he sided with the Royalists. He held the rank of Colonel and surrendered to Lord Fairfax on 23 July 1645. His property was seized by Parliament, and he was imprisoned at the Gatehouse of Westminster.

On 28 October 1645, his petition before the Commission of Compounding with Delinquents was granted. This commission had been formed to inquire into the financial, religious, and political affairs of people who were considered delinquents. (A *delinquent* was defined as someone who had fought against Parliament or who had contributed money or other aid to the Royalists against Parliament.) Those found guilty were fined an amount equal to two years' value of their estate.

On 26 June 1646, Walrond was fined £350, was released, and had his estates returned. This committee was hearing another petition to compound from his wife when it was informed that Humphrey Walrond had sold his estates and gone to Barbados. The date was 3 February 1650.

My first reaction was to wonder why Humphrey had thought it necessary to sell his estates and leave the country, and my second was to ask why he selected Barbados as his destination. My original quest for information about my name and a link between England and Barbados now led two new puzzles. The answer to the first question seemed obvious: He did not want to live in a country whose parliament had imprisoned him, seized his estates, and executed the monarch. The second question — that of why he chose to go to Barbados — necessitated a lot more research.

Chapter 7
Westward Bound from the Mediterranean

Throughout history, the progress of humanity has been invariably linked to human movement across the face of the earth. Perhaps Humphrey Walrond was motivated by this impulse as well. My own life so far was proof of the strength of this urge.

It was not long before it became clear to me to that the countries bordering the Mediterranean Sea, as well as the islands that lay in its waters, had played a very significant role in the eventual answer to the question of why Humphrey Walrond went to Barbados.

This large sea was so named because it is located in the center of what was then the known world. Until the construction of the Suez Canal, seagoing access was gained only through the Strait of Gibraltar. Over the years, Carthaginians, Etruscans, Celts, Phoenicians, Greeks, Mesopotamians, Egyptians, and Romans lived in the countries that bordered its shores. These peoples were all travellers. Its waters were and still are peaceful, as over the centuries the many inhabitants of these countries carried on their respective water-borne businesses. The lands that surrounded the sea were not as peaceful though, as the residents invaded and raided each other's lands and settled on their neighbours' territories.

In time, the Romans dominated the area. They even went so far as to rename the sea *Mare Nostrum,* or "Our Sea." The Roman Empire was founded on commerce and relied on its Mediterranean naval power for its existence. The empire stretched from the Atlantic outskirts of Iberia to the eastern Mediterranean area known as Levant, a name which means "rising," referring to the sun.

The Islamic invasion and occupation of Catholic Spain began in 711 and its occupation lasted for over 700 years. During this time, the Jewish, Catholic, and Islamic faiths coexisted in this relatively small country. It is difficult for me to even imagine what the course of history would have been without this religious tolerance. Also as long-lasting, though, was the struggle by the leaders of the fractious Spanish kingdoms to oust the invading Muslims. At first this was a futile struggle because during this period Spain was made up of several warring kingdoms.

In 1085, the Kingdom of Spain was finally cohesive enough to begin a systematic attempt to oust the Muslims. Finally, in 1492 Ferdinand and Isabella, the Spanish monarchs, were able to accomplish this.

During this struggle to regain Spain, other events were taking place. These events profoundly influenced the course of my story and especially helped to shed light on the reason why Colonel Humphrey Walrond went to Barbados in 1649. To fully grasp the import of these events, we must go 10,000 years further into the past and thousands of miles farther east than the Levantine shores of the Mediterranean Sea.

More than 10,000 years ago, the inhabitants of the island of New Guinea discovered and domesticated a grass. In fact, it was a weed. The inhabitants of the island simply chewed the succulent stalk of this plant to extract its sweet juice. It was perhaps the world's first organic candy.

This plant was sugar cane. Soon it was being grown and used in Southeast Asia, then in southern China, and not long after, in southern India. Here, in about 350 CE, it was discovered that by boiling the juice, then letting it dry in the sun, crystalized granules were formed. These grains were called "sugar," and they represented a portable and more useful form of the juice. By 650 CE, the Chinese had acquired the skills of crystallization. The resulting crystals looked like gravel, so the Sanskrit name *sharkara* ("gravel") was given to this product. The Chinese also use the name "gravel sugar" to describe what is still known elsewhere simply as sugar.

This product soon made its way along the Silk Road from China to the Mediterranean area, where it formed part of the trade in this region of the world. Although the Romans and Greeks had known and used sugar since the first century, this was only as a medicine. By the time of the Muslim expansion, the Arabs were using sugar manufacturing processes from India in the first sugar mills and had even established plantations for cultivating the canes. Because the sugar cane plant needs a lot of water and Arabia is mostly desert, the Arabs used artificial irrigation to enable farmers to operate these early plantations.

By the 12th century, the canes were also grown in parts of southern Italy and southern Spain, and sugar was being used as a sweetener in many countries. Evidence of sugar cane cultivation also exists in Mesopotamia, on the eastern shores of the Mediterranean Sea, and on the larger islands in the Mediterranean Sea, notably Cyprus. It was not long before sugar cane cultivation spread to the Madeira archipelago, to the Canary and Cape Verde Islands. These Atlantic countries were all under Portuguese control. Sugar cane had become firmly established as a trading crop, and sugar was an important element in the cuisine of the entire Mediterranean area.

The problem with sugar production is that it required a tremendous amount of labour. Sugar cane stalks, when harvested, are heavy. They must be taken to the manufacturing plant to be processed. There, the stalks must be crushed and the juice, extracted. The juice then has to be boiled, purified, and concentrated. Crystallization is the last step of this long process. Only after this final stage of sugar manufacturing is the real value of the plant realized. As time went on, people invented machines that simplified the manufacture of sugar. However, the problem of human labour for the cultivation and harvesting of the sugar cane remained.

On the island of Cyprus, plantation owners solved this problem by importing slaves from the Black Sea region. Later, they brought in slaves from Africa. At the time, sugar production was low, and not many slaves were needed. When sugar cultivation spread to the Atlantic island regions of Portugal, the number of slaves needed rose because the native population of these areas refused to do the menial work.

Starting in 1390, there was an explosion of sugar manufacturing in the Mediterranean area. Andalusia in Muslim Spain and the Algarve region of Portugal became major sugar-producing areas. Madeira soon surpassed Cyprus in sugar production.

In the Spanish Kingdom of Castile, African slaves worked on the sugar plantations. There was to be no turning back; the cultivation of the sugar cane plant and the manufacture of sugar became inalterably associated with the use of African slave labour. This bond was to last a long time.

* * *

Just before the end of October 1451, Christopher Columbus was born in the Mediterranean town of Genoa. His father was a wool weaver who also owned a cheese booth where, as a young lad, Christopher sometimes worked as a helper.

In 1473, Columbus began an apprenticeship as a business agent for three very important Genoese families. He made trips to Northern Europe — to Bristol in England and to Galway in Ireland. In addition, between the years 1482 and 1485, Columbus traded along the western coast of Africa, as far south as the Coast of Guinea. As a trader, he was well-versed in the importance of sugar as a commodity. As he travelled, Columbus became very familiar with the Atlantic Ocean currents and their westerly and easterly flow from and to the Canary Islands located 300 kilometers off the coast of north-western Africa. He also studied and understood the strength and directions of the prevailing winds in the latitudes of Europe.

As time went on and his knowledge and experience grew, Columbus became convinced that it was possible to sail west and still reach India and China and all other countries of the Orient. These eastern lands were the source of a lot of the products that he dealt with. By 1485, he had dreamed up a plan to achieve his goal of sailing west to find the east.

However, although many of his contemporaries believed that he was mistaken about the distance between Europe and the East via a western route, they all agreed that such a voyage would be over an uninterrupted and dangerous ocean. And yet, sailors of his time knew that if such a route were discovered, it would be most desirable because trade with Asia still depended on travelling over land through parts of the Middle East and then over the Indian Ocean, a long and tedious journey.

It is important to note that in addition to his navigational interests and accomplishments, Columbus also studied history, geography, and astronomy. He could read Latin and spoke Portuguese and Castilian. He was also a devout Christian and was very interested in the Bible and its prophecies. He was, in short, a very learned man.

Columbus' wisdom strengthened his belief in a western route to the east, and in 1485 this intrepid sailor went to Portugal and secured an audience with King John II. Columbus was clear in his objectives. He requested help in the form of three well-built ships and 12 months within which to sail west across the Atlantic, find a western route to the Orient, and return to Portugal. Columbus also requested that he be made Great Admiral of the Ocean and Governor of all lands he discovered and that he be given 10 percent of all revenue derived from those lands. The king duly presented Columbus's proposal to his experts, who rejected it.

In 1488, Columbus again went to the king of Portugal and made another proposal. Again it was rejected. This was probably because even as the proposal was being considered, the navigator Bartolomeu Dias returned to Portugal with news that he had rounded the Cape of Good Hope at the southern tip of Africa. This discovery rendered more feasible an Eastern route to Asia via the south of Africa. A trade route across the Atlantic became less urgent.

Having been twice rejected by Portugal, Columbus went to Genoa, his home town, and also to Venice. He received no promise of help from either of these cities. In the meantime, he had also sent his brother Bartolomeu to the court of Henry VII of England to ask for help in his endeavors. This visit was also fruitless.

Columbus saw Spain as his last hope. He would appeal to the king and queen of this country for help. By this time, the country had become unified and was occupied with trying to oust the Muslims from its lands. Spain's success in this regard seemed close. Finally, in 1492, Ferdinand and Isabella were able to capture Granada, the last outpost of Muslim rule in Spain, and the country was once more Catholic. It was only then that the Spanish monarchs could think of other things, including the ideas of Columbus — ideas that had been presented to them several times before.

On 1 May 1486, for example, Columbus had received permission and duly presented his proposals to Queen Isabella, who referred them to a committee. The members considered the proposition for a while and returned a verdict that the idea was impractical. They believed that Columbus had greatly underestimated the distance between Europe and Asia in a westerly direction.

However, on reflection, the Spanish monarchs knew that perhaps there was some merit to the idea of sailing west, and they did not want Columbus to approach other sources of assistance. But they were still too preoccupied with the Muslim problem. They decided to put him on a "retainer" of 12,000 maravedis (a coin of the realm at the time) and later on, in 1489, gave him a letter that ordered all cities and towns in their kingdom to provide him with food and lodging at no cost. (I wonder if this was the start of the welfare system that some governments still use.)

In 1491, with the help of a monk from the monastery of La Rábida, Columbus was able to have another audience with the queen. Yet again, his proposal was rejected, and he left Granada for Cordoba. He planned on visiting France and on making an appeal to the king there.

Reports say that at this point, King Ferdinand shrewdly sent messengers after Columbus and brought him back to Granada. The monarchs didn't really believe that Columbus would return from such an overseas endeavor. At the same time, they didn't want to risk the possibility of another country benefiting from any discoveries which might be made.

It is possible that because of this doubt, the monarchs readily agreed to his demands of 10 percent of all profits, elevation to noble status, and the governorship of all and any new territories being awarded to him and to his descendants. The monarchs believed that these demands were but a small price to pay for the possibility of new commercial gains for Spain. Besides, the possibility of finding new converts to Catholicism was also uppermost in the minds of these Catholic monarchs. And so, on 17 April 1492, Ferdinand and Isabel signed an agreement with Columbus. The deal was done.

The persistence of Columbus and the timing of the recapture of Spain from Islamic rule combined to shape the course of history in general and of my story in particular. To fully develop this idea, I find it expedient to describe his voyages in some detail.

Once the agreement was signed with the Spanish monarchs, Columbus wasted no time. He had already selected his partners: two brothers from the ship-owning Pinzón family. He was given three ships. Two small caravels, one square-rigged and one lateen-rigged, had a complement of 18 men each. These were the *Niña* and the *Pinta*. They were captained by the Pinzón brothers, Martín Alonso and Vicente Yáñez. Caravels were shallow ships. When rigged with lateen sails, they were very manoeuvrable, especially in strange waters. With their shallow keels, they could come very close to shore. Columbus's flagship was the *Santa Maria*. This vessel could carry 100 tons of cargo and had a crew of 52 men. Columbus was well-equipped, though some of his crew weren't too sure about what they were in for. They showed little enthusiasm for the journey ahead.

On 3 August 1492, Columbus set sail from the previously insignificant port of Palos on the Atlantic coast of southern Spain. The fleet sailed for the Canary Islands, where they made a stop for food and other supplies. On 6 September, they set sail on a westerly course. By 10 October, some of the crew had become worried. They feared that after 34 days, they were going to fall off the edge. A mutiny was at hand.

This is when Columbus is reported to have said, "Give me, my men, but three days." It worked. They agreed. The very next day, green tree branches were seen floating on the water. Land was near. On 12 October 1492, Columbus made landfall on Guanahani, a chain of several islands now known as the Bahamas. He planted a Spanish flag and claimed the land in the name of Spain.

On Christmas Eve 1492, the *Santa Maria* ran aground off the coast of modern-day Haiti, on the island of Hispaniola. He was sure he had reached India. With the help of some native inhabitants, Columbus's crew removed the supplies, dismantled the ship, and built a settlement which he named La Navidad, meaning "The Birth." Thirty-nine crewmen were left behind at the settlement. They included a barrel-maker, a tailor, a physician, and other professionals.

Columbus arrived back in Spain early in 1493 aboard the *Niña*, with the *Pinta* following close behind. He docked in Palos on 15 March to a hero's welcome. Celebrations and feasting honoured him. A crown committee was immediately set up to prepare for other expeditions.

Columbus set sail again in September of 1493 on his second voyage. This particular voyage is of supreme importance to my story. He commanded 17 ships and a complement of 1,200 men. On this occasion, all his crew members were excited at the thought of wealth and riches. Again, he stopped off in the Canary Islands for supplies. Among these were sugar cane cuttings. Remember, Columbus was well-experienced and knowledgeable about the growing of sugar canes and about the manufacture of sugar crystals. He knew very well the value of these cuttings. He planted them on the island of

Hispaniola. This island harvested its first crop in 1501, and by 1509, sugar cane cultivation on the island was well-established and very profitable.

Sad to say, however, the second voyage was somewhat less successful than the first. He had established a second settlement, also on Hispaniola, called La Isabella. Of the 1,200 men who travelled with Columbus, some of whom were apparently passengers (tourists?), 300 died from disease during the year 1494. Some of these passengers could have been mapmakers. The custom of sending cartographers on overseas trips had already been well-established. Columbus's physician, a Dr. Chanca, did what he could to help the ailing, but medical supplies were short. To add to Columbus's troubles, in 1495 a severe hurricane destroyed all the ships in the harbour at La Isabella.

Columbus barely made it back home to Spain. He had to use timbers from the wrecked ships to create one ship seaworthy enough to make the trip back. He arrived in Spain in 1496. His men were angry that the riches they were expecting did not materialise. None of their expectations had been met. To top things off, there was no hero's welcome; instead, they received a somewhat icy reception from the Catholic monarchs.

The third voyage of Columbus was in 1498. It was in many ways even more of a disappointment. The main objective of this voyage was to bring supplies to the settlements and to explore the more southerly areas of the new lands. Columbus left Spain from the port of Sanlúcar on May 30 with only six vessels, a few volunteer sailors, and some convicts who were being expatriated as colonists.

Before he left Spain, Columbus dedicated his third voyage to the Holy Trinity. After a stop in the Canary Islands, three ships sailed directly for the settlement of La Isabella, and the other ships, led by Columbus, headed in a more southerly direction. His ships spent a lengthy period of nine days becalmed in the area known as the Doldrums. On the tenth day, his little fleet sailed on. With food and supplies running short, he spotted land on 31 July.

As luck would have it, this first land he saw was in the form of three low but definite hills. To fulfill his promise of dedication, he called the island *Trinidad*, a Spanish word meaning "Trinity." He replenished his supplies, spent eight days in the Gulf of Paria, and saw the coast of South America. By this time, his health was failing, so Columbus headed for Hispaniola and arrived there on 19 August to find a settlement rife with discontent and on the point of mutiny.

The settlers were angry at the small amount of gold that had been found. Complaints had been sent to Spain while Columbus was further south. In response, Ferdinand and Isabella had sent a regal representative, Francisco de Bobadilla, of even higher rank than Columbus, to investigate. He arrived in 1500 and promptly arrested Columbus, who was put in chains and, along with his two brothers, was sent back to Spain, charged with mismanaging their responsibilities as Royal Governors of the Spanish Colonies. Although the prisoners were released immediately upon arrival in Spain, the sovereigns did heed the complaints of the colonists. Columbus and his brothers were stripped of their authority to govern.

The final voyage of Columbus was made under very different conditions from the other three. Although the monarchs did allow him to make this voyage, it was done without their help or partnership. They allowed him to keep his title of Admiral, but he had no governing authority on any of the islands he might discover.

In 1502, Columbus left on his last voyage to what he still considered the East. With just four ships, he sailed along the coast of South America, still looking for a breakthrough to China, Japan, and India. When he returned to Spain on 7 November 1504, it was as a thoroughly defeated man. His glory and honour had evaporated, and his reputation was tarnished beyond recovery. He died in 1506, suffering from gout and arthritis, still believing that he had found India by sailing west across the Atlantic Ocean.

* * *

There is no doubt that the voyages of Christopher Columbus were of monumental importance to the course of my history. It must be remembered that when he came ashore on the island of Guanahani, his first step was on a continent (or at least on part of a continent) that most Europeans had absolutely no idea was there. He did not in reality discover these lands, because they were already inhabited (perhaps his voyages should be classified as being of more of an uncovering by Europeans rather than a discovery).

Columbus's landings and claiming of the lands, in the name of Spain, unleashed a centuries-long sequence of further travels, exploration, conquering, colonization, and exploitation of a vast continent. The inhabitants of these "new" lands were the descendants of hunters who had migrated from the mainland of Asia across the land bridge at the Bering Strait. This earlier migration had taken place between 40,000 and 25,000 BCE. By 1492, when Columbus arrived on the Bahamas, the population of all the Americas would have been, conservatively, about 45 million.

These indigenous people constituted a great number of tribal and cultural groups. But Columbus thought that he had reached India, so he called the first inhabitants who welcomed him on Guanahani "Indians." The name stuck. Only in recent years have they been called *aboriginals*, a word that means "from the beginning." Many present-day descendants still prefer to be called *indigenous people*.

I cannot help but wonder if Columbus's return to Spain at the end of his third voyage did not presage the voyage made by so many Africans across the Atlantic Ocean, albeit in the opposite direction, for so many subsequent years. Doubtlessly, these Africans, shackled as they were, and deprived of much more than just physical movement and self-determination, faced a fearsome and unknown fate.

Chapter 8
Slavery: Its Origins and its Nature

It is unfortunate that one of the most immediate results of the discovery of the new lands by Christopher Columbus was the establishment of the transatlantic slave trade. It is even more unfortunate that Humphrey Walrond ended up a plantation owner in Barbados. Of course, if he had not, then I would have no story to tell. Indeed, I would not be.

In the years immediately following his voyages, tremendous developments took place in the construction of ocean-going ships and in the technology of navigation. The preparing and printing of maps and charts, for example, had a lot to do with the ease with which ships sailed across the Atlantic and down the western coast of Africa.

These improvements meant that newer ships were better able to cope with the Atlantic storms and tidal currents. Travel across the ocean became routine. The old motto *nec plus ultra* ("nothing else on the other side") no longer applied to the Strait of Gibraltar. Within a few years, trade between the European powers and the West Indies was well-established, and the transportation of African slaves was an important element of this commerce.

While looking for information about the transatlantic slave trade, I came across this quotation taken from the book *Collected Essays*, by James Baldwin, a 20th-century African-American writer: "I think that the past is all that makes the present coherent, and further, that the past will remain horrible for exactly as long as we refuse to assess it honestly."

In his essays, Baldwin goes on to emphasize the importance of looking into the past because this helps one make sense of the present. Looking at the past, he says, no matter how scary or painful it is, helps create a clearer picture of what someone or something might be in the future. I could find no better way to explain what I am trying to do in this section of my book.

Over countless years, many people and institutions have tried to come up with definitions of *slavery*. All these attempts have, in my opinion, resulted in a jumble of legalistic phrases which simply confuse what most people already know.

I came to the conclusion that slavery was a common factor in just about every ancient civilization. This includes the Sumerians, the Ancient Egyptians, the Ancient Chinese, Assyria, the Akkadian Empire, Ancient India, Ancient Greece, the Roman Empire, the Islamic Caliphate, the Hebrews, and even in pre-Columbian America. Slavery did not begin with Columbus.

We have to remember also that slavery and religion were not mutually exclusive. The Roman Empire was a Christian Empire for the last part of its existence. The Hebrews of Palestine had slaves, and the leaders (Caliphs) of Islam held slaves. Even the caste system of Hinduism is a form of slavery.

Slavery, one can summarise then, has existed for as long as human history. It also appears that movements to free slaves have existed for just as long. But great care must be taken to distinguish between movements to free slaves and movements to stop trading in slaves. This is important because there is no point in freeing slaves if trading in slaves is allowed to continue.

The rising prevalence of movements to free slaves quickly led to the practice known as the *manumission* of a slave. This word comes from the Latin verb *manumittere*, which literally means "to send off by hand." Manumission would take place when an owner gave a slave a friendly slap and declared him or her free. Conditions, of course were attached. For example, manumission was by no means an absolute discharge of ownership. In ancient Rome, a slave who was "freed" by manumission still had specific service obligations towards a former owner. Failure to perform these duties led to immediate re-enslavement.

* * *

The development of slavery on the western coast of Africa was hampered by an area of dangerous reefs. This region lies just south of the Canary Islands, on the Atlantic coast of Western Sahara. Sailors of old gave it an Arabic name. They called it Abu Khajar, which means "The Father of Danger." Seafaring men dared not go past it. It was not till 1434 that a Portuguese navigator named Gil Eanes successfully navigated this area and opened up the region to its south to exploitation.

In 1441, another Portuguese navigator called Dom Henrique led a few ships into the area. The crews landed on the African Coast, looking for gold, but found none. Some of his captains, however, captured twelve Negros. The captives, which included men, women, and children, were taken back to Portugal. Henrique presented ten of them to the king as a gift. This was the start of what became known as domestic slavery. (Capturing slaves for work on the sugar plantations of Madeira, Cyprus, and the Canary Islands was already well established. This was called agricultural slavery.)

Notwithstanding his apparent generosity towards his king, Dom Henrique had an ulterior motive. He wanted to demonstrate to the king that it was easier to sail down the west coast of Africa and procure slaves for a much lower cost than buying them off Arabic and other European slave merchants on the Mediterranean Sea who did their business from the northern shores of Africa.

Dom Henrique went on to Rome, where he offered the two remaining slaves to the pope. The pope was so impressed that he immediately granted the Portuguese permission to trade in slaves on the west coast of Africa. He also offered advanced absolution to any person who would die in the struggle to obtain slaves in countries on the West African coast. This effectively ended the Arabic monopoly on slave trading through the Sahara and on the southern coast of the Mediterranean Sea and established the Portuguese as the main slave traders of western Africa.

By 1481, the Portuguese had built their first fort on the Gold Coast of West Africa. Called El Mina ("the mine"), probably in reference to the name Gold Coast, it was the physical beginning of what was to become the Atlantic slave trade, and this was to last 300 years.

* * *

The history of slavery on the continent of Africa is as old as the history of the continent itself. Slavery was an important part of the social structure of Africa, and to best understand the reason for this, one must compare the legal systems of Africa with those of Europe.

In Europe, the basis of the legal systems was the ownership of land. Private ownership was the main source of revenue to the landowners. Land was used to produce income-generating products such as food or timber. In addition to this, in Europe, land was handed down to members of the same family. Its revenue-generating properties could sustain many generations of the same family — like the descendants of Waleran Venator. Land could be bought and sold, resulting in the increase of revenue. Land was taxed by governments and crown to realise revenue for their coffers.

In Africa, on the other hand, people, not land, were used as the source of revenue and as the basis for the production of wealth. People were used, through labour, to create wealth and revenue. The political and economic elites of African societies relied on the trading of people for their personal income and wealth. In Africa, this complicated institution of the ownership of people led to widespread slavery and slave trading.

When, after the landing in America by Columbus in 1492, the Portuguese and other European traders arrived along the coast of West Africa, they found in place a well-established and efficient system of slave trading. The Europeans simply tapped into it with a voracious appetite. Whether the slave trader was African or European did not matter. The business of slavery just went on as usual, and it was sustained for centuries.

It seems to me that the establishment of slavery in the new world of the American continent was a combination of both the European and the African systems of revenue and wealth creation. The European system was used to buy land in the new world, and the African system provided human beings for labour. Although this union did last for a very long time, it is to my mind inconceivable that it could have lasted forever.

* * *

The transatlantic slave trade began in the 16th century and lasted till the 19th century. It was fueled by the greed and avarice of the economic systems of the times. The *triangular trade,* as it was called, is well-documented. I will not recount the horrors and abasement suffered by the Africans on the Middle Passage and on the plantations of the West Indies and American continents in graphic detail here.

Suffice it to say that the Middle Passage was a horrible one. The bodies of the many slaves who died were thrown overboard. Some committed suicide by throwing themselves overboard. I suppose they were the ones who knew without a doubt that there was a fate worse than death. The slaves were scared, believing that they were going to be eaten. They were given little food until they neared their unknown destination, when they were fattened so as to command better prices at the slave markets. A good trip lasted 40 days. Others, depending on the weather, took as long as 150 days.

The greatest number of these slaves worked mainly on sugar plantations. Many others worked on coffee, cotton, tobacco, and rice plantations, depending on the country to which they were shipped and the time of their enslavement. The sugar plantations of the Caribbean and Brazil demanded the highest supply of slave labour.

It was not long before the islands of the Caribbean were populated with these unhappy Africans who laboured long and hard in the fields of these new lands revealed to the Europeans by Columbus.

Chapter 9
Barbados

Of all the islands of the Caribbean, Barbados is of special interest to me. Ever since I found out that several of my paternal forbears had come from this island, I began to look upon it as a sort of ancestral home. Of course, I knew that in the final analysis these forbears would have all come from Africa, but that continent seemed too distant. Barbados was a closer and more certain source of my immediate heritage. Perhaps because of this affinity, I wanted to find out as much as I could about the island.

All the Windward Islands of the Caribbean, including Trinidad and Tobago, lie between 61 and 62 degrees west of Greenwich. All the other islands, including the Leeward Islands and the larger islands of Cuba, Hispaniola, Jamaica, Puerto Rico, and the Bahamas and Virgin Islands, all lie still further west. Barbados, on the other hand, lies further east than 60 degrees longitude. This island is a mere 21 miles in length and 14 miles at its widest. The island is considered to be just outside the main Atlantic hurricane belt (although strong winds have been experienced on occasion; in 1780, a hurricane killed more than 4,000 people).

It was Christopher Columbus who brought the sugar cane plant to the Caribbean area. For some reason, Barbados is not on the list of islands visited by Columbus. Whether Columbus saw the island or not, the fact remains that he did not land on Barbados and as a result this island was not claimed by Spain or even Portugal. The island was originally inhabited, at least in the 9th century, by peaceful Arawak Indians. They were supplanted by the more warlike Caribs by the 13th century. This pattern of the cannibalistic Caribs conquering and sometimes eradicating the Arawaks is one that was repeated throughout the Caribbean islands.

When Portuguese traders landed on the island, they were attracted by the bearded fig trees that they saw there. They called the island Los Barbados, meaning "the bearded ones." In 1511, King Ferdinand of Spain made a reference to this island, and the name was first seen at this time on Spanish maps. However, Portugal did not claim the island as its own.

By 1625, when an English ship called the Olive Blossom arrived in the Barbadian area of Holetown to take on water and other supplies, the Caribs had disappeared. (Holetown was named after a hole in the ground out of which bubbled a stream of clear water.) It is speculated that the absence of indigenous people was due to the fact that in 1511, the Spanish government had allowed Carib Indians to be seized and transported as slaves to other Caribbean islands, most notably to the island of Puerto Rico.

As a result of this 1625 landing, Barbados was claimed in the name of King James I of England. In 1627, a group of 80 English settlers arrived to colonize the island. They grew cotton and tobacco. Around 1636, the failure of the cotton and tobacco crops forced the planters to find another crop. The planters then imported sugarcane cuttings from the state of Pernambuco in Brazil.

It was not long before the value of this crop had surpassed that of the former ones. The hot, humid climate and the coral formation of the island were the ideal conditions for the cultivation of the sugar canes. It was estimated that an acre of land yielded three times as much profit from sugar as from cotton.

This prosperity led to an influx of settlers from England, and in 1639, the Barbadian House of Assembly was established. The island thus became the third-oldest Parliamentary Democracy in the world, after Britain and Bermuda. By 1643 —spurred on, no doubt, by the English Civil War — more than 40,000 white landowners and over 6,000 Africans were working on the many sugar plantations that had been established in Barbados.

It was the unqualified success of the transition from cotton and tobacco to sugar cane in 1636 that resulted in the Africans' being brought to Barbados. Not only did they work in the fields, but they were also trained to work in the factories, boiling houses, curing houses, and distilling houses. Many became skilled carpenters, blacksmiths, and other craftsmen.

By 1650, there were 6,000 enslaved Africans in Barbados working alongside 24,000 whites. The number of blacks was increasing at a furious rate. Most of the whites were domestic servants transplanted from England. In 1649, a plot was uncovered. The white plantation workers intended to rise up in revolt, cut the throats of their masters, and seize control of the island. It was brutally aborted. After the discovery of this intended revolt, the plantation owners began to build their homes to look like forts and bastions.

After the 1650s, many of the white settlers in Barbados had migrated to the British colonies on mainland America, Virginia being a popular destination. This migration left a small group of elite white plantation owners who were referred to as a Barbadian plantocracy. Among the members of this plantocracy was Humphrey Walrond.

* * *

In his book *The History of the Rebellion and Civil War in England (1702–1704)*, the Earl of Clarendon wrote, "The Barbadoes, which was much the richest plantation, was principally inhabited by men who had retired thither only to be quiet and to be free from the noise and oppression in England, and who had no ill thoughts towards the King." Humphrey Walrond was one of these retired men who arrived in Barbados in 1649. His brother Edward, a lawyer, either accompanied him or had arrived a bit earlier.

Richard Dunn, in his book *Sugar and Slaves: The Rise of the Planter Class in the English West Indies,* lists Walrond as one of a group of newcomers to Barbados in the 1640s. They were described as able and aggressive men anxious to get in on the ground floor of the sugar business. Similarly, Sir Hilary Beckles, in *A History of Barbados: From Amerindian Settlement to Nation-state,* lists Walrond as one of the leading family names in 1673.

In their book *No Peace Beyond the Line: The English in the Caribbean, 1624–1690,* Carl and Roberta Bridenburgh report that in the 1650s, the Walronds built Fontabelle in St. Michael's Parish. This was a large and elegant structure. This building was later rented out to the Assembly, who used it as the Governor's Residence. The rental fee was £500 a year.

Life at this Walrond estate seems to have centered on the sea. Fontabelle is located on the Caribbean side of Barbados, not far from the capital Bridgetown. The Bridenburghs also recorded that Colonel Walrond was one of the few "seaside" plantation owners who maintained a crew of fishermen and provided them with a seine (fishing net). To add credence to this claim, in chapter 12 of his book *Barbados: Food and Drink through the Ages*, George Hunte states that at Fontabelle, "Humphrey Walrond invariably offered his guests mullet, mackerel, parrot fish, red and grey snappers, cavallos, terbums (*tarpon*), crabs, lobsters, conyfish, and other sorts of seafood for which there were no names."

There is no doubt in my mind that Colonel Walrond enjoyed the advantage of living within a short distance of the sea. George Hunte gives this description:

> His cellars were kept stocked with wine of all kinds, oil, olives, capers, sturgeon, meats, tongues, anchovies, caviare, botargo [*salted and cured fish roe*] and all sorts of salted meats, flesh and fish, such as beef, pork, English peas, ling, haberdine [*salted and dried cod*], cod, Poor John [*a small fish similar to cod*] and Jerkin Beef.

Richard Dunn reports that Fontabelle was torn down in the late 1700s.

Carl and Roberta Bridenburgh have also given a very competent description of how the most popular type of sugar — Muscovado — was made. They describe the final step in the process, called *knocking*, as a most important one. This is when the sugar is gently tapped out of its cone. The best sugar, Muscovado, is formed in the center of the cone. The less desirable sugar, still containing too much molasses, sticks to the side of the cone. The description ends this way: "Colonel Drax, Colonel Walrond, Mr. Francis Raynes, and a few other major planters performed all the steps in the knocking process with great care."

It would seem that Walrond took his sugar manufacturing seriously.

Carl and Roberta Bridenburgh also write about Walrond's treatment of his servants:

> When, towards 1650, as "discreeter and better natur'd men" came to rule, some commentators thought that the miseries of white servants eased somewhat. Possibly a stronger reason

for less heartless treatment was the marked decline of the servile white population brought about by heavy mortality and migration which left the ranks of the insular militias much depleted. In any case, on some of the great plantations servants now slept in hammocks slung in warm, dry rooms and those who came in wet had a shift of shirts and drawers. Colonel Humphrey Walrond, seeing his servants all wet through with sweat or rain, sent over to England for "rug Gownes" such as poor people wear in Hospitals. The Cavalier planter, and others, were learning too that by feeding their servants fruit, vegetables, salted beef, and a little Irish butter several times a week they got more work out of them.

Such concern on the part of Walrond won him the devotion of his grateful laborers, but enlightened treatment of this sort had not become the general rule by the end of the period, because the small planter, who actually lived little better than his servants, could not afford it.

In another chapter, the Bridenburghs state that

The "Cavees" or Cavaliers who arrived in 1646 brought ample money and credit with them, as well as the habit of remaining gentle and showing establishments for the rest of the populace to see and admire. Dignity, taste, good manners, *noblesse oblige,* a certain imperiousness, culture — the contributions of the Walrond brothers, Thomas Modyford, and above all others, Richard Ligon, turned out, with the passage of time, to be more lasting and more important in the civilisation of the Caribbean colonies of England than their economic and political activities.

In his book *Slavery on the English Island of Barbados,* Richard Ligon tells of this rather strange encounter between Humphrey Walrond and his slaves:

When any of them die, they dig a grave, and at evening, they bury him, clapping and wringing their hands and making a doleful sound with their voices. They are a people of a timorous and fearful disposition, and consequently bloody when they find advantages (opportunities). If any of them commit a fault, give them present (immediate) punishment, but do not threaten him; for if you do, it is an even lay, he will go and hang himself to avoid the punishment. What their other opinions are in matter of Religion, I know not; but certainly they are not altogether of the sect of the Sadduces *(A Hebrew sect — 2nd century A.D., that rejected the belief in the resurrection of the dead).* For they believe *(in)* a Resurrection and that they shall go into their own Country again and have their youth renewed. And lodging this opinion in their hearts, they make it an ordinary practice, upon any great fright or threatening of their Master, to hang themselves.

But Colonel Walrond, having lost three or four of his best Negroes this way, and in a very little time, caused one of their heads to be cut off and set upon a pole a dozen foot high; and having done that, called all his Negroes to come forth and march round about this head and bid them look on it, whether this were not the head of such an one that hanged himself. Which they acknowledging, he then told them 'that they were in a main error in thinking that they went into their own Countries after they were dead; for this man's head was here, as they all were witnesses of; and how was it possible the body could go without a head.' Being convinced by this sad yet lively spectacle, they changed their opinions; and after that, no more hanged themselves.

There is no doubt that Humphrey Walrond was a competent and logical plantation owner. After exploring this aspect of Colonel Walrond's life, I turned my attention to another aspect of his life in Barbados. I found that in contrast to his social and plantation life, which seemed to be quite private, the more public and political history of Barbados seems to have revolved around his name for many years after his arrival.

* * *

Colonel Humphrey, a staunch Royalist, was only one of many men who left England at the time of its civil unrest and went to Barbados. Some were Royalists, and some were Roundheads.

English emigration to Barbados had started as early as 1627, when 80 settlers arrived with their ten African slaves, whom they had captured at sea. By the late 1640s, when Walrond arrived, the island had prospered through a massive accumulation of capital, which was generated through the cultivation of sugar cane. Led by the more prominent planters, Barbados had developed its own socio-political consciousness. Above all, these planters did not allow the turmoil and disputes in England to ruin their peaceful and quiet lifestyle, to say nothing of their class authority. The island also maintained a free trade policy, especially with the Dutch traders.

The Barbados House of Assembly, the governing body established in 1639, had adopted a neutral position of home rule and independence in the face of the conflict between king and Parliament in England. It was this façade of neutrality that worried Walrond and his group of Royalists.

When King Charles I of England was executed by Parliament in January 1649, however, the plantation owners were sent into disarray. For at least ten years, the Cavaliers and Roundheads of Barbados had coexisted and prospered. They had all kept their political feelings to themselves. With the royal execution, attitudes began to change.

Incited no doubt by the "bravery" of the mother Parliament, the Roundheads no longer hid their support for Parliament and could no longer tolerate the neutrality of the Barbados House of Assembly. At the same time, they did not want to see the self-government enjoyed in Barbados fall apart.

The Royalists, on the other hand, reacted negatively to the *Commonwealth,* as the new, non-royal government in England was called. The first thing they did was to declare Charles II to be the legal King of Barbados.

Both sides of the political fence were now in full evidence, and it was not long before civil war became a part of Barbadian life.

The Royalist planters, led by none other than Humphrey Walrond tried to influence public sentiment in Barbados against the Parliament in London. The House of Assembly passed "an Act and an Oath" which simply stated that anybody who vilified or opposed the local Barbadian government was to be considered an enemy of the island. It did not help matters when the aforementioned plans for an uprising were discovered.

In 1650, Francis Lord Willoughby arrived in Barbados to take over the governorship from Captain Philip Bell, who had held the post for about ten years. Willoughby was appointed by Charles II, who was in exile. When the new governor arrived in Barbados on April 30, Walrond was not overly pleased. Willoughby was once a Roundhead but had objected to the extremists of that group and became a Cavalier, or Royalist.

Walrond wasted no time in using this fact to his advantage in the House of Assembly. He reminded the Assembly of this volte-face and succeeded in delaying the acceptance of Willoughby's commission as governor. Earlier in April 1650, Walrond and his supporters had spread a report of a plot to kill all Royalists on the island and confiscate their estates. The House of Assembly blacklisted 122 individuals (some of them planters), fined them, and banished them from the island. On their arrival in London, they went to Parliament and asked this body to call Barbadians "rebels and traitors."

Willoughby, it must be remembered, came to Barbados as governor. But he was also a representative of the king, Charles II. In addition, he had a commission appointing him lieutenant-general of the "Caribbee Islands." No doubt, he was an important man and desired nothing more than moderation between the islands and England.

Humphrey and his brother Edward literally ruled the Assembly. They all wanted to enjoy the results of their action against the Roundheads. But at the same time, they could not defy the commission of their king, Charles. Willoughby, on the other hand, did not have an army big enough to enforce any decision that he might make, which would undoubtedly be against the wishes of the Walrond "faction" — in other words, the Assembly.

Willoughby was also Lieutenant-General of the Leeward Islands, so he decided to leave Barbados in the hands of the Assembly and the Walrond brothers and to visit these other islands. It was in his absence that the leading Roundheads were rounded up and either fined and or banished, and their estates were confiscated. This group included the famous Colonel Drax (who was one of the largest landowners on the island), Colonel Alleyne, and about 100 others.

In August of 1650, Willoughby returned to Barbados. Included in his policy of government was moderation between the two political parties on the island. He therefore set about to win the confidence of the Moderates, who were led by Colonel James Modiford (Modyford).

Since Willoughby's aim was reconciliation, the first thing he did was to deprive the Walrond brothers of all the military and civilian offices that had rendered them powerful. This effectively put an end to their rule over the Assembly and therefore over the island. Willoughby then annulled the act that Walrond had passed to confiscate the land of the banished Roundheads. However, when he found out that the Parliament in London intended to overrun Barbados by force, Willoughby reinstated the order.

In October 1651, a Commonwealth force led by Sir George Ayscue did arrive in Barbados and created a revolution of sorts. On 4 March 1652, the Assembly passed an act to banish Walrond and some others for a year. He was later forbidden to return without a license from Parliament or the Council of State.

For the next eight years, the whereabouts and activities of Humphrey Walrond are obscure. It is thought that during this period, he enlisted in the service of Spain, probably staying in the Caribbean area. The Anglo-Dutch wars were being waged, and Spain was dependant on Holland. To side with Spain was a mistake on the part of Walrond, but he did it anyway. On 5 August 1653, Philip IV of Spain publicly acknowledged Walrond's activities by creating him Marquis de Vallado, Conde de Parama, Conde de Valderonda, and a grandee of the first class.

When Charles II was restored to the throne in 1660, Willoughby became governor of Barbados again. It seems, though, that Willoughby's attempts at moderation and reconciliation knew no bounds. In 1660, he appointed Humphrey Walrond governor of Barbados and left for a while. Colonel Modyford, who was governor at the time, went back to being Leader of the Opposition in the Assembly.

However, when Willoughby returned to Barbados to reassume his post as governor, he immediately relieved Walrond of his duties and had him arrested. He was imprisoned on a warrant, accused of receiving and accepting money from Spain in return for trading favours during the period of his disappearance. Willoughby also confiscated Walrond's estate. This fact probably accounts for the total absence of records of either land ownership or agricultural activity in his name after this date. (The name does show up on a 1673 list of eminent planters of Barbados. It shows Mr. Henry Walrond Jr. as holding 200 acres and Col. Henry Walrond as owning 400 acres. These men were descendants of Humphrey Walrond.)

Humphrey Walrond, for his part, refused to follow orders. On 4 November 1663, he was deemed armed and at large, and he was accused of moving from place to place inciting the public to riot and rebel. He escaped from Barbados and made his way to London, where he made an appeal to King Charles. There he was confronted with new accusations, for which he apparently had no response, and he was ordered committed, since he had contracted over £30,000 worth of debt. Because his creditors were after him, Humphrey left England again.

On 8 April 1668, his wife petitioned for a reversal of the commitment order, but the results of this remain unannounced. After his withdrawal from England, his whereabouts were not known. It is presumed that he returned to the Caribbean and sought refuge among his Spanish friends. He appears to have died not long afterwards.

At his death, or perhaps his disappearance, Humphrey Walrond had no estates to bequeath to his descendants. All he had to offer as a legacy was his hereditary Spanish title Marquis de Vallado. It was passed on to his descendants. (The last known holder, fittingly enough, was a Henry Humphrey Walrond, who held it from 1862 to 1940.)

Humphrey Walrond did, however, leave a legacy of sorts in the Caribbean. His first son, George, lost an arm fighting for Charles I and succeeded to his father's Spanish titles. His second son, John, became secretary to Lord Willoughby. His third son, Henry, became Speaker of the House of Assembly of Barbados, then Chief Justice of the Court of Common Pleas, and still later Governor of Barbados. Some of Humphrey's descendants were for a long time prominent on the island of Antigua. I have also been in contact with descendants in Australia and South Africa.

* * *

After reading about Humphrey Walrond, I found it difficult to come to a reasonable conclusion as to what type of man he really was. Politically, as many historians have pointed out, he was fiercely fanatic. He was loyal to his sovereign, almost to a fault. Yet I believe that it was this apparently unbridled allegiance which led ultimately to his loss of property and social standing. He reminds me of modern-day politicians who keep getting elected, become (in their own minds) more important than the jobs they were elected to do, and eventually end up being dismissed in a blaze of ignominy.

From the point of view of his politics, he leaves the impression that he was his own man. The French have an expression which I think sums up his character: *Un homme comme il faut.* Humphrey Walrond was certainly a man who did what he thought necessary to maintain the political status quo of his country.

His treatment of his slaves convinced me that he cared very much for their wellbeing. This aspect of his character made me wonder how widespread this practice was among the other plantation owners. In addition, the care and attention he gave to the manufacture of sugar revealed him as a sound businessman.

The description of the different types of seafood with which he regaled his guests indicated a love of life which surprised me. I did not think that plantation owners of his time were that interested in such luxuries. Or were they really luxuries?

I was forced to conclude that had Humphrey Walrond not gotten involved in the politics of his time to the extent that he did, perhaps my story would have been different in some respects.

For a while, as I thought about this man, I mentally berated him on some of his actions. But I soon softened my opinions. "Why should I be even a bit angry with such a man?" I asked myself. "After all," I mused, "he is the one who gave my family its name and which my ancestors have borne for many generations." And really, he did do his best at all times. But I still had one question left to answer.

* * *

A chain, it is said, is as strong as its weakest link. Having discovered what I believed was all I could about Humphrey Walrond, I was still faced with the enigma of how the name Walrond, a very European name, as I have shown, got transferred to so many people of African origin. The more I investigated, the more convinced I became that this link between Europe and Africa was the weakest in this long and interesting chain of people, events, places, and times that led me from 7th-century Germany to 20th-century Barbados. There was obviously a lot more to be discovered.

I found some answers from Jerome S. Handler and JoAnn Jacoby, who, after intense research, wrote an article entitled "Slave Names and Naming in Barbados." Here is an excerpt of that article, which was published in Volume 53 of the *William and Mary Quarterly*, dated 1996:

> How slaves adopted or were assigned surnames is another issue. Writing in the early nineteenth century about the growth of the freedom population (free blacks and mulattoes) in Barbados, J.W. Orderson, a white Creole, reported that most slaves who purchased their freedom were already baptised; when they were manumitted, they added their Christian names to that of their owner's family.

Illustrations of Orderson's observation can be found in *The Newton Plantation Records*.

It is important to remember that when a person is baptised, only "given" names are used, not family names or surnames. These given names become their Christian names. The *William and Mary Quarterly* article cited earlier is an excellent source of information on the way in which slaves in the Caribbean, especially in Barbados, acquired their surnames.

It seems that some slaves simply adopted the name of their owners. If they did not like their owners but were partial to another plantation owner, they took his name instead. Other slaves were ascribed names by other people, and these names became a permanent part of their identity.

I had to conclude that there is no consensus on the way or ways in which slaves acquired their surnames. All I am left with is the undeniable fact that in the year 1649, there was one Anglo Walrond plantation owner in Barbados, and by the late 1980s, there were hundreds, if not thousands, of Afro Walronds living on this island, all or most of whom were descendants of plantation workers. It is also very possible there are some Anglo Walronds still living in Barbados.

To do justice to the question of how slaves got their names, certain facts have to be considered. Humphrey Walrond arrived in Barbados in 1649. He owned two plantations and disappeared in 1663. How many slaves he had on these two estates is unknown to me, though I am reasonably sure that the number could be ascertained. Let us for a moment assume that they all took the name Walrond.

A 1673 list of prominent plantation owners shows Mr. Henry Walrond Jr. and Colonel Henry Walrond both owning estates. These men were descendants of Humphrey Walrond. I would like to suggest that some or all of the slaves on these two other estates also adopted the name Walrond. Again, the number is unknown. It is also safe to assume that of all these Afro Walronds, some would have been women, who would have probably changed their last name if they got married.

I have drawn the conclusion that those Afro-Barbadians who acquired the name Walrond through being slaves on these different estates would have done so between the years 1649 and 1807, when the slave trade ended. Any offspring of these early Walronds would also of course have inherited the name.

But this also introduces another fact that would give a slightly different complexion to the issue of last names. If any of the Walrond plantation owners fathered offspring through African women, we can also assume that these children would adopt the name Walrond. The plantation owner would not officially pass on his name to a child because that would be the same as saying that the child could inherit his estate. Finally, there is the scenario that some slaves from other plantations may have liked one or other of the three Walrond planters and may have opted to use this name. The net result of the naming process is that in Barbados, Walrond is now just another name.

Of course, all of these ideas would have to be considered in conjunction with one other important question: Who would have recorded these births?

A baby born on a sugar plantation was considered a nuisance, a bag of human impedimenta carried on the back of the new mother as she laboured in the fields soon after delivery. And this happened only if there were no older women, long past the age for heavy labour, available to look after the newborn.

Also to be considered is the fact that the ledgers and record books of plantation owners did not include the lineage of slaves: just their cost, date of purchase, provenance, and perhaps how many years of service they provided before death overtook them. In addition, plantation owners did not usually pass their name on to any children they may have fathered with women slaves. This would have set a bad legal and moral precedent. The slaves themselves were not literate enough or socially motivated to keep their own records of deaths, births, and marriages. Nor did they have the time to do so before emancipation. After emancipation, the churches may have either started or continued to register some of these events. Once freed, however, many slaves began to move around from plantation to plantation in search of better-paying jobs. This would most probably have caused problems of accuracy for any record-keepers.

Perhaps if I describe a ratoon, you will understand the complexity of the links between people who share the same last name. The name *ratoon* is given to the root system of a fully matured sugar cane plant. It is a jumbled mass made up of one primary root, several large secondary roots, more multiple roots called sett roots, and many other shoot roots. It is a large system that penetrates deeply into the soil to gain a solid foothold. (There is little wonder that the sugar cane plant is considered to be a very tolerant one.) Sometimes two or three ratoons are clustered together to form one even larger — and confusing — root system. And finally, a plantation would have thousands of these plants growing on it. I think that if the lineages of all the Walronds of Barbados could ever be brought together, they would resemble a plantation of ratoons, all prospering and multiplying.

Chapter 10
The Slave Trade
Expands and Dies

To gain an understanding of the reason behind the increase in the number of Afro-Barbadians and consequently of persons named Walrond on the island, I began to take a close look at the history of the slave trade between Africa and the Caribbean. As I read through the many pages of information relating to this, I became convinced that although the Portuguese and the Dutch were the first to trade slaves across the Atlantic, in the final analysis, only the British could ever have stopped this abominable practice.

As I researched, I found myself going back to 1562 in order to put several things into perspective. This was the year in which England joined the slave trading business. True, it was reported that in 1555, an Englishman by the name of John Lok brought a few slaves to England from the West African country of Guinea. And another Englishman, William Towerson, returned to Plymouth with slaves in 1556 and again in 1557. However, these forays were not considered truly transatlantic, and the slaves involved had not been traded.

The Englishman who is widely considered to have started the Atlantic slave trade is John Hawkins. In 1562, 70 years after Columbus, Hawkins left England with 100 men and three ships, bound for Sierra Leone. There he loaded his ships with 300 slaves and other goods. He crossed the Atlantic and sold his cargo on the Spanish island of Hispaniola. When he returned to England, Queen Elizabeth I was very impressed. Hawkins had established a working formula. He had also found a new partner: the queen. It was the English version of Christopher Columbus's voyage.

In 1564, Hawkins left Plymouth, England, again for Guinea and the West Indies. For this trip, Queen Elizabeth I was one of his benefactors. On this second voyage, Hawkins took somewhere between 400 and 500 slaves. Again, they were sold in different Spanish colonies in the Caribbean Sea.

On 2 October 1567, Hawkins departed on his third voyage. On this occasion, he took along his cousin Sir Francis Drake. The queen was again a sponsor. The British navy supplied two ships, and Hawkins supplied another four. The six ships and a crew of over 400 sailed on to Guinea. They arrived there on 18 November after being battered by a storm.

Hawkins proceeded to raid and burn villages and capture Africans. He finally sailed for the West Indies with about 400 slaves. Drake was put in command of one of the ships. Upon arrival in the Caribbean, trading began. Some slaves were traded in Dominica, but most were traded on the Spanish Main (the mainland of Spanish America).

By the end of July 1568, trading was over, and Hawkins got ready to return to England. Reports say that he was now in command of eight ships. July, of course, is the start of the hurricane season in the Atlantic. In mid-September, after having had to seek safe haven on the Florida coast, the men were forced to take refuge for a second time, this time in the port of San Juan de Ulúa on the coast of Mexico.

The Mexicans were not hospitable to Hawkins and his men, and the fleet was ambushed. Three ships escaped. Many of Hawkins' men suffered terrible fates. Finally, on 22 January 1569, one of Hawkins' ships sailed into Plymouth. Another arrived in Mount's Bay on the 25th. Apparently, the third managed to reach Ireland in February 1569. Of the 400 men who left Plymouth in 1567 in six ships, only 70 men returned in three vessels.

As was to be expected, the city of Plymouth desired retaliation for the atrocities that had been inflicted on Hawkins, Drake, and their men. England was at war with Spain, and Hawkins and Drake used this conflict to earn their reputation as Sea Dogs, or pirates, as they wreaked their revenge.

In 1571, Hawkins was elected Member of Parliament for Plymouth and was appointed Comptroller of the Navy in 1573. He was instrumental in upgrading the British Navy, which later led to the victory against the Spanish Armada in 1588. In 1577, Hawkins left Plymouth on board a ship named the Pelican. He formed a convoy with four other ships and 150 men and sailed around the world — the first Englishman to do so. When he returned to Plymouth in September 1580 with 59 men, his ship was renamed the Golden Hind. The next year, he was knighted by Queen Elizabeth.

I have to admit that, as a Caribbean student of British history using textbooks written by English historians, I knew very little about the slaving activities of Hawkins and Drake. I happen to own a copy of the West Indian Reader that was used in my elementary school. I consulted it and found that their slaving exploits were covered in one short paragraph. By contrast, a lot was written about Hawkins' trip around the world, his defeat of the armada, and his other heroic deeds. I am sure that most readers will agree with me when I say that written history is at times biased.

During the period of Hawkins and Drake, England had no colonies in the Caribbean. All lands were Spanish, Portuguese, or Dutch. Hawkins and Drake had sold their slaves mostly on the Spanish Main. These two men simply proved that profits could be made from a well-organised slave trading system. They did this in only three voyages, the last of which ended in disaster.

During the 40 or so years following Hawkins' last catastrophic voyage, England contented itself with trading goods between Africa and the West Indies. In 1607, England established its first New World colony, but it was on mainland America. This colony, Virginia, was soon followed by another, Plymouth Colony, in 1620.

However, these two were not the colonies that swept England back into the slave trade. The number of English possessions in the West Indies was increasing rapidly. The Atlantic island of Bermuda was colonized by the British in 1612. St. Kitts became British in 1624, and Barbados, in 1625. Antigua, Nevis, Montserrat, and the Leeward Islands were under British rule by the 1630s. Jamaica was captured from Spain in 1635. England now controlled most of the islands of the Caribbean.

The immediate result of this colonization was the decimation of the indigenous Carib peoples of these islands. They had been forced to do manual labour, the likes of which they had never seen and to which they were not accustomed. The importation of other labour was seen as the only alternative. Naturally, the plantation owners looked to Africa as the source of this labour.

While this colonization was going on in the New World, England was also busy establishing trading posts all along the coast of West Africa. Soon, there were more than 60 fortified holding places along the coast from Senegal to the Cameroons. At first they were used for storing the goods that England was trading with the West Indies. However, before long, due to the demand for labour in the new colonies, England was fully entrenched in the slave trading business. Africans were added to the list of goods being stored for shipment to the West Indies.

This renewed endeavour on the part of England was in direct competition with the Dutch traders, who had become the biggest slavers in the business. In 1621, they had been granted Spain's trading monopoly called the Asiento, after that benefit was taken away from Portugal. In other words, England was not supposed to be transporting slaves. All the slave-trading done with Hawkins and Drake was totally illegal.

In order to protect its markets, which had now increased considerably, the English Parliament passed what they called Navigation Acts. As a result of these monopolistic laws, foreign ships could not enter and trade in the English colonies. England thus became the largest slave-trading nation.

Meanwhile, in America, the tobacco plantations could not rely on the continued supply of white indentured labourers from England. So they, too, turned to Africa as a source of labour. To do this, they relied on the English ships and slavers to supply their needs. By 1689, London shippers alone had transported over 89,000 slaves from Africa to the West Indies and America. Beginning in 1700, Plymouth was also fast becoming another English slave-ship port.

It was not long before the English transatlantic slave trade was flourishing. Almost simultaneously, the plight of the African slaves during the Middle Passage became public knowledge. This was not the first time that the misery of the slaves had come to the attention of caring and concerned people.

* * *

While still in elementary school, I was issued a new history book. One day, as I sat thumbing through it, I came upon a drawing of the deck a slave ship. I stared at the image. The description "like sardines in a can" came to mind as I looked intently at the black blobs that represented the shackled bodies of the slaves. One of those figures represented, to me, an unknown ancestor. I hated that picture. More than anything I have read, it represented the horrors of the slave trade.

For almost as long as there has been slavery, there were people who thought it should not exist. I decided to take a look at the efforts of the English to end transatlantic slavery. As I have said, England was the only country that could possibly have accomplished this, and the English people wholeheartedly accepted the challenge.

George Fox was one of the first Englishmen to speak out against the many inhumane aspects of slavery. He was born in 1624 and was the founder of a group called The Religious Society of Friends. They later became known as Quakers because their fervour during prayers caused them to quiver. Fox also travelled a lot in Europe and across the Atlantic to the New World, where he made his views known.

In 1671, on a visit to Barbados, he met for the first time with some African slaves. He was interested in them, and together they discussed their condition as agricultural labourers. He concluded that plantation owners should treat their slaves as family members, and he thought that planters should treat their slaves gently and should not be cruel towards them. He also believed that after a certain number of years of service, slaves should be set free.

These sentiments became part of Fox's preaching in the New World and in England. By the 1780s, regular Quaker meetings were calling for the abolition of slavery. Anti-slavery material was being printed and passed around. Pamphlets with titles such as "The Care of Our Fellow Creatures — the Oppressed Africans" were distributed to important and influential members of the English public.

In November 1781, all of England was shocked by the story of the slave ship Zong. This ship sailed from Liverpool, by then an important slaving port, and headed for Jamaica with about 470 slaves. Because of the cramped conditions, by the time the ship got to the Caribbean, severe illness had taken hold. Sixty Africans and seven crew members had perished. The captain of the Zong ordered 133 sick slaves to be thrown overboard to drown.

When the Zong returned to England, the owners made a claim from their insurance company, stating that the sick Africans had posed a threat to the remaining cargo and crew. They further alleged that the ship's water supply was low and could not be wasted on the sick cargo. Although the ship's owners won the case, the incident served to bring to the attention of the general public the awfulness of the slave trade and the callousness of the slave merchants. It was also revealed, after the judgment, that the Zong was actually carrying 420 gallons of water when the slaves were thrown overboard. This revelation greatly increased the anger directed at slavery.

In 1784, so intense was the feeling against the slave trade that the vice-chancellor of the University of Cambridge chose as the title for the annual Latin Essay competition "Anne liceat invitos in servitutem dare?" (Can men be lawfully made slaves against their will?). In response to this challenge, a 24-year-old divinity student by the name of Thomas Clarkson wrote an essay that he hoped would be useful to injured Africans. The essay won resounding approval from the many deans at the university.

Sometime later, Clarkson realised that if the contents of his essay were true, then the atrocities of slavery should end. At that moment of inspiration, Thomas Clarkson dedicated his life to this cause. He became "the slave of the slaves." His essay was translated into English and widely publicized. In 1785, he was introduced to the anti-slavery movement, which set up a committee to convince Members of Parliament that the movement was a worthy one.

One sympathetic member of this group was the Member of Parliament for Hull, William Wilberforce. He was acquainted with Thomas Newton, who had been a midshipman aboard one of Her Majesty's Ships. Newton had deserted but was found and thrown into the guardhouse. He later turned to slaving, gave that up, and joined the clergy. From his personal experience aboard a slave ship, he was able to convince Wilberforce of the evilness of slavery and of the worthiness of the anti-slavery movement. In 1785, Wilberforce became a member of the abolitionist movement, which now had a voice in the House of Commons.

On 22 May 1787, the anti-slavery movement made a concrete step forward when a committee was formed in England to work towards the abolition of the slave trade. It was made up of twelve members, including nine Quakers, Thomas Clarkson, and Granville Sharp. These men needed evidence of the evils of slavery that Wilberforce could present in Parliament. For the next seven years, Clarkson travelled throughout England looking for such evidence.

In Plymouth, he found a leaflet published by the Committee for Abolition of Slavery. It showed the interior deck plans of a Liverpool slave ship, the Brookes, with no fewer than 454 Africans crammed and stretched out on board. This pamphlet was to have a great impact on the movement. The drawing in my history book and the one on this leaflet were the same. Now that I understood the role this image had played in the abolition of the slave trade, I was able to look at it with a newer, more thankful attitude.

Clarkson continued to travel around England, especially visiting the ports on the southern coast, gathering evidence and eyewitness accounts of atrocities related to the slave trade. He was dogged, and his successes inspired his continued actions.

Meanwhile, supporters of slavery mounted their own movement. They proposed that England's commercial success as well as the very survival of the colonies depended on slavery, even suggesting that it should be increased. However, most of their arguments were published anonymously and, happily, were largely ignored.

As the abolitionists continued their relentless struggle, the fight started to take a toll on the leaders of the abolition movement. Thomas Clarkson retired from the movement in 1794. Although still a young man, he was tired and very much overworked. William Wilberforce was getting on in years, but he continued his work in Parliament. He had introduced an abolition motion in Parliament every year starting in 1791. Every year it was defeated, but he carried on. His first speech lasted four hours.

Filibustering and delaying tactics started to cause even more frustration to the members of the Committee for Abolition of Slavery. One such manoeuvre came about in 1797 after Trinidad became a British colony. This island had a lot of land available for the cultivation of sugar. It was estimated that the island needed one million slaves. William Pitt, who was the Prime Minister at the time, suggested that any new slaves for Trinidad would have to be brought in from the other islands. The abolitionists did not like the idea however, noting that if Pitt's suggestion were accepted, more slaves from Africa would simply replace the ones sent to Trinidad from the other islands. In other words, slavery would continue. The stonewalling continued until 1799, when a new element had to be factored in: The price of sugar started to fall.

At the same time, Cuba had increased its sugar production to such an extent that the Americans were exporting it to Europe. This put sugar from the British colonies at an economic disadvantage. To add to the economic problems of West Indian cane sugar, beet sugar was becoming more and more widespread and was also increasingly cheaper to buy in Europe. The net result of all this was that the demand for sugar from the colonies dropped, and the call for new slaves was heard no more.

During the May and June session of Parliament in 1804, the House of Commons finally voted in favour of Wilberforce's Abolition of the Trade Bill during all three readings. The bill was sent on to the House of Lords, where the bill was stalled all through 1805. However, by the summer of 1806, the bill had finally passed through both Houses of Parliament.

In 1807, a new Abolition of Slavery Bill was presented in the House of Lords first. It was passed on 4 February. The bill was then referred to the House of Commons and was passed there as well.

This Abolition of Slavery Act came into force on 25 March 1807. According to this Act, the trading and purchasing of slaves was prohibited in the United Kingdom and its colonies, slaves ships were banned, and captains of ships caught transporting slaves were fined £100 per slave. The removing of slaves from the African continent was also banned. To enforce these provisions, a strong navy was needed.

By the time England had become Europe's largest slaving nation, the other continental governments were not in a position to contemplate ending the trade. France was at war with itself, and Spain's navy had been eliminated in 1588. The English population, led by the Quakers and the other abolitionists, was the only group motivated enough to carry on the long struggle that the cause needed. Towards the end of the fight, it was the collapse of the English sugar trade that precipitated the end of the slave trade. Finally, the British Navy was strong enough to enforce the Abolition of the Slave Trade Act.

Considering that George Fox first planted the seed of better treatment of Africans in 1671 and that the Abolition of Slave Trade Act came into force in 1807, the struggle was indeed a long and tedious one. What Drake and Hawkins had seemingly established within six years really took many men and 134 years to end.

* * *

After the passing of the Abolition of the Slave Trade Act, attention was turned to the plight of the slaves and to slavery itself. So far, only the trade had been banned.

Starting in 1820, all around England, several Anti-Slavery Societies came into existence. In contrast to the members of the abolitionist movement, women now took the lead in these newly formed societies. In many ways, these societies led to the women's rights movement.

One of the primary ways in which African women brought to public attention the horrible plight of their existence as slaves was simply to run away. Mary Prince, a slave from Bermuda, was brought to England by her owners in 1828. She promptly escaped. The Abolition Society contacted her and helped her in the writing and eventual publication of her story, which was called *The History of Mary Prince, a West Indian Slave. Related by Herself.* She said she wrote it because she wanted the good people of England to hear from a slave what a slave had felt and suffered. Mary Price reminded me of the pioneering role played by Rosa Parks during the American anti-segregation movement of the 1950s.

In 1824, it was estimated that there were over 200 branches of the Anti-Slavery Society in England. This growing support was taken as a favourable omen for the fight ahead. There were also other signs that changes were coming with regards to workers in general.

* * *

The abolition movement wasn't the only form of social upheaval in the world at the end of the 18th century and the beginning of the next. In fact, the period starting around 1780 was one of tremendous economic and social development in all of Europe and in the West Indies.

The French Revolution was perhaps the first to bring the problems of the working class to the forefront of public concern. The War of American Independence lasted from 1776 to 1783, and between 1793 and 1802, there was war between England and France. Between 1803 and 1815, all Europe had to contend with the efforts of Napoleon Bonaparte.

There were also revolutions in Haiti and Santo Domingo, which shared the island of Hispaniola. The stories of the lives and accomplishments of men like Toussaint L'Ouverture, Henri Christophe, and Jean-Jacques Dessalines in Haiti are well-documented.

Not to be left out, several of the British West Indian colonies were scenes of revolutions as well. Perhaps the most important, if not dramatic, conquest of the time was the capture of Trinidad from the Spanish. Trinidad, though a colony of Spain, had been severely neglected. At the start of the French Revolution, many French royalists went to Trinidad to wait out the conflict in their homeland. At that time, land was being granted to settlers on the basis of the number of new slaves brought into the colony, a policy that gave rise to rampant slave-stealing. The island had also become a haven for privateers and buccaneers.

The British wanted to rectify this problem, which was detrimental to their trade monopoly in the Caribbean. When, in 1796, Spain declared war on Britain, Sir Ralph Abercromby received his commission. He was to attack Trinidad, and if his forces were not large enough, he was ordered to hold the island till he could destroy all military stores and then arrest the malefactors and ship them off to England.

In 1797, Rear-Admiral Harvey and Abercromby sailed from Martinique with 3,000 men in five well-armed ships. Shortly before their arrival, a fleet of four Spanish sailing ships and a frigate had arrived in Trinidad with Admiral Apodocca in command. They were on their way to Cartagena on the Spanish Main. Don José María Chacón, the governor of Trinidad at the time, asked him to stay awhile.

The British fleet arrived off Port of Spain at sunset on the evening of 16 February. The Spanish fleet was in the harbour at Chaguaramas Bay. At 2:00 the next morning, lookouts on the British ships reported that the Spanish ships were on fire. The Spanish Admiral had considered the British force too powerful and had set fire to his ships as his men went ashore at a point now known as Invaders' Bay, just west of Port of Spain. The next day, Chacón surrendered the island of Trinidad to the British.

* * *

In 1808 — the year after England called for an end to the slave trade — there was a slave revolt in the colony of British Guyana. It was known as the Demerara Revolt. On 17 August 1823, there was another even more serious revolt. Slaves on the east coast of Demerara found out that their masters were about to deny them benefits that the British government had ordered. They got together at their regular meeting place, which happened to be a chapel belonging to the London Missionary Society in the charge of Reverend John Smith.

After discussing the issues, the slaves decided to revolt. The governor was informed of the impending riot, and the armed guards were called out. Martial law was declared, and in two days, the revolt was over. Unfortunately, the Methodist minister was arrested, blamed for the uprising, charged, tried, and sentenced to death. However, he was ill and died in prison.

News of this revolt, and of the treatment and subsequent death of John Smith, reached England in due course. These incidents added to the growing list that was used to promote the freedom of slaves in the colonies. Similar revolts took place in Barbados in 1816, in Jamaica in 1824, and in Antigua in 1831.

As these revolts in the British colonies strengthened the resolve of the different branches of the anti-slavery movement in Britain, planters in the Caribbean and their supporters in England continued their demand for the continuance of slavery. This demand sometimes brought violence, and in some instances, missionary churches in the Caribbean were burned by the plantation owners. Of course, these atrocities added impetus to the calls for the freedom of the slaves.

While the cries of the Anti-Slavery Society were being heard in the public domain, men like William Wilberforce carried on the fight in Parliament. (Women were not allowed to run for election to the House of Commons, and the House of Lords, was, of course, made up of men.) For several years after the Abolition of the Slave Trade Act was passed, there was little progress in Parliament. Different slave codes aimed at improving the lot of slaves were passed but were never implemented. William Wilberforce began to think that perhaps a clean and clear-cut emancipation of slaves would be better than a more gradual approach.

There seemed little hope that Parliament would turn its attention to solving the problems of the slaves in the Caribbean. The Napoleonic wars had ended, and in England there was growing unemployment. The problems created by the French Revolution were over, and the returning soldiers were not happy. The British Parliament was quite occupied with the country's internal struggles.

Wilberforce, in the meantime, was growing old, and his health was deteriorating. He wanted to find a younger man to take over the reins of the struggle to free the slaves. He found such a person in Thomas Fowell Buxton, who was elected Member of Parliament in 1818. Buxton immediately began to campaign for reform of prisons and also for the reduction of the severity of criminal laws. He also hated slavery and had always supported the abolitionist movement.

By the end of 1822, the economic and social conditions in Britain had settled down, and the abolitionists thought it was time to renew the fight and begin a fresh campaign to help the slaves. Wilberforce and his other colleagues approached Buxton and asked him to be the leader of the movement in Parliament. He agreed immediately. The movement now had a more powerful force of influential men, in and out of both Houses of Parliament.

In March of 1823, Wilberforce began the attack in Parliament with a petition from the Quakers. Some short time later, Buxton made a forceful speech that ended with a motion that slavery was a repugnant state and should be gradually abolished throughout the British colonies. To the surprise of Parliament, the Foreign Secretary replied that slavery would be abolished.

Opposition from the planters was immediate. However, the British Parliament decided to tackle the situation first in the newer Crown colonies, like Demerara, Berbice, and the islands of St. Lucia and Trinidad, which were all ruled by a governor and a council appointed by Britain. The home government began to pass laws aimed at improving the condition of the slaves in these colonies, in the hope that the older colonies like Barbados, Jamaica, and Antigua would follow suit and enact similar laws. The plan backfired. Riots took place in Berbice, Jamaica, and Barbados. The cause suffered severe setbacks during this time.

In May 1830, there was an important anti-slavery meeting in London. Wilberforce opened the proceedings with his usual motion that "slavery be abolished at the earliest possible period." The crowd was not impressed with this motion. There was an amendment that "slavery be abolished immediately." This amended motion was carried. The stage was set.

The following year brought a dramatic change of power in the British Parliament, and the newly elected Whigs sent a recommendation to the Assemblies of the older colonies, Jamaica, Barbados, and St. Lucia. The Assemblies were more defiant than ever. More riots broke out. Needless to say, the Assemblies were on the side of the planters.

The great irony of the entire situation lay in the fact that the planters, and perhaps the Members of the Assemblies, did not know that the sugar from the Caribbean was no longer an important product in Britain. Sugar from Bengal and other places was being imported into Britain at a lower cost than sugar from the Caribbean. England could also buy sugar more cheaply from Cuba and Brazil. Still, Britain had to do what it could to protect her colonies, so an import tax was put on foreign sugar.

To add to the problems, over the years, the planters in the British colonies had not been improving the quality of the land on their estates. They were, for the most part, absentee landlords and had no real idea of what was going on in the islands. Their resident agents had allowed production costs to rise. This lack of care and concern on the part of the plantation owners and managers simply added to the gravity of the situation. The net result was that in Britain, sugar had become a scarce and expensive luxury product.

By 1829, the British public had had enough of slavery and wanted it abolished. If slavery could not supply them with cheap and plentiful sugar, there was no point in having it. The planters had in fact destroyed themselves. Sugar was no longer king.

By May of 1833, the Colonial Secretary notified the House of Commons that his government intended to free all slaves in the British Empire. Twenty millions pounds would be given to the planters as compensation. The Emancipation Act was passed on 29 August 1833, four days after William Wilberforce had died. Slavery would end on 1 August 1834.

The Emancipation Act of 1833 was not an easy one to formulate. The first act before Parliament called for unconditional freedom for the slaves and a compensatory loan of up to £15,000.00 to each plantation owner, depending on the number of slaves owned. It also proposed to enforce slave labour for "a certain period of time." It was rejected by both the Cabinet and the colonists.

A second act was presented in Parliament on 5 July 1833 and was passed with two small amendments. This act proposed that there be a period of time between the end of slavery and absolute freedom. This period was to be called an "apprenticeship period." It would last for six years for field workers and four years for house servants. Slaves would work as unpaid servants for three-quarters of the work week. The £15,000 loan was kept as compensation for the loss of one quarter of the free slave labour. This amount was later raised to £20,000, and it was decided that the money should be a gift, not a loan. A total of £20 million was paid out to planters as compensation.

The slaves were granted certain rights and protections related to their spare time and to their rent-free provision grounds or gardens, where they could grow their own food. They could also sell some of this food, and with money so earned, they could buy their freedom before the apprenticeship period was over.

The actual Emancipation Day was set for the 1 August 1834. During the year before this date, many planters took the initiative to improve the working conditions of the slaves. However, it was the tireless work of missionaries that did a lot to ensure that the important day would pass without the riots that many planters feared and predicted.

Throughout the British colonies, the evening of 31 July was a sombre and emotional one. After a hurriedly eaten evening meal, some slaves climbed to the top of the nearest hill to wait for sunrise on 1 August. This was going to be their "Dawn of Freedom." Some slaves dressed in their finest and headed for their churches and chapels, which had been decorated with flowers, branches, and palm fronds. Once there, they sang hymn after hymn, in praise and thanksgiving, while keeping an eye on the clock. At midnight, the ministers gave the message "You are free."

The 1787 Josiah Wedgewood anti Slavery Medallion

Ignatius Sancho (c. 1729–1780) symbolized to the British abolitionists the humanity of Africans and the immorality of the slave trade.

The Symbol of Freedom

Chapter 11
A New World

I was now overwhelmed by a feeling of satisfaction regarding my knowledge about the efforts to abolish the slave trade and to free the Africans who still laboured on the sugar plantations of the West Indies. I felt that I could now go on with finding out why my family migrated from Barbados to Trinidad. My interest was reinforced, and my efforts were redoubled.

Emancipation was set to take place on 1 August 1834. It was to be followed by a six-year period of apprenticeship. Colonist planters and the British government had therefore no more than six years to solve any problems that would or could arise before the emancipated slaves were to be given their complete freedom. The main question was what would happen if the majority of the slaves did not want to remain on the plantations as paid workers. In the islands where there was still a lot of crown land, the slaves would be able to squat there and make a living on their own. The planters wondered what would happen to their production of sugar and their trade with Britain if this occurred — and they were sure it would.

The other major issue was that of the wages to be paid to the freed slaves if they decided to remain on the plantations. What would these wages be? Who would set the levels? Would freed slaves have to have a contract to work a set number of days or weeks per year? Would the slaves' cottages on the plantations be rent-free or not?

Other unanswered questions dealt with the care and concern for the old and ailing former slaves. This had formerly been the charge of the plantation owners. Consideration would also have to be given to the cost of educating the freed slaves. Here again the decision as to who would pay for this aspect of their future demanded close scrutiny. The plantation owners and the local governments had hoped that these issues would have been addressed in some form or other before the actual emancipation of the slaves.

The colonies each had specific additional problems to overcome as well. The island of Barbados, for example, had an overall population of about 99,000, of which 80,000 were former slaves. However, almost all of the land in Barbados was cultivated. What was not had become towns or villages. Plantation work was the only kind available. There was therefore no shortage of labour, but the workers tended to wander around looking for better wages. As a result, Barbadian planters had to offer competitive wages, along with free housing and some free land for workers to grow their own food.

The colonies of Guyana and Trinidad also warrant close consideration. At the time of emancipation, Guyana had only 222 sugar plantations, wages were as high as in Trinidad, and labour was as scarce. The island of Trinidad was and is the most fertile of the British Antilles, and it's the largest after Jamaica. The soil was so rich that sugar canes, once planted, continued to send up shoots year after year. It was not necessary to plant new canes every two or three years as was needed in the older colonies. Trinidad's challenge was the lack of labour. There were only about 17,400 slaves in Trinidad at the time of emancipation. Guyana also needed more labourers.

It was clear to the British government that something had to be done to improve the supply and stability of the labour force in Trinidad and in Guyana as well. As early as 1834, a few indentured labourers, 44 in all, arrived in Trinidad from the Azores, islands located in the Atlantic Ocean about 1400 kilometers off the coast of Portugal. In 1839, some more Portuguese immigrants landed. Soon after, about 670 French and German nationals took up residence. Between 1840 and 1842, even more French, German, and Irish workers migrated to Trinidad. However, these attempts at increasing the labour force were not successful, because many newcomers died from the intense tropical heat. By 1846, the labour situation began to improve because inter-island immigration became more prevalent. Because of the availability of jobs and higher wages, many people moved to Trinidad and Guyana from Barbados, and a smaller number came from Grenada, St. Vincent, and St. Lucia.

The Assembly in Barbados became alarmed at the drainage of its labour force and passed an Act that required would-be emigrants to obtain an exit certificate, thereby assuring the government that no dependents were being left behind in Barbados. Although this act was vetoed by the British government, the result was that some entire families emigrated from Barbados. In spite of this inter-island migration, however, the need to augment the supply of labour for the sugar plantations of Trinidad and Guyana was still urgent.

* * *

At this point, I found it expedient to take a look at the composition of the population of the Caribbean countries around 1834. In addition to whoever remained of the indigenous peoples, there were Africans, Europeans, and Asians. Among these peoples, some were voluntary inhabitants. This latter group included the merchants and traders who settled there, travellers who loved adventure and stayed, and people who migrated for religious, economic, and social reasons (in other words, because of a desire for a better life).

Other members of the general population included the involuntary inhabitants, foremost among whom would be the freed slaves and some criminals who had been deported, mostly from Europe. Finally, there were the Africans who were liberated from latent slave ships, those slaves who had escaped prior to emancipation and were fugitives, Sephardic Jews who had been expelled from Spain and Portugal, and sundry other refugees of war. The entire Caribbean area had become a veritable melting pot of cultures and peoples from many other countries.

* * *

As the results of emancipation took hold, several questions still remained unanswered. From a purely personal point of view, I was especially curious about those who migrated from Barbados to Trinidad. Who were they? Were they just freed slaves who simply went looking for a better-paying job? Did they offer something new and perhaps even different to Trinidad? What did they know of the social conditions in their new prospective homeland? Did they care? Did they know what social and economic conditions they were likely to encounter? In short, what was their motivation, and what were their expectations?

So I kept on looking. Fortunately, I did not have far to go. Many years ago, on a visit to Trinidad, I had purchased a rather handsome book called — would you believe it? — *The Book of Trinidad* (Paria Publishing Co, 1992). It holds a special place among my somewhat extensive library. In my research for this book, I had all but ignored it. Now, however, I took a much closer look at it. Written and edited by Gerard Besson, an advertising executive, and Bridget Brereton, a history professor, it contains many articles by these two authors and by several other Trinidadian authors and personalities. These diverse items were written at different times throughout the history of the island. It is a veritable compendium of interesting data, photographs, anecdotes, and drawings.

In a comparatively short article entitled "British West Indian Immigrants," Brereton offers a wealth of data that answered my many questions. For example, there seems to have been two distinct periods when workers moved to Trinidad from the other Eastern Caribbean Islands after the Emancipation Act was passed in 1834. The first was from 1839 until 1849, when approximately 10,000 new settlers arrived in Trinidad. Later, between 1871 and 1911, around 65,000 more new inhabitants arrived. By 1897, however, it was estimated that about 14,000 Barbadians had permanently established themselves in Trinidad.

Before delving into the question of their character, it is necessary to describe, even briefly, the society into which these new immigrants settled. They joined what has been called the Trinidadian Rural Creole establishment. It was important for me to find out the significance of these two terms, *rural* and *creole*.

First, the term *rural*. Christopher Columbus, as we know, saw Trinidad in 1492, and the island was claimed in the name of the king and queen of Spain. In 1795, Trinidad was surrendered to the British. During those 303 years, the Spanish government constructed one road. It went in an almost-straight line across the island from Port of Spain to Arima and, eventually, to Balandra Bay on the Atlantic or east coast, a distance of about 30 miles. At the Amerindian district of Tunapuna, a little less than halfway across the island, a branch road led due south to a Catholic mission called Savana Grande another 30 miles away. At this village, another branch went west to

San Fernando, a city founded in 1792. Yet another branch led further south and then west to another mission, that of Siparia. This comprehensive road system was called the Camino Real, or "royal road." This road was, in fact a slightly improved aboriginal footpath through forest and across bushy plains. Mobility throughout the rest of the island was by means of more rustic footpaths.

Other than Port of Spain and San Fernando, there were no towns as such but rather areas and villages where small pockets of population existed around sugar, cocoa, and other plantations. These villages were scattered throughout the island. To be sure, a capital city, San José de Oruña, had been founded in 1592, a hundred years after Columbus. However, in 1593 (some historians say 1595), this city was burned to the ground by Sir Walter Raleigh as an act of revenge against the then Spanish governor. In 1649 (some historians say 1640), the struggling city was again burnt by the raiding Dutch. Though St. Joseph, to use its English name, was a small town, it was centered on the prerequisite public square, governor's house, town hall, church, and prison. Although this first city did survive the ravages of time, the capital was later moved to Puerto de España, now known as Port of Spain. Still, by the time of emancipation, Trinidad remained largely rural in nature.

Creole refers to persons of mixed ethnicity. Every country in the Caribbean area as well as those on the South American continent, including Brazil, has its own particular blend of Creoles. In Trinidad, as elsewhere, they formed the middle social class. They were of a mixture of English, Spanish, and French extraction. Most importantly, they all spoke a patois which was also a local combination of French and English, with some Spanish thrown in for good measure.

France and Spain were and are predominantly Catholic countries. As a result, although the Spanish government did not build many roads, they did allow churches and missions to be established wherever they thought that the local population warranted such actions.

Against this background, it is easier to place the migrating Barbadians. Several traits set them apart from the local Trinidadian population. The primary difference was that the Barbadians were a much politicized people. By 1639, at least 200 years before emancipation, Barbados had evolved into a country governed by an elected Assembly. These newcomers to Trinidad had been exposed to politics and fully understood the importance, and above all the power, of policies, of politicking, and of politicians. Barbadians could advocate for themselves, and they deferred to no one. The local landowners referred to this character trait as "insolence." Barbadians were even considered to be agitators whenever they stood in defence of the rural Creoles.

Another important difference between the Trinidadian labour force and the Barbadian workers was that the new settlers were all Protestants. For the most part, they were either Methodists or English Catholics. They were not Roman Catholics, as the patois-speaking Creoles of Trinidad were. The Barbadians spoke, read, and wrote English. This facilitated communication between them and the British-appointed government officials. The men especially were skilled workmen, and their craft as carpenters and mechanics put them in good stead in towns and on sugar estates, where they commanded positions of authority. But the women were also very capable workers as housekeepers, cooks, and seamstresses and in other domestic occupations.

As a result of their abilities, the Barbadians were more socially confident than the local Trinidadians. They were also very well-educated. This combination of political awareness, ease of communication, social confidence, and education made them a very mobile force. Some of them became policemen, office clerks, and teachers.

With this last point in mind, I find it necessary to expand a bit on the state of the education system in Barbados. It must be remembered that formal education is the primary gateway to social and economic self-determination. The information I garnered helped me put in proper perspective a lot of the material in the report "Historical Developments of Education in Barbados, 1686–2000." It was prepared by the Planning Research and Development Unit of the Ministry of Education, Youth Affairs and Culture and is dated November 2000. The information I gathered is summarised as follows:

1688–1785	Six wealthy Anglo-Barbadians funded the establishment of schools. Sir Christopher Codrington donated two estates for the creation of a college for the training of missionaries. Called Codrington College, it is still in operation.
1818–1827	Three different schools for coloured children were built by churches.

1835–1845	The British government made annual grants to all its colonies in the West Indies towards the education of former slaves. The various churches started schools all over the island. By 1844, there were 48 Anglican schools, 4 Moravian schools, and 4 Wesleyan schools. There were also 149 private schools. Altogether, these schools enrolled about 7,150 students.
1846	The Barbados legislature made a grant of £750 towards education. It was their first such grant. The first attempt to train elementary school teachers was made by the principal of Codrington College.
1850	Barbados passed its first Education Act, providing for an Education Committee with a part-time inspector and an increased grant of £3,000.
1858	A second Education Act allowed for a full-time Inspector of Schools.
1874	The annual grant was increased to £9,200
1878	The annual grant was increased to £15,000
1880–1894	Many schools were upgraded and formally recognised by the Board of Education.
1894	The Alexandra School was founded.
1900	One hundred sixty-nine elementary schools with an enrollment of 24,145 children were in operation. There were also three first-grade schools and five second-grade schools with 532 children on roll. Elementary school fees ranged from one to three pence per week. Over £1,000 was collected per year. Secondary school fees ranged from £5 to £15 per year.

There is no doubt that education was an important element of life in Barbados before and after the emancipation of slaves. It came as no surprise to me that the emigrants from Barbados to Trinidad in the post-emancipation period were so self-confident.

The preceding data also demonstrate that from 1686 to 1827, education in Barbados was at the mercy and goodwill of wealthy planters, who offered financial support, and of the religious interests of the churches: Anglican, Wesleyan, and Methodist. The schools that had been established were for the benefit of white children, mostly boys. This initial preference of students was no accident. It coincided with the period when slavery was still the only way of life for Negro children. However, the churches must be recognised for the effort they did make to educate some of the children of slaves in the period immediately preceding emancipation — in other words, when the writing was on the wall, so to speak.

When emancipation did finally arrive, the efforts of the churches resulted in schools being built close to the established church buildings. It was clear that education and religion were to be closely linked to each other: spiritually, mentally, and physically.

Even when the Barbadian government, aided by efforts of the British government, did get involved in education, the close association of church and education was maintained. Finally, it must be acknowledged that this unity of effort was perhaps the most important aspect of early education on the island. I was later to discover that Trinidad also benefitted from this precedent as well.

Whether they remained working-class labourers or lower-middle-class employees, these new Barbadian immigrants to Trinidad were upward bound. They tended to be more accomplishment driven, more ambitious, and much more politically aware than other groups. However, they did not migrate only to Trinidad. Their counterparts who migrated to Guyana were just as well-respected, appreciated, and successful as the ones in Trinidad. In both countries, new labour was still needed, and these immigrants provided it.

* * *

Barbadians were not the only people who migrated to Trinidad or to Guyana. In January of 1838, two ships, the Whitby and the Hesperus, sailed from India to Guyana. These voyages were not government-sanctioned, and the vessels carried 405 men, women, and children.

This first attempt at Indian immigration was in fact a renewal of the African slave trade in that the immigrants were for the most part involuntary. Travelling conditions from Asia were just as bad as on the Middle Passage endured by the African slaves. Eighteen of the Indians died during the journey, two of whom were suspected suicides, since they drowned. There were no further attempts at immigration for a few years.

On 19 October 1843, a group known as the West Indian Body wrote to Lord Stanley, the British Member of Parliament for Hindon (and later for North Cheshire). The letter asked Lord Stanley to allow Indians to immigrate to the West Indies as a means towards achieving a steady supply of labourers. His reply was that he was attempting to get Africans from New Brunswick and Nova Scotia in Canada to go to the Caribbean. He did not agree to emigration from India.

Twenty-three days after this first response, however, on 29 November, Lord Stanley finally understood the difficulties being faced in the West Indies, and he took the initiative to write to the Governor General of India and ask that the restrictions placed on Indian Immigration to the West Indies be lifted. Discussions followed, and the terms of an agreement were eventually reached among the British, Indian, and Trinidadian governments.

Restrictions were relaxed, and large sums of money were made available. The primary target for this new program was Eastern Indian workers. Immigrants were offered three-year contracts, and each contract had to have a government stamp attached to it. A member of the Assembly was appointed as Protector of Immigrants. It was his job to ensure that the terms of the contract were carried out. The money collected from the sale of the stamps went to defray the emigrants' passage from India. They were free to return to India at the end of five years. This term was later extended to ten years. If an immigrant wanted to stay in Trinidad and not return to India, a grant of money and land was made. Although these new regulations were put in place, the journey was still a horrible experience.

As a result of these successful negotiations, on 16 February 1845, the clipper ship Fatel Razack weighed anchor in the Indian port of Calcutta. On 30 May, this first official immigrant ship arrived in Trinidad. On board were 225 survivors of what was indeed a dangerous journey. Some of the immigrants were as young as 15 years. Some reports give slightly different numbers and ages. In addition, there are conflicting reports as to when this ship docked in Trinidad. One report lists the arrival date as 10 May 1845.

When the ship docked at Nelson (Nielson) Island, one of the Five Islands in the Port of Spain harbour, the immigrants were quarantined for a while. The ship, food, and blankets were inspected by the Protector of Immigrants before permission was given for the immigrants to land. The healthy were sent off to estates, and those who needed medical care were sent to a health institution for necessary treatment.

The immigration scheme that started in 1838 with the arrival of the Hesperus in Georgetown, Guyana, and in 1845 with the arrival of the Fatel Razack in Trinidad initially lasted until 1848, when it was suspended by the Indian government. The reason given was the high mortality rate of Indians during the long and hazardous journey. The program was begun again in 1851, and it lasted until the Indian government permanently suspended the program under the Defence of India Act of 1917.

During this period of Indian immigration (1845 to 1917), 319 voyages were made to Trinidad, and 147,592 registered indentured Indians, Hindus, and Muslims came to Trinidad. They were assigned to sugar, cocoa, and coconut plantations throughout the island. There is no doubt that without this influx of Indian labour, the plantations would not have survived. W.G. Sewell, in his book *The Ordeal of Free Labour in the British West Indies* (1861), wrote this about the Indian immigrants to Trinidad: "Not only has the island been saved from impending ruin, but a prospect of future prosperity opened to her such as no British island in these seas ever before enjoyed under any system, slave or free."

* * *

Thirty-two years before the Whitby and Hesperus made their ill-fated voyages to Guyana, the ship Fortitude left China carrying immigrants from Macau, Penang, and Canton. The boat docked on 12 October 1806 with 192 Chinese, although some reports say there were 194 men alive. When the ship left port, 200 men were on board.

In 1806, the abolition of the slave trade to the West Indies was very much a topic of conversation. The planters in the Caribbean feared that sooner or later, their source of cheap labour would no longer exist.

This first attempt at immigration from China was a result of this threat. It was nothing but an experiment, spearheaded by a Portuguese captain, at setting up a peasant colony of farmers and labourers using a new source of workers. The journey to Trinidad took eight months. The survivors were established at the Surveillance Estate located in Cocorite, near Port of Spain.

Because there was not much farm land in this area, the Chinese immigrants requested that they be allowed to find work as labourers, not as farmers. They established themselves in their own little village called Speculation Estate. They were under the supervision of Mr. Ayo, who bought a fishing boat and is said to have introduced the seine method of fishing to Trinidad. He taught these first immigrants how to use these nets. Others became butchers, market gardeners, shopkeepers, carpenters, and shoemakers. Some reports suggest that selling crabs, oysters, and charcoal were also included as occupations.

The 1806 experiment was considered a dismal failure because of the 192 immigrants who arrived, 17 had died within one year. Sixty-one of them returned to China when the Fortitude sailed in July 1807. By 1810, only 22 men remained, and in 1834, a mere 7 were still alive. These first immigrants were not in the best of health to begin with and were not prepared for the arduous labor expected of them.

In 1853, Chinese immigration was again tried. This time, it was organised by the British, Chinese, and Trinidadian governments. Most of these immigrants came from the province of Guangdong where the cities of Macau, Hong Kong, and Canton are located. The immigrants included both indentured labourers and free Chinese who came voluntarily. For the indentured labourers, the terms were similar to the ones that governed the Indian indentured labourers.

The first set of Chinese immigrants to Trinidad came on three ships in 1853. The Australia arrived on 4 March; the Clarendon, on 23 April; and the Lady Flora Hastings, on 28 June. Together they brought 1,100 Chinese male labourers (women were not allowed to immigrate until 1862). On 3 July 1862, the ship Wanata brought in a further 467 immigrants from Hong Kong. Between 18 February and 25 May 1865, 600 more Chinese arrived in Trinidad. Between 12 and 24 February, two vessels, the Dudbrook and the Little Red Riding Hood, also landed more immigrants.

This wave of Chinese immigration lasted until 1866, when the Chinese government insisted on free passage for those labourers who wanted to return to China. The British government thought that this would be too costly, and the program was ended.

Between 1862 and 1866 when the program ended, 309 women landed. Between 1853 and 1866, the number of immigrants who arrived in Trinidad ranges from about 2,500 to 2,837 and includes 7 babies who were born at sea. All immigrants came from Macau, Amoy, Canton, and Hong Kong.

Those immigrants who were indentured labourers finished their terms and left the estates. Some of them returned to China, but most of them chose to remain. They set themselves up in business as shopkeepers, garden farmers, restaurant owners, fishers, carpenters, butchers, and traders or merchandisers. Tailoring and laundry operators were also among the businesses they started. Many of their shops were in rural areas.

Soon these immigrants had established a reputation for being hard workers and thrifty but generous tradespeople. They introduced the system of "trusting," by which a customer could take goods, usually food, on a promise to pay later. These items of credit were duly noted in a book. Payment could be made in installments.

Organised Chinese immigration ceased in 1866. However, Chinese immigrants continued to come to Trinidad on a smaller scale. In 1911, because of unrest in China, a larger scale of immigration to Trinidad began. This movement peaked around 1949.

* * *

From the time of their arrival in Trinidad, the Chinese have made an important contribution to life in the island. On 6 March 2013, I received an e-mail from my friend Paul in Trinidad. Attached was a note about Dai Ailian, the Trinidad-born ballerina who is acknowledged as being the Mother of Modern Chinese Dance. She was born Eileen Isaac on 10 May 1916 in the town of Couva. Her father planted sugar cane and coffee and owned a shop that sold food supplies, cloth, and stationery.

His shop was located at a ninety-degree corner of the Southern Main Road, which connected Port of Spain with San Fernando, the second largest city on the island. At this corner, another road led eastwards to the village of Balmain and to other rural inland villages. Another street, called Isaac Street, continued southwards. To the west was the continuation of the Southern Main Road. This very busy and important intersection is still known as Isaac Junction.

When Dai's great-grandfather arrived in Trinidad, probably in 1853 aboard the Clarendon, he was given the surname Isaac. This naming was a common practice, especially for Chinese immigrants who wanted to be businessmen. By the time Dai was born, the family had prospered, and her parents had enough money to give her a good education.

At age 14, she was sent to London to learn ballet and modern dance. There, after many ups and downs in her life, Dai went to China, first to Hong Kong and later to Beijing. Her trip to China was sponsored by the British government, who wished to repatriate any Chinese. I was amazed at Dai's accomplishments, especially because when she arrived in China, she could speak neither Cantonese nor Mandarin. She was, in effect, an immigrant. In London, she had faced financial shortages and discrimination as a Chinese immigrant from Trinidad. In China, she faced language problems. But she persevered, survived, and achieved her dreams. She died in Beijing on 9 February 2006. She was 90 years old.

Dai's international importance to the world of dance and ballet was recognized when a statue of her was unveiled in the reception hall of the British Royal Academy of Dance in London. Her statue is one of four female dancers who were honoured at the same time. Her story revealed to me the fact that there could be something which I call reverse immigration.

* * *

I had never known about Dai Ailian, but I knew she had a nephew named Adrian, and I was very familiar with the area in Trinidad where her family lived. I too was born in Couva. The e-mail and its reference to Isaac Junction in Couva rekindled a host of memories for me. My friend who sent it to me did not know that I came from Couva.

When I was about 3, I lived for a while with my family in the upper level of a house directly across the street from Dai's father's corner shop. Though a small child, I remember looking through the spaces of the banister that ran the length of the verandah, which overlooked the street below. From this viewpoint, I could see the Isaac shop. I could also place a chair beside the railing and climb up to see even better. (My parents did not like this, of course.) Living in this house is one of my fondest childhood memories.

I know we spent at least one carnival in that home. The Trinidadian carnival takes place on the Monday and Tuesday before Ash Wednesday every year. Its origins lie deep in the French Catholic tradition of having a masquerade ball before the start of the stringent Lenten season. I looked down and saw the costumed masqueraders perform their dances to the noise of drums and other musical instruments, mostly improvised, and all very local in provenance. The colours of the revellers' costumes were as spectacular as their shouts, and screams were deafening.

Most mornings, I was treated to the crash, clang, and clamour of the many delivery trucks that serviced the building in which I lived. The ground floor was occupied by a cheerful lady named Mrs. André. She ran a parlour and specialized in sandwiches, pastries, soft drinks, and what today would be called fast food.

Trucks brought in the soft drinks, notably Coca-Cola, Pepsi, and 7Up. But there were also locally bottled soft drinks that carried other brand names such as Solo, Ju-C, and above all, Sun Crest. These were all bottled in Port of Spain, mostly by the Canning Bottling Company. The Joseph Charles Bottling Company, for example, produced the Solo brand. The rattle of the empties being loaded onto the trucks seemed to have its own rhythm. Incidentally, I recently found out that Joseph Charles was the son of an Indian immigrant. He had to change his name in order to succeed in business.

When that truck left, the Stauble's Bakery truck would arrive. Oh, the smell of fresh bread! What a delight! The bread provided by this company carried the brand name Holsum. It was not till many years later that I realised that this name was a takeoff on the word wholesome.

Yet the odour of fresh bread was nothing compared to that of the cakes, pastries, buns, and other sugared confectioneries that were delivered by yet another vehicle. If ever there was a heaven on earth, this was it. Its every arrival awakened in me an alert sense of the delicious. (Remember that this was in the days before the concept of vacuum wrapping.) This truck would also reclaim the unsold products from the days before. Supplies were therefore always fresh. Years later, when we lived in another house, an uncle of mine was employed by the bakery on this delivery run. Sometimes, on his way back, he would stop off at our house. Some of the day-old cakes that were being returned never made it back to the bakery. Need I say more?

If you ever wanted to know what was done with the returns, you simply had to buy *a bellyful*. This was a cake, in truth a bit of a delicacy, which was simply a reconstitution of the day-old cakes. New ingredients such as eggs, spices, and flavourings were added to create a unique taste. These new cakes always looked the same, and they were very tasty. This was recycling at its most delicious. And the name was very appropriate as well. One bellyful was all the average person could eat.

The parlour below was also furnished with some chairs and tables at which patrons could rest while partaking of the varied and delicious fare. (Ask any true born Trinidadian what a "currants roll" is. Mmm!) Lively and heated conversations could also be heard rising to the floor on which we lived.

In the hot climate of the island, the arrival of the ice truck was always a welcome relief. "The ice truck come yet?" was a frequently heard question. Its late arrival was a hardship few rural Trinidadians could often tolerate. A negative answer was always followed by a *cheups*, sometimes called a *steups*. This sound is a uniquely eternal Trinidadian oral gesture of total disapproval, caused by the inhalation of air through clenched teeth, but with lips open. Try it!

And then the day came when my older sister and I were taken to the Port of Spain General Hospital to undergo operations. We had both been born with hernias which needed to be repaired. Days later, we looked forward to going back to the house at Isaac Junction. Imagine my surprise and sadness when the car — it was a taxi — turned the corner but did not stop. I could not understand what was going on because the house was still there.

We went instead to another house located on Edgar Street. My family had moved while I was in the hospital. If I had to select the saddest day of my life, it would easily be that one. Sad because I never got to say goodbye to my favourite childhood home. Most of all I missed being able to look out and see the Isaac house and the street below. I also missed seeing Adrian and his bicycle. My family had 'migrated' to a larger house beside sugar cane fields. As it turned out, one set of pleasures was replaced by different but equally enjoyable ones. As usual, moving meant improvement.

Chapter 12
The Walronds of Trinidad and Guyana

As I did more research in my quest to discover all I could regarding the history of my family, I was reminded once again that the history of humanity is in fact a chronicle of migration. From the very early exodus of mankind from the confines of Africa upwards and outwards over Europe, Asia, across the Bering Strait, and down into the Western Hemisphere, it seems that people in general have forever been seeking to improve their standards of living, and they did this by moving.

Sometime around 1887, two families left Barbados in search of a better life. One family — the Walronds — was made up of three brothers and two sisters. From this family, one of the two brothers, Sam "Pappy" Walrond, went to Guyana, where he established himself as a skilled craftsman, working in wood. The other two brothers, Charles and Joshua Walrond, along with their sisters Clem and "Dear Aunt," made Trinidad their home.

Charles Walrond was born on in 1863. His first wife, Julia Stoute, was also from Barbados; she was born in 1861. Sadly, she died in 1935, and Charles married Angelina Straker. Charles died in 1958; Angelina, on 4 October 1974.

The other family that left Barbados around 1887 consisted of a father, mother, and two daughters. The Chandlers — Joseph and his wife Mary Williams, plus their daughters, Gertrude and Mathilda Mariah Phillipa — also went to Trinidad.

The Walrond family and the Chandler family were united when Joshua Walrond married Mathilda Chandler. Joshua, my grandfather, was born around 1864, and Mathilda was born on 2 October 1868. They had nine children: Clementina, Maude, Frank, Agatha, my father Randolph, Olga, Daphne, Nora, and Horace. Unfortunately, Nora died when she was in her 20s.

Gertrude Chandler married a man whose last name was Alleyne. His first name is unknown, and he too may have come from Barbados. They had three children: Edith, Leonora, and Aubrey. Of special interest to my story is Aubrey Alleyne. He married a woman whose last name was McGowan. Her first name is unknown. They had four children: Enid, Dorothy, Edna, and Carlton.

The story of Dorothy Alleyne is a case study in migration and upwards mobility. She married Dr. David Pitt, who had migrated to Trinidad from Grenada. He was born in 1913 and in 1933 left for Edinburgh University to study medicine. He returned to Trinidad in 1939 and began a practice in San Fernando. He and Dorothy were married in 1943, and they both went to England in 1947, where he continued his medical work. They had three children: Bruce, Phyllis, and Amanda.

His efforts and achievements in his field were so much appreciated that in 1985, he was elected President of the British Medical Association. Prior to that, in 1975, he was granted a life peerage by Queen Elizabeth II, became Baron David Pitt of Hampstead, and took his seat in the House of Lords in London. His work in England also included advocating against racial discrimination in England and in the Caribbean. He died in 1994 and was buried with full honours on his home island of Grenada.

The stories of Dai Ailian, Dorothy Alleyne, and her husband, David Pitt, are not the only interesting ones revealed by my research. As I wrote these pages, I could not help but remember the information that I had gathered regarding the qualities and attributes of those intrepid Afro-Barbadians who had migrated to Trinidad, since evidence of these character traits permeated the lives and careers of my family members.

* * *

My great uncle Charles Walrond married Julia Stoute on 15 December 1894. He was 31 years old, and she was two years his junior. On their marriage certificate, he is listed as being a police constable and a carpenter, residing at the police barracks in Port of Spain. Julia is listed as being a servant, residing in Woodbrook, a suburb of Port of Spain, not far from the police barracks.

When I first met Uncle Charlie, I was very young, no more than 9 or 10. He lived at the corner of Francis Street and the Eastern Main Road in the town of Curepe, not far from the first capital of Trinidad, St. Joseph. The Eastern Main Road leads from Port of Spain in the West clear across the Island to Arima and eventually to Balandra Bay on the east coast of the island. This main road follows the route of the old Camino Real that was built by the Spaniards during their earlier tenure in Trinidad.

Uncle Charlie's was a small house built about 4 feet off the ground. Most houses in Trinidad were built this way to allow air to circulate under the structure and keep them cool. Because the Eastern Main Road, or EMR as it is called, was a busy main thoroughfare, visitors usually entered through the rear of the house. I remember doing so on the two or three occasions that I visited him with my parents, or with just my father on one occasion.

I still remember, though, that Uncle Charlie always led us children through the house to the small living room. It was elegantly but simply furnished in what I later came to know as the Victorian style. I can still remember the fact that most of the furniture was of French-polished mahogany, with not too many upholstered pieces. The word *austere* comes to my mind as I think about it.

In this front room, he would reach up onto a shelf and take down a small tin, probably a cigarette tin. He would open it and offer us a dinner mint. We were allowed only one. This routine was followed on each visit. After that, he would converse quietly with my father till it was time to leave.

By the time I met him, Julia Stoute had died, and he had married Angelina Straker. She was born in 1894 and died on 4 October 1974. I was living in Canada at the time. We all called her Aunt Angie. She was a very kind lady whom we visited not often enough. I am sure, however, that my father kept in close contact with her.

When Charles Walrond died on the 8 June 1959 and his will was probated, his assets were as follows:

1. All and singular one lot of land situated at corner of Francis Street and Eastern Main Road, Curepe, in the town of St. Joseph in the Island of Trinidad with a building thereon valued at $5,500.00
2. Five acres, 1 rood, 28 perches situate at Mont Plaisir, Cunupia, valued at $2,000.00
3. Burial lot valued at $25.00

* * *

I had all but given up hope of ever finding out anything about Sam Walrond when on 3 January 2012, I received an e-mail from a cousin in Edmonton. She had been in contact with a gentleman named Grantley Walrond. She was wondering if this newfound friend was in any way related to us. I replied saying that I had no idea. However, I attached all the information that I had collected about our family, including the mention of Sam "Pappy" Walrond and that he had moved to Guyana. This information was new to my cousin, but nonetheless she forwarded it to Grantley.

Within a few hours, a message was sent out by Grantley Walrond, and it was copied to me. In part, it said

> Notwithstanding, I am most pleased to tell you that Sam "Pappy" Walrond is my grandfather. He settled in Guyana, building boats and other things and had five children: Eva, Walter, Andrew, Frederick and Trim Benjamin, my father. Incidentally, he lived to the ripe old age of 104 years and is buried at Auchlyne Church of Scotland Cemetery on the Corentyne, here in Guyana. At last count, about 150 of us will be gathered here for a period of reflection and celebration as we meet to fellowship and to explore the richness and blessings of the family. The theme for the gathering will be "The Family as a Resource."

Needless to say, this message immediately filled an enormous gap in the lineage of the Walronds who migrated from Barbados to Trinidad and Guyana after emancipation. I hope one day to be able to attend a reunion of this branch of the family. Until then, just keeping in touch would be important.

* * *

Although not much is known about Joshua Walrond, the following documents will give some idea of the times in which he lived. The first is a bill dated 8 October 1906 showing the amount due by Joshua on the lease of some property. The final amount due is $189.00. The last line, in red, states that a settlement was requested on or before the 12 October 1906.

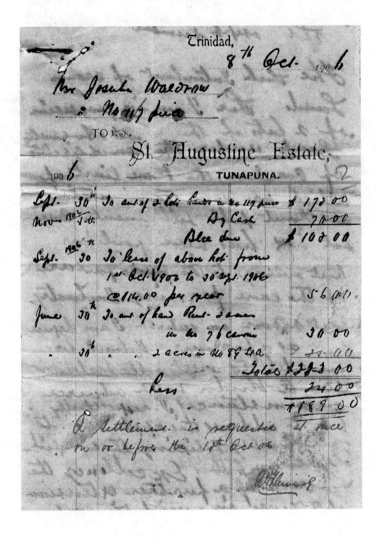

These next two documents show his reply.

St. Joseph, Trinidad
The Sub Intendant of Crown Lands,

Sir, I am in possession of 2 lots of the St. Augustine Lands under an Agreement of Purchase, the time limit of which has now terminated without full settlement. One lot has been paid for but owing to the failure of the cane farming industry last season on which I am dependent as a farmer, I have been unable to meet the balance. Under such adverse circumstances I respectfully beg to address this application to you humbly soliciting the consideration of His Excellency the Governor of a further extension of 2 years in which time I hereby promise to pay.

11 October 1906

To the Manager of St. Augustine Estate,

Nine months after the date of my letter, I promise to pay to the Manager in behalf of the Government of Trinidad and Tobago the sum of one hundred and eighty-nine dollars for value received, and for the said sums I do pledge one tapia building covered with galvanize on one lot of land leased from above estate in lot No. 116 and as further security one lot of land purchased by me in said No 116 for $70.00 [**Note:** Tapia is a building material akin to adobe.]

Reading and contemplating the second and third of these three documents, I could not help noticing the clarity and style of Joshua's handwriting — clearly that of an educated person. The humility and respect he showed to the government and estate officials as he so eloquently pleaded his case were evidence of his awareness of how politics worked. Through it all, he reminded his addressees that he was simply a cane farmer and that he was at the whim and fancy both of the cane farming industry and of the government.

He subtly reminded them that his abode was a humble one and that he leased the property on which it stood. He also declared ownership of another lot that was valued at $70.00. I believe that he used this other lot as a small sugar cane plot, as he also described himself as a cane farmer. I am sure that he succeeded in convincing the officials of his honesty and straightforwardness.

The next document is of extreme importance to me.

Caroni Estate, March 16th 1911

As requested by him, I state that I have know Joshua Walrond for more than one crop. I know him to be sober and a steady worker and consider him a competent panboiler. I have know him to boil very good molasses sugar in the crop 1910 (yellow) under none too easy conditions. As I think, he is a thouraughly competent man in his profession, I wish him the best for his future, and shall, on application, be always open for further reference, if requested.

Hugo F. Klatt Dr.-Ing.
Chemist.

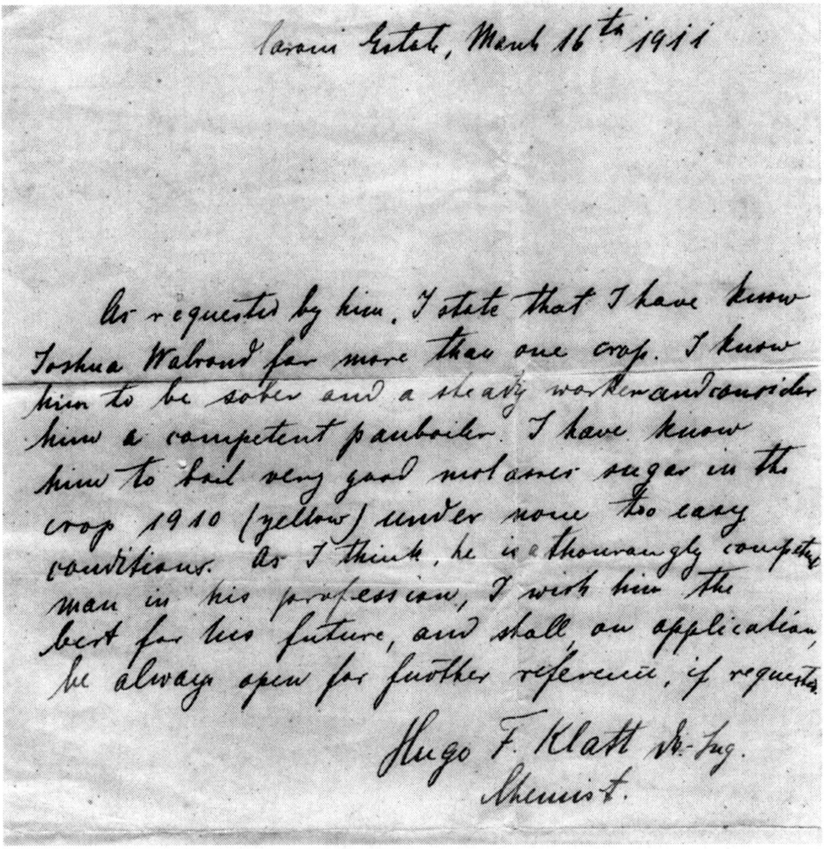

Caroni Estate 16 March 1911

As requested by him, I state that I have known Joshua Walrond for more than one crop. I know him to be a sober and steady worker and consider him a competent panboiler. I have known him to boil very good molasses in the crop 1910 (yellow) under none too easy conditions. As I think, he is a thoroughly competent man in his profession. I wish him the best for his future, and shall, on application, be always open for further reference, if requested.

Hugo F. Klatt, Chemist

After I had read this note a few times, a lot of memories came flooding back to me. As children, when we asked Daddy what his father did for a living, the reply was always the same: "He was a panboiler." We were, or at least I was, left with an image of my grandfather, whom I had never seen, sitting in some kind of kitchen tending a large pot with a fire beneath it. Inside the pot was a collection of smaller pans which he boiled.

Later on, through what process I cannot now recall, I realised that a panboiler was a sugar maker. I was therefore very happy when I came across the preceding note. In an instant, I knew so much more about my grandfather and was very proud of him. The facts that it was signed by the Chemist of the Caroni Estate, that it was dated 16 March 1911, and that it described my grandfather as a "thoroughly competent man in his profession" were all very significant to me. This document is over 100 years old, yellow with age and very fragile. It is perhaps the most valuable piece of paper in my possession.

* * *

In 1946, when I was about 4 years old, my family moved from Isaac Junction into a house on Edgar Street in the little town of Couva. We lived there until December 1956. The lot on which the house was built bordered the sugar fields of the Caroni Estate, from which it was separated by an estate trace and a shallow drainage ditch. In the center of the back line of the property, as you faced the fields of sugar canes, was a tall coconut tree. To its right, at the very edge of the lot, were two large trees growing side by side. One was a mango tree, and the other was another coconut tree. The trunks of these two trees came together at the ground. I used to place a piece of wood between them at about 18 inches high to form a seat. The only other vegetation on the property, not counting the numerous weeds, was a clump of sugarcane, which we kept growing for our own use. We were not allowed to cut the canes in the fields of the Caroni Estate.

As I grew up, I loved to climb among the branches of the mango tree, as high as I could, to get at the fruit on the coconut tree. I used a long bamboo rod to coax the nuts to the ground. It was a very effective relationship among the coconut tree, the mango tree, and myself. My mother will tell you that my favourite drink is still coconut water. Sometimes, perched among the branches of the mango tree, I would see and hear the passenger and freight trains rolling by on their way to and from San Fernando, for the tracks lay less than a mile away.

My fondest memories of these ten years were the times when I would simply wedge myself into a spot where three branches of the mango tree came together. There were two spots where this happened. I was able to stretch out on the lower branch while the other two side ones held me in place. It was very comfortable, especially if I remembered to bring a cushion with me. Often I would sit there and read. Mostly, I would just look out over the cane fields at the Caroni sugar factory, which lay just beyond the distant train tracks. Sometimes I would pretend that my perch was the cockpit of a plane, or a helicopter, and I would fly off to get a closer look at the factory or to other unknown faraway places. My imagination was very active but was assisted by the fact that the sugar factory used a helicopter and a small fixed-wing aircraft to spray insecticides over the canes. DDT was popular in those days. Occasionally, these aircraft would fly over the canes, their deadly cargo spewing out in a mist behind them.

Sometime during the years that we lived in that house, the factory grew from a one-chimney to a two-chimney operation. From my seat in the mango tree, I could actually see the tiny figures of men working on the side and at the top of the new chimney as it was being built. In the stillness of the nights during the harvesting season, I could hear the throbbing of the machinery as the canes were ground and the sugar was made. In the mornings and in the evenings, one could hear the wailing of a siren as it blew the workers on and off shifts.

Most of all, at the height of the "crop season," when the canes were being harvested and processed, it was the smell of the cane juice and the molasses that was the most powerful sensory experience. One could almost taste them. How I longed to see the inside of that sugar factory! And eventually, I did.

One of the most exciting memories of living in the house on Edgar Street was the harvesting of the canes every year. The cane fields were by my estimation about a quarter of a mile square and were separated from each other by access traces about 20 feet wide. These traces were used by the workers and various machines for the cultivation and harvesting of the canes.

The canes were harvested during the dry season, which began in early January and lasted till the end of June. At Christmas-time, the mature canes would burst into bloom. A long shaft, upwards of 3 or 4 feet, would sprout from the top of the canes, and they would be covered with smaller shafts of flowers. They looked much like a corn plant, only more graceful as they waved and danced in the wind. I found out later that sugar cane and corn are genetically related.

It was my habit, on coming home from school, to take up my perch in the mango tree and look out over the cane fields. On occasion, perhaps every two years, just before the sun set, off in the distance, a sudden plume of smoke would rise swiftly into the air. It would be followed closely by a sheet of flames that would shoot 15 feet or more into the sky. Then could be heard the crackling of dried cane leaves as they burnt. Bits of leaves and charred ash would be lofted upwards by the dense, smoky updrafts that spread quickly across the entire field, consuming all that was flammable. In about 40 or 50 minutes, all the dried leaves of the entire cane field would be consumed. Some not-so-dried leaves would also be burned due to the intense heat. All that would be left would be the stalks of sugarcane and the very green leaves at their tops, now charred and wilted. The smell of the burnt canes was very powerful. Watching a cane field go up in flames was a colourful display that would warm the heart of the most devoted pyromaniac.

This seasonal event served many purposes. The leaves of the sugar cane plant are razor sharp. Destroying as many of them as possible reduced the risk of injury to the workers. The ash that was left on the ground supplied nutrients to the soil. The heat and smoke purged the field of any noxious vermin, of which there would be many after a growing period of 15 to 18 months.

Early next morning, just before the sun was up, I could hear the rumbling of a large piece of machinery coming from the field area. A crane was being brought in to assist in the harvesting of the crop. It would be located at the junction of four fields, whenever possible. Once a field had been burnt, the canes had to be harvested as soon as possible, for the juice would have been cooked to some degree. Sometimes two fields would have been burnt the night before, heightening the effect of this aspect of the harvesting process. The other two would be fired as time went on and the harvesting progressed.

A little later in the early morning, just as the sun was rising, the chatter and laughter of the harvesters could be heard in the street as they made their way to the traces and eventually to the field that had been readied for harvesting. These workers always dressed in at least three layers of loose clothing:

long skirts or trousers and long-sleeved blouses and shirts. The remaining cane leaves would cut their garments to shreds in short time. The layers offered more protection to the workers' limbs. Hanging from their shoulders and hips would be a bag containing their daily ration of food along with several files to keep their machetes or cutlasses sharp. These were usually kept in a scabbard or sheath.

There was also one other piece of equipment that most if not all cane-field workers carried. This was a *bowlie*, made from the dried and evacuated fruit of the calabash tree. It was a spherical object that was used in many tropical countries as a water carrier. It was the original organically grown water bottle. Once the fruit had dried, a small hole was cut through the top of the now very hard shell, and the inner seeds and dried pulp were extracted. The inside of the shell was scraped clean and washed. A short, stout stick attached at its middle to a strong wire was inserted through the hole, and the wire was pulled up. The stick was thus lodged on the inside of the sphere, and the wire was looped around another piece of wood to form a handle. The bowlie was ready for use.

Being organic in nature, bowlies did not last forever. Having a calabash tree in one's yard was an asset, especially if one were a cane field worker. The use of this fruit goes back in history and is as old as human migration. It is one of the first plants to be cultivated. The variety used as water containers are called calabash gourds. These can also be cut in half to form bowls (hence the name bowlie) used for food preparation and serving. Some varieties are used for making maracas. In Trinidad, we call these musical instruments shack-shacks, from the sound that they make.

Once at the edge of the burnt field, the workers would start working their way along the furrows of the field. From my perch in the mango tree, I would watch each person take hold of a sugar stalk in one hand and, with a deft stroke, sever the cane not less than 6 inches or so from the ground. With a swift twist of his or her hand, the worker would turn the leafy end to the cutlass and slice off the top. The now-bereft cane stalk was thrown to the ground, and the worker would reach out for the next cane stalk.

Following closely behind this vanguard of cane cutters was another team of workers leading draft animals — mules, oxen, or donkeys — pulling carts. A chain would be placed crosswise over the tray of the cart. The attending worker would gather the canes off the field and lay them lengthways on the cart, the sides of which were furnished with upright stakes to keep the canes from falling off. Once these carts were filled to capacity, the chain would be thrown over the top of the canes and the ends of the chain would be hooked together. The carts then made their way to where the crane had been stationed.

At this juncture, one by one, huge tractor-trailers would pull up beside the crane. A chain would be lowered to the cart, and a hook would be attached to the chain holding the canes together. Up went the load of canes, and with a tug on a rope hanging from the hook, the chain would be loosened, and the canes would drop into the high-sided trailer. Once full, the trailer would rush off to the factory.

At the end of a day or two, depending on how many workers had been assigned to the field, the field would be bare again. The green tops of the canes would lie strewn on the ash-darkened field to compost and become fertilizer, and the low stubs of the cane roots would be scarcely visible along the furrows of the field.

At times during the day, an overseer would arrive to check on the progress of the harvest. Sometimes he would be mounted on horseback, dressed in khaki, with a pith helmet as protection from the sun, and looking as officious as ever. He would ride in along the furrows to observe, perhaps stopping now and again to talk with the workers. Other overseers drove a green Land Rover emblazoned with the name Caroni Estates Limited. They observed the operation from the comfort of their many-horsepower vehicles.

As they harvested the canes, they were not silent, these workers. From time to time, their carefree chatter as they discussed the latest gossip and their raucous laughter as someone told a joke would waft across the field to my ears. They all seemed satisfied with their lot as field labourers. They were well-paid, and in later years they belonged to a union that advocated for their welfare. They represented, in their own way, the dignity of hard work.

The morning procession of workers would be repeated in the evening, this time in the opposite direction. The earlier chatter would be a bit more subdued, the clothing of the workers would be decidedly darker and more ragged, their swagger reduced to a more sedate crawl. The day would soon be over for these hard-working labourers, who were for the most part immigrants or descendants of immigrants from India or from Barbados.

What a difference they presented compared to the life led by the slaves on the Barbadian plantations of a hundred years before. Then, and there, the sound of the drivers' lash would silence any whispering among the slaves. There was no laughter, only the screams resulting from the brutal punishment by the slave drivers. The European method of using land to create wealth worked in unison with the African custom of using slaves to produce riches: The plantation owner's wealth provided the capital, and the impoverished slaves were forced to supply the labour.

Watching the cane-harvesting process when I was a child was interesting. The crop season, as it was called, always coincided with the dry season. By the time the wet season came around in June or July, the fields would be green once more because the roots, or ratoons, would have sprouted again. In about 15 to 18 months, the harvesting process would be repeated. If the field were not destined to regrow from the ratoons, then it would be plowed over and re-graded into furrows. New pieces of sugar cane, about 1 foot long, would be stuck into the ground at an angle of about 45 degrees. The buds would be visible, and because they were at the same angle, the new stalks would grow perpendicularly to the ground. It was all very scientific.

A very pleasant family excursion was an afternoon walk along the traces that separated the fields after the canes had been cut. (It was safer at that time because bogeymen could hide among high canes. At least, that was what we were told.) I used to enjoy taking this walk just to see the huge cranes that were used. The model of choice was the Jones KL44. These machines had a distinctively robust but simple look. They were the workhorse of the industry. They were so popular that toy manufacturers in England still make a model for sale.

* * *

As I said before, I did eventually manage to visit the Brechin Castle Sugar Factory that was operated by Caroni Limited. This company was a subsidiary of the large Tate and Lyle company that was headquartered in Britain. The Tate faction of this large company built the Tate Museum in London, which I also once had an opportunity to visit.

The manager of the factory lived in a large Spanish Colonial style mansion called Brechin Castle, set atop a low but prominent hill on the outskirts of

Couva. The buildings there included his residence and a series of chemical labs where sugar testing and other experiments were carried out. The private residence was called Sevilla House.

My father was friend and mentor to St. Clair Jones, a young Barbadian who also lived in a bungalow at Sevilla House and worked as a chemist in the labs. My father would visit him to play chess, and sometimes I came along. I amused myself by wandering over the grounds, peering into the labs at the countless numbers of test tubes and other paraphernalia, the use of which I would never know. My father was also acquainted with the manager of the estate.

One evening I overheard my father say that he was going to visit the sugar factory the following evening. I asked him if I could come. This was in 1954, and I was not yet 12 years old. He hummed and hawed, and I persisted. He finally agreed to let me accompany him. When we got to the factory and reported in, our guide was surprised that such a young person as myself was included in what was supposed to be a tour for one. They never allowed people under 12 into the factory, he explained. When he found out that I was going to be 12 in October, he allowed me to come along. I had to promise to stay close and not wander off.

Our tour started at the point where the canes were brought in from the fields on the tractor trailers, unloaded, and washed with powerful and noisy jets of hot, steaming water. The next step was the crushing of the canes and collection of the juice in channels located below the huge rotating cylinders. The desiccated stalks went off to be dried and later become either fuel for the factory or insulating panels used in the ceilings of houses.

Next we visited the rooms where the juice was purified, boiled, and concentrated. The boilers were fired by the dried cane stalks. On and on the tour progressed. We climbed along gangways and walkways and looked down into machine rooms, all the while observing the processes involved. Everywhere there was heat and noise, and always the sweet smell of molasses.

Finally we came into a room in which the molasses was actually turned into sugar. This chamber was very hot and humid. The noise was overwhelming, and the smell of the boiling molasses assaulted our senses. One could almost taste the sweetness of it all, so intense was the entire operation. Four or five huge, shining, cylindrical vessels with lids stood there. The bottoms of these vats were set below the floor of the room, and we could easily see into them, for the lids were of glass.

The attendant explained that these vats were like huge washing machines. Inside each vessel was another tub with very fine holes on its side, looking very much like a perpendicular cylindrical strainer. It was in reality a circular upright strainer with a top and a bottom, both of which could be opened.

The worker demonstrated the process for converting the boiling molasses into sugar granules. He began to press buttons. A volume of brown seething molasses poured in, and the transparent lid was closed. The inner cylinder began to rotate slowly at first and then at tremendous speed. Another button allowed a controlled jet of hot water to spray the molasses, which had climbed up the side of the spinning drum. We watched in amazement as the hot water turned the molasses from dark brown to a light brown and the spent liquid was sucked out through the tiny holes in the side of the centrifuge and was channeled away. This liquid was eventually distilled into rum. Left behind, stuck to the side of the drum, were the granules of brown sugar. The holes were much smaller than the crystals.

Another set of buttons slowed down the speed of the inner bucket and opened the lid. The attendant used a large, flat spatula and scraped the sugar off the side of the barrel as it turned at a much slower speed. A trap door at the bottom opened, and the sugar was carried off. This system of sugar manufacturing was known as the *vacuum pan method.*

The sugar crystals were taken on a conveyor belt to a large holding area, where they were unceremoniously dumped onto the floor. There, a few moments later, as we looked on from above, front end loaders shovelled the sugar into huge piles. Another conveyor belt, one protected from the elements, transported the raw sugar from this room directly into the holds of ships waiting in the dedicated sugar port not far away.

It was after this tour that I fully understood, making allowances for the changes in technology, what my grandfather did as a *sugar boiler.* Maybe my father should have answered, "Your grandfather was a sugar manufacturer." But then, perhaps my curiosity would not have been persistent, and my knowledge as to what went on in the factory across those fields would not have been satisfied. I know I went home that evening a happier boy.

Years later, when my father had a house built and we moved away, I really missed those two trees. They had entertained and amused me more than can be imagined. Once, and once only, many years later, I visited the area. The two trees were still there.

I thank my grandfather Joshua for these memories. Though I have never seen him, through the experience of living close to the sugar factory and the chance to visit it, I feel that I have met him.

Part III: My Father's Life

Chapter 13
The Memoirs of
Randolph Osric Walrond

As I wrote several pages back, my grandparents — Joshua Walrond and Mathilda Chandler — had nine children. Joshua was born in or around 1864 and died on 25 January 1915. Mathilda was born on 2 October 1868 and died on 31 March 1957. I was 15 years old at the time of her death.

She was a short woman, robust and energetic, though the years had taken their toll on her mind. I am sure the loss of her husband so many years before was a contributing factor. I first met her when I was about 3 years old. By that time, she had begun to suffer from a form of dementia. She spoke to herself almost incessantly, in a strong Barbadian accent. Her favourite topic was a childhood friend named Bertha Moore.

At the time I knew her, her hair was quite short, the result of a very peculiar incident. It occurred when my father was living in Princes Town. She had gone to live with him for a while, and one morning, after he had left for school, the house in which they lived caught fire. She got out safely, locking the door behind her. When the firemen and neighbours came to help, she steadfastly refused to give up the key so they could go in and put out the fire. As a result, they lost everything. Throughout the episode, she is reported to have said nothing and in effect showed no emotion. A few days later, most of her hair fell out.

Yet, in her younger days, as we will see later, she must have been a dynamic lady who looked after her children as best she could, considering the fact that she was a single mother for over 40 years. She was an accomplished seam-stress, a craft she must have learnt in Barbados. In 2013, my mother told me that Granny was so good that she was employed by the Trinidad government and worked at Government House as a seamstress.

She lived in her house at the corner of the Eastern Main Road and Scott Street, one block over from where her brother-in-law Charlie lived. I lived in that Scott Street house for a short while when I was about 3. I have fond memories of living there, and I will share some of them with you later on as well.

My father, Randolph Osric, was the fifth child of Joshua and Mathilda Walrond. Most of my memories of him cover a short period of his long life. What I mean by this is that I was born when he was 42 years old, and I lived with my family until I was almost 22. He died when he was 97. I lived with my parents for only 22 years.

I am very fortunate, however, in that when he died, my father left behind, among other intangibles, a box full of documents. There were file folders crammed with sheets of paper. There were several envelopes stuffed with notes and letters. There were bits and pieces of foolscap on which were cryptic scribbled notes, as if he were trying to jog his memory about some long-forgotten event. Some of the notes and letters seemed to be copies or first drafts of ones he may have written to a friend, or perhaps they were just items that just never made it to a mailbox. There was a diary, along with receipts for purchases such as a wire gate and bottles of milk. Several receipts came from a shop that specialized in women's hats. There were two exercise books in which he had started to write his memoirs. There were several con-tracts between workmen and his mother regarding the construction of the house in which she lived. There were references to invitations from friends. He threw away nothing that he considered of lasting value.

After I inherited these items, I looked through them cursorily and set them aside. They sat for many years in my home, neither hidden from sight nor forgotten, in a box clearly labeled "Family History." When at last I began to sort through them in a more analytic manner, they began to tell a very interesting story.

As I read and studied these documents, as I sorted and arranged them by subject matter and eventually by date, I had the eerie feeling that my father was speaking to me through these fragile bits of paper. I felt that he was telling me, "Son, these important pieces of paper are evidence of lives, mine and others'. They are my legacy to you all. Do not destroy them. Use them."

By means of these papers, I was able to fill in blanks that were created by the difference in our ages and the distance between us after I moved to Canada. They also allowed me to recall memories of this important figure in my life. Of primary importance to this process were his diary and his memoirs.

As I read and reread these two particular documents, although they were very interesting to me, I still somehow felt a bit detached. I could not relate to some of his comments. I finally realized that I needed to put these documents into a context.

It soon dawned on me that my father's writings primarily described his life as a pupil, student, pupil teacher, assistant master and head master at different schools. In other words, the education system of the island of Trinidad was the background against which his life unfurled.

I decided to explore the system of education as it existed in Trinidad at the time. Once I was able to come up with this suitable backdrop, many of his descriptions and comments took on a new life. So too did his actions and achievements. It was not long before I could see their full relevance to his writings. At that point, his life — both as I knew it and as it was revealed to me — began to mean more to me. Then and only then was I able to remember and accept him for what he really always was: a teacher.

My mother often said that when they started a family, our father was only really interested in us children after we learned to read and write. (I am not sure what she meant by "interested in us.") His relationship with us then became and has always remained one of pupils and teacher. Although this might be a bit exaggerated, it is basically sound.

* * *

In the very early years that followed the colonization and settlement of Trinidad, there was very little that could even remotely be considered formal education. The Spanish settlers, and later the English, led lives that were socially separate from the working class. The African slave population was even more socially isolated from the middle segments of the local population.

The original Amerindians were soon decimated by the effect of the rigorous regimen of forced labour exacted from them by the Spaniards.

The British capture of Trinidad that took place in 1797 came after almost three centuries of Spanish domination. During this period, the Roman Catholic Church had tried to establish some comprehensive schools that included both primary and secondary levels of education. There were also some attempts to establish private institutions.

In 1825, records indicate a grand total of six schools on the island. These consisted primarily of three French-run day schools in Port of Spain along with one English boarding school for women. There was also a Cabildo-run school that specialised in teaching English and another small day school in one of the Amerindian villages where Spanish was taught. (The Port of Spain City Council was still being referred to as the Cabildo, which was the Spanish name given to the organisation that administered the city; in other words, it was City Hall.)

I rather thought that these efforts amounted to what we kids used to call "playing school," because I had trouble discerning whose interests were being served under this early system of education. I concluded that each of these schools existed to promote the interests of those churches or agencies that set them up in the first place.

In 1838, four years after emancipation was proclaimed in Trinidad, it was estimated that more than 20,650 slaves had been freed. Of these, no more than about 15 could read and write. There is no doubt that these freed individuals led a rather uncertain and perhaps insecure existence, at least for a time. They had become the largest segment of the society in which they lived.

The churches, in their desire to convert as many souls as possible to Christianity (and this even before emancipation), had begun to show some level of concern for education. In 1845, the British government appointed Lord Harris to be Governor of Trinidad. When he assumed his post, more than 50 primary schools were operating in Trinidad. Many of these were non-secular schools.

As governor, Lord Harris was also head of the colonial government. His term in office marked the beginning of deep-seated and positive changes to the education system of the island. He was considered a visionary when it came to governing, and his ideas extended into the realm of education.

From the point of view of local government, Lord Harris enlarged upon the "Quarter" system that the Spanish had instituted and divided the island into eight counties, which were further subdivided into 29 wards, each with a warden's office, courthouse, and even police station.

These wards also formed the basis of what Lord Harris called a State School System. He proposed that each ward should have at least one primary school that would be secular (not under the control of religious denominations). He passed an ordinance in 1851 which allowed for this. This law also created a board of education with paid school inspectors. However, in spite of the secular nature of his system, it also allowed for clergymen of the faith that was most represented in the ward to visit the school and provide religious instruction. Parents were free to withdraw their child or children from such instruction if their faith were not the predominant one. In many ways, his system was similar to the one that had been used in Barbados for several years.

The act also allowed the creation of what Harris termed a Normal School. This was in reality a training school for prospective primary school teachers. Closely associated with this Normal School were two Model Schools, one for boys and one for girls. These two schools provided locations where the teacher trainees could practise their craft. They were later named Tranquility Boys' and Tranquility Girls' Schools.

This, in brief, was the foundation for Lord Harris's vision of mass primary education. He considered this regimen necessary for the freed slaves and their children and their children's children.

To be sure, there were problems to be overcome. By 1870, only 30 new schools had been built. Then there was the problem of language. Most, if not all, of the pupils spoke a French-derived patois, while English was the language of instruction. Human nature being what it is, it was not long before the population became bilingual. This lasted until English became the dominant language.

A final concern was the physical condition of many of the buildings in which education was supposed to be an uplifting experience. It is extremely interesting to me that the education system in Trinidad is still being discussed, with no probable end in sight to its many problems and challenges. These concerns include the conditions of some of the schools. It seems that not much had changed.

Secondary schools started to be established as early as 1836. The first was opened by the Sisters of Cluny, a Roman Catholic order. Located in St. Joseph, the old capital of the island, and called St. Joseph's Convent, this school still provides excellent education for girls. It was so successful that in 1859, the colonial government established the Queen's Collegiate School for boys. This school was renamed Queen's Royal College (QRC) in 1863, and in 1904, it moved to its present location on Maraval Road, facing the Queen's Park Savannah. Queen's Royal College is so named because at its founding, it received a special Royal Charter from Queen Victoria on the occasion of her birthday. I'm happy to say this school is my alma mater.

In the same year, 1863, the Catholic Church opened the College of the Immaculate Conception (CIC), a secondary school for boys. It is located in Port of Spain. Also in 1863, the Canadian Presbyterian Church established the Naparima College in San Fernando.

After the advent of secondary schools, a complicated and racially oriented system of *exhibitions*, or free secondary education scholarships, was established in 1872. These exhibitions were available to only a few, a very few, well-chosen individuals. They were at first for study only at QRC or CIC. Also available were post-secondary scholarships valid at selected British universities in one of two fields of study: law and medicine. Very few of these scholarships were available, and they were hotly contested.

At first, these exhibitions and scholarships were available only to white students. However, these exhibitions and scholarships provided the only immediate and very important avenue towards secondary and tertiary education for non-white students. Through persistence, determination, and hard work, these non-white students proved themselves equal to the task of winning these prized exhibitions and scholarships. Success led to success, and the non-white students have never looked back.

As late as 1894, the principal of QRC, William Miles, was still not prepared to accept the fact that non-white boys should be allowed "free education." He was of the opinion that what he called the "tone" of the institution would be lowered by such possibilities. In fact, he made it difficult for them to advance into the one class (of which he was the master) that allowed these students to write the university scholarship exams.

This racially motivated aspect of secondary education brought to my mind the motto of Queen's Royal College, which is *Certant Omnes, Sed Non*

Omnibus Palma. This Latin observation translates as "All may strive, but the prize is not for all." Although this motto was adopted in 1918, I rather guess that it would have had a different meaning in the old days.

In any event, by 1872 elementary and secondary education in Trinidad had a solid foundation on which to build. It is clear, too, that this base included the necessity for well-organised training schools for teachers.

This, briefly, was the education system into which Randolph Walrond was born, and into which he entered. His progress, as he described it in his memoirs and diary, followed closely the steps prescribed by the Department of Education.

With this backdrop in place, I had a deeper appreciation for the legacy of writings and papers that my father left. Together, they presented a three-dimensional image of his mental, geographical, and social mobility within his ever-changing and sometimes demanding lifetime — a lifetime which I finally came to appreciate and understand.

* * *

My father began his memoirs with this rather simple sentence: "I was born on 13 June 1899, at King Street, St. Joseph in the island of Trinidad."

When I first read this line around 1993, several thoughts flashed through my mind. The most salient, though, was the date 1899. I considered myself very lucky to have had such a close relationship with some who was so old, still in possession of all his mental faculties and very wise.

I began to think of all the technological and social changes he would have witnessed. In the area of transportation alone, he would have gone from the horse-and-buggy days to the age of the jet plane. This is the only technology story I can relate: My brother had installed a fax machine in the family house at Champ Fleurs, Trinidad, and showed my father how to use it. Shortly after his return to Canada, my brother phoned my father and asked him to fax a document to him. The document arrived, and all seemed well. About three minutes later, the same document was transmitted and received again. Thinking this was due to some mechanical malfunction, my brother ignored it. However, when within five minutes a third copy arrived, my brother phoned to find out what the problem was. My father said, "Well I put the paper in as you showed me and pressed the buttons, but it came out at the other end, so I put it in again and it came out again. So I thought I would try it one more time."

All was explained and understood. Years later, someone asked my father what was the most fascinating invention he had witnessed. His answer was the fax machine.

Another thought that entered my mind when I read where my father was born centered on the town itself. St. Joseph, as I have said, was the first capital of Trinidad. I never visited it until I was about 15 years old. In 1957, my family moved from Couva to our house in Champ Fleurs. This area was the site of an old sugar estate of the same name and is located not ten minutes' walking distance from St. Joseph.

Shortly after we moved into the house, my father took me and some of my siblings to visit two very old ladies. They lived on King Street in St. Joseph in an old but tidily kept house. Their last name was Peter, and one of these ladies had been my father's piano teacher. After the visit, we drove along King Street — which branched off of the Eastern Main Road — to Abercrombie Street (a distance of about six blocks), turned right, came down a hill back to the Eastern Main Road, turned right, and went home. We had gone around the block, so to speak.

That was my first glimpse of the old capital of Trinidad. Obviously, I wanted to see more of it. I had inherited an old bicycle from one of my elder brothers, and I used to go riding and exploring on weekends. Naturally, St. Joseph became my next target. It was an enjoyable experience to ride up to the top of Abercrombie Street and then continue on along into the beautiful green Maracas Valley.

The road followed the twisting and crystal-clear St. Joseph River for most of the way. As a matter of fact, an alternate part of this valley road is called Riverside Road. The main road up the valley is called the Maracas Royal Road, and it's lined with old cottages clinging precariously to steep hillsides.

The valley was famous for its cocoa, coffee, and sugar plantations of old, but some of these areas are now filled with beautiful villas and larger houses of the rich and famous, Trinidad style. The road leads eventually, via a long forested footpath, to the highest waterfall on the island: Maracas Waterfall. I still enjoy visiting this lush and peaceful valley and the old historic town.

When I first visited the town, I noticed an ancient cannon that was placed as part of the wall around one of the houses that overlooks the city square. I am happy to say that when I last visited the area in 2013, the ancient cannon was still there. It is now painted silver, and a plaque on the house names it as the Silver Cannon House.

I was saddened by the fact that my father did not give the number of the house in which he was born. In 2013, I went looking for the old house that Miss Peter lived in. It had been replaced by a still unfinished brick house.

* * *

One of the earliest memories my father mentions is of being intrigued by the activities of a couple of carpenters who were building a family house at Scott Street in the Curepe area of St. Joseph. He was especially interested in the tools they were using but confessed that he failed to recognize the result of their labours. He was a toddler at the time.

I was able to sympathize with him. When I was about 13 years old, my father asked me to help him. He got together some pieces of wood and some tools. He measured and marked several bits of wood. My job was basically to hold down pieces of material as he used a tenon saw to cut them to the required dimensions. He used a plane to trim the pieces before he sanded, fitted, and then glued and clamped the bits together. I had no idea what he was building. When he was finished, it turned out that he had built a wonderful table at the top of which he placed his chess board, held in place by a raised lip. He could lift the board out if he needed to take it to a friend's house to play a game. My father was, in fact, an accomplished woodworker. I never realised until much later that while I was helping him, he was teaching me.

Later on, as a student at Queen's Royal College, I enrolled in the carpentry class and learnt even more. I am still an ardent woodworker. In each room of my home there is at least one piece of furniture that I have built. But there is still something which I do not know, even to this day: Where and when did my father learn his skills as a carpenter? Nowhere in his writings did he even give a hint about this.

* * *

My father began his schooling at the St. Joseph English Catholic (E.C.) School, but he quickly changed to the St. Joseph Government School where the head teacher was from Barbados. He then moved to the E.C. School in Tunapuna, the next village along the Eastern Main Road after Curepe.

He lived with his grandfather, Joseph Chandler, with whom he had a very close relationship. My father described his grandfather as "a man of advanced age who worked as a meat man in the Tunapuna market, selling pork; who was careful and methodical at his job, soft-spoken and polite to all his customers; who was respected by all who came to his stall and who was always addressed as 'Mr. Chandler.'"

My father described his life at his grandfather's home as lonely but added that it gave him the time to devote himself to his studies. He moved into the Grade 1 or Standard 1 class at this school. He was about 7 years old at the time. One day, a visiting clergymen came to examine the students on the topic of Religious Knowledge. When it was his turn, as my father put it, "I answered the questions so well, the clergyman said to my teacher, 'This boy might become a local preacher.'"

One Sunday evening sometime after 1947 — I cannot remember how old I was — my father took me to church with him. I do remember, though, that shortly before the service was due to begin, my father disappeared from the pew where we were sitting. The service began almost immediately. I later learned that it was an Evensong service.

The officiating members of the clergy exited the vestry and proceeded along the aisle to the area before the altar. Imagine my surprise when the man dressed in a minister's robes and leading the procession turned and faced the congregation. It was none other than my father, Randolph Walrond. He began the service and at the appropriate time went up to the pulpit, where he delivered a sermon. I remember saying to myself something along the lines of "Good heavens! Daddy is a priest." Of course, as I learned much later on, he was not a priest but a lay reader. He had, in fact, become a local preacher.

Further along in his memoirs, my father described a most interesting, almost alarming event. He was in the third standard class at the time and was one of the two top boys of the class. The other was William Wilbert Besson. At the end of the year exam, Wilbert took the first place in proficiency, and my father was ranked second.

On the last day of school, the head teacher, Mr. W.A. Jordan, another Barbadian scholar, silenced the school and began announcing the names of children, promoting them the higher classes. When he began promoting the children from the third standard class, Besson was sent to standard five, and my father was sent to the fourth standard class. As the promotions were announced, the students would take their place among the others of the new class.

When the principal was finished promoting the children of standard three, my father went to the fifth standard class, held Besson by the hand, and took him to the fourth standard class. The school was struck with surprise, and the teacher of the level four class sent my father to the headmaster's table. This procedure meant that some sort of discipline was in the offing. The headmaster took no notice of my father, much to the surprise of the whole school, and with dignified composure, he continued the promoting of the children of the remaining classes of the school. When he finished, he gave a short address to the children and then dismissed the school for the end-of-the-year vacation, and, as my father wrote, "then silently sent me home without chiding me about my misconduct."

I am not sure what motivated my father to do what he did. Was it because he thought that the principal had made a mistake? If he did, and this is really the only reason I can think of, where did he get the bravery to react the way he did? I am sure that my father learned a lot about tact that day. I believe that the principal himself was probably so taken aback that he could not find the words to express his reaction. I do know, however, that this incident reminded me very much of the letter I received from a grade eight student in 1969 after my teaching practicum was over.

There is an epilogue to the story. Sometime during the next school year, William Besson transferred to Tranquility Government School in Port of Spain. From there, he was awarded one of the coveted exhibitions and enrolled at Queen's Royal College. He later won a Government scholarship and studied to become a doctor. I think the lesson my father may have learnt is that sometimes coming second is just not good enough.

When he finished the fourth standard, my father transferred to Richmond Street Boys E.C. School in Port of Spain. Here again, the principal was from Barbados. This school was one of the top schools in Port of Spain. The reason for his transfer was to give him a better chance at winning an exhibition to a secondary school, perhaps Queen's Royal College. This was in 1911.

Unfortunately, his grandfather, Joseph Chandler, died suddenly that year. I believe that my father was so grief-stricken that he was unable to concentrate on his studies. In any case, he was not one of the two lucky students to win an exhibition that year. He returned to St. Joseph and enrolled at the Anglican school there. He also began taking typewriting and bookkeeping at a commercial school in Port of Spain.

In 1914, before the school year came to an end, a new principal was appointed to the St. Joseph Anglican School, and he encouraged my father to become a teacher. This school is also called the Curepe E.C. School. At 15 years old, my father accepted the challenge and became a student teacher.

It was not long before another misfortune befell my father. At the end of January 1915, his father suddenly became ill. On his death bed, Joshua made a silent plea to my father that he look after his youngest sibling, a 2-year-old boy named Horace. My father accepted the challenge, and in his words, he "honored it." I believe that it was at this point in his life that Randolph may have begun to give up his hopes of pursuing a career in medicine.

After the death of his father, Randolph concentrated on his studies leading to the pupil teachers' examinations. In 1919, he wrote his third class teachers' examination — a three-day process — which made him eligible to be appointed vice principal of a large school. Student teachers from all over the island took this exam. When the results were announced, my father was ranked third.

Prior to this, he had started taking courses and passing examinations in several areas, all part of his training to become an effective teacher. These areas included religious subjects, hygiene, and physical training. He was also awarded a certificate from the Diocese of Trinidad in general religious knowledge.

In 1920, my father described himself as a pupil teacher drawing a salary of about nine or ten dollars a month and was concerned about where his career would lead him. His younger brother, Horace, whose education he had promised to supervise, would have been about 8 years old and in school. However, I don't know anything about him, at least at this point. I assume that the other siblings were also doing their parts in looking after Horace.

My father described a rather interesting event that took place at this point in his career. He was still employed as a pupil teacher at the St. Joseph Anglican School when, one day, on his return towards the end of the lunch break, he noticed a visitor had arrived at the school. He greeted the visitor, welcomed him into the school, and seated him at the principal's table. He then sent a student to inform the principal, Mr. Henwood, that a visitor was waiting for him at his desk. Once assured that the visitor was comfortable, my father went about his preparations for the afternoon session.

Mr. Henwood arrived and sat talking with the visitor for a short while. Before classes resumed, my father was asked to join the conversation. It turned out that the visitor was the principal of the Couva Anglican School, and he had come, with the permission of the manager of his school, to offer my father the position of assistant principal of his school.

My father immediately accepted the offer, subject to the approval of Mr. Henwood. The appointment was effected immediately, and so on 1 November 1920, my father set out for Couva with, as he put it, "a fair amount of self-assurance."

Couva, in 1920, was a small town that grabbed your attention no matter from which direction you approached it. At the time, it had a population of 2,667. It was not a blink-your-eyes-and-you've-missed-it town. The town was centrally located, almost midway on the island on a north-to-south axis. Although not far from the west coast of Trinidad, it was not considered a coastal town, being about 3 or 4 miles from Carli Bay on the Gulf of Paria.

Surrounding the town were the vast Caroni Plains. Couva owed its prosperity to sugar cane, which grew profusely on these gently sloping lands. The large Caroni Sugar Estate built its factory there. As one approached Couva along the Southern Main Road, from either direction, north or south, one had to make a 90-degree turn to the right. Exactly 1 mile after the first turn, a visitor would turn sharply to the left, another 90 degrees, and bid goodbye to Couva. The corner at the east end of the town became known as Isaac Junction, and the western one is called St. Andrew's Junction.

Not far from either junction, along the side of the road that led into and out of the town, there were extensive sugar cane fields. They were that close. Along the 1 mile of paved road that formed the main thoroughfare of the town were found all the major buildings that comprised any town worthy of the name.

There were shops, dry goods stores, drug stores, grocery stores, and cafés. There was a police station next to the courthouse, and set between these two was a jail. There was a Catholic church, and in fact every other denomination was represented in the small town. Each major religious sect had built its own school as well. There was a post office, a reservoir, and a railway station, a telephone exchange station and a fire station. The north-south railway line bisected the mile-long town. Every conceivable amenity or utility was there. There was even a recreation ground, with a grandstand and cricket pitch, of course. I loved this town and have many fond memories of living there. But that was 22 years after my father first arrived there.

The self-assurance with which my father took up residence in Couva came as no accident. The principal of the Couva E.C. School was Christopher Evans Patrick. This was a name that, over 20 years later, we had grown accustomed to hearing as children.

With unusual care and concern, Mr. Patrick had made arrangements for my father to have as seamless a transition as possible into his new surroundings and to life in Couva. He arranged for a house for my father to rent, for a small boy to run errands for my father, and for a place where my father could have meals. As my father wrote in his memoirs, "All these arrangements were happily maintained during the three and a half years I spent at Couva. It was truly a life at home away from home."

My father described the school as a building that had withstood the test of time. This description reminded me of what Mr. Keenan, an employee of the British government, said in his report on the education system in Trinidad in 1869: "The school buildings would bring discredit upon any country that recognizes civilization as a principle of government."

My father simply said that his school was an old residence in which a couple of sheets of galvanized iron kept the rain and afternoon sun from entering a hole in its western wall. It was run by a staff of six teachers, including the principal. It was operated under the aegis of the department of education but was greatly influenced by the Church of England.

St. Andrew's Church, to which the school was spiritually attached, was located at the junction that shared its name and was but a few minutes further along the main road from the school. The recreation ground that was used by the school on occasion was about halfway between these two buildings.

My father's memoirs reminded me of several things. As children growing up in Couva, one of the first names we heard mentioned on several occasions was that of Mr. Patrick. Suddenly, the reason became very clear. The relationship between Mr. Patrick and my father was deep-seated, sincere, and long-lasting. The more I read about Mr. C. Patrick, the more I wondered what he looked like.

In March of 2013, in an effort to satisfy my curiosity in this regard, I wrote to Paul, a friend in Trinidad who sends me many e-mails, and asked him to speak with another friend, David. I wanted Paul to find out whether David was in any way related to Christopher Patrick, because they both had the same last name. I suspected they were but was not sure how. Paul and David were both former classmates of mine at QRC back in 1955.

Before long, I had the information I needed. Christopher was, indeed, David's great-uncle. I also found out that Christopher's grandson, Errol, lived in Toronto, Canada. I was given his telephone number. Shortly after, I called Errol, and we had a really interesting chat. The happiest outcome of this was a picture of Christopher Patrick. To make this story even more interesting, I found out that Errol Patrick had been the youngest guest at my parents' wedding in 1937. When I checked the newspaper report of the wedding, I saw his name.

Much later, perhaps in the late '40s, I met two of the staff members my father mentioned in his memoirs. One was Mrs. Mariah Valentine, who lived on the main road not far from the school, opposite the Couva Recreation Grounds. I also had the pleasure of meeting Mrs. Mary Drayton, whom I especially remember. She was a kind, elderly lady at the time, at least 25 years older than when my father first taught with her. She lived in a small house near the end of a side street close to the school I attended. In front of the house, to the right of the steps that led to a small entrance porch, there grew a vine that, in its season, produced a translucent fruit, somewhat like a large blue-green grape. The inner seeds could be seen through the skin and flesh. These fruits were very tart, but I enjoyed munching on them. Mrs. Drayton was not sure of the name of these fruits; she just called them "gooseberries."

There is no doubt in my mind that my father took his first job very seriously. Not many 21-year-old men would have had the opportunity he had. The fact that he was asked to assume these duties speaks volumes in favour of his abilities and reputation. He was appointed to teach the fifth standard class and was responsible for the administration of the school in the absence of the head teacher. In addition, it was his duty to assist the pupil teachers in their studies for their annual examinations leading to their qualification as teachers. He had not too long before completed his examinations in this regard. He also had to instruct the boys in their study of horticulture in the school garden.

In addition to these responsibilities in the school, he had to take part in the work of the parish. He had to be present at morning and evening services and at any evening weekday services. He joined the choir and became a Sunday school teacher.

At the end of the month, he would travel to St. Joseph to visit his mother and family, returning on Saturday evenings. On one occasion, he missed the Sunday service. During the following week, he was approached by the parish priest, the Reverend G.H. McEachrane, whom my father described as "a man of striking personality and an excellent preacher held in high esteem by all."

"Walrond," said the minister, "I did not see you in church on Sunday."

My father explained the circumstances of his absence from church on Sunday. As my father wrote, "He looked at me steadfastly and said, 'You may do this once too often. Once too often.'" This was enough warning for my father.

* * *

Thanks to the many details left by my father, I was able to have a good idea of what he called his social life. He learned to play contract bridge with a group of Mr. Patrick's friends. The manager at the railway station and the husband of one of the teachers at his school taught my father to play chess. He studied this game assiduously from books, as there were not many persons in town with whom he could play.

At the end of his first year at Couva, he accompanied Mr. Patrick to the annual concert and dance held by the Government School in California, another small village about a mile away along the Southern Main Road to San Fernando. Mr. Thesiger was the head teacher of that school. They left Couva during the late afternoon and arrived in the vicinity of the school having time to visit the home of the Bains family, parishioners of the St.

Andrew's Church, before going to the function, which they thoroughly enjoyed.

Another public function that my father started attending was the annual Corpus Christi Athletic Sports meet held at the close of the sugar manufacturing season. The meet was held on the recreation ground and was a very popular social event of the Couva Recreation Club, of which Mr. Patrick was the secretary.

One year, Mr. Patrick invited my father to come to his home to help sort, match, and label the donated prizes against the list of races. With him was an employee of Salvatori and Co. Limited. This dry goods store was located in Port of Spain and was one of the regular patrons of this school sports event. Now and again, Mr. Patrick and Mr. Chambers would go into an adjoining room for a few minutes. During one of these adjournments, Mr. Chambers said to Mr. Patrick, "Why don't you call the young man to have a drink?"

Promptly, Mr. Patrick said, "Randolph, come and have a drink. If you don't want to, say 'No!' Let no man force you."

My father's assessment of the event is as follows: "I did the right thing. I went and had a drink; but the admonition that preceded the request stood me in good stead always after that night."

Every year, after the sports on Corpus Christi Day, a dance was held to raise funds for the building of a new E.C. School. This was a function that overseers and clerks of the Sugar Company and residents of the town would attend. The almost nonchalant statement about a new school on the part of my father proved to be very significant many years later.

At this point in his written memoirs, my father stated that he was happy to have been drawn out of the life of a pupil teacher in a school in St. Joseph and confirmed into the life of an assistant head teacher of a school in a little town far from his home — and moreover to have been introduced into the social, Christian, and recreational life of the residents of his new community. He added that he was forever grateful for this opportunity.

* * *

I could almost sense the pride with which my father related the following story. This incident has to be one of my father's major accomplishments as an assistant teacher. I know he considered the event a very important one in his career.

When my father started at the Couva E.C. School, Adeline "Del" Sargent was a student in a class one or two below the one he taught. Very often this child would make a sudden outcry that rang throughout the school, bringing it to silence. Immediately afterward, the teacher would send Adeline to the principal's desk to be disciplined. My father silently noted the incidents and determined that when that class passed into his control, he would put an end to it.

Sure enough, the next year the class in which Del was a pupil was posted to my father's care, and he made sure to be on the lookout for the strange behavior. It was not long in coming. One day, the class was set an assignment, and my father sat at his table correcting some written work. He kept a wary eye now and again on the class. The children sat three to a desk. He saw Del Sargent and another girl talking happily. Suddenly there came the loud outburst from Del.

My father looked at her with mock surprise on his face. She stared at him with a look of expectation, waiting no doubt to be sent to the principal to account for her behavior. My father waited until she in turn looked surprised that she had not been sent to the principal. He then motioned her to come to him. When she did, he asked her why she had made such a loud outburst, disturbing the school and stopping it from working.

Del answered that the girl next to her was disturbing her. The other girl was called and questioned. She explained that she was talking to Del, who suddenly and without cause cried out. My father then informed the two girls that he had observed them talking for a long while instead of doing the work they were given.

Fortunately, the third girl seated at the same desk was a pupil of exemplary conduct. She was called and appointed to be in charge of the occupants of the desk with these instructions: "Anyone talking must be told to stop. If they don't, tell them to go to Mr. Walrond. If anyone asks you to explain any of the work they don't understand, do so. If you can't, send them to me." She was then told to take the two girls back to the class and sit in the center of the desk. There were no further outbursts from Del Sargent.

* * *

My father's social life was also winding its course. Apparently, romance was not out of order for my father. On his first visit to the nearby village of California to attend the dance at the Government School, he was introduced to the Bains family. He came to know the daughter, with whom he developed a very cordial friendship.

She was a member of the staff at the Couva Post Office, but after a short while, she was appointed to the staff of the Princes Town Post Office. They kept in contact for about two years. However, when my father was transferred to Port of Spain in 1923, the friendship ended.

* * *

My father's efforts at the school were winning the appreciation of the head master, staff, and manager. During the second year of his tenure at the Couva E.C. School, he had to write the Second Class or Final Teacher's Examination, which usually took place on a fixed date during the latter part of the year. However, that year it was fixed to take place during the first half of the year. He wrote the exam on the appointed date.

On Holy Thursday or Corpus Christi of that year, a close friend and student contemporary, Ben Sealey, came to Couva to compete in the Couva Recreation Club Athletic Sports. They met at the Railway Station, where my father was told that he had passed the Second Class Exam. His friend Ben was referred to take Arithmetic the following year.

In 1923, my father was appointed as assistant master of the Richmond Street Boys Anglican School in Port of Spain, where he had been a student years before. The headmaster was Mr. Egbert B. Grosvenor. My father was proud to write that he carried with him a testimony from the headmaster of the Couva E.C. School, Christopher Patrick. In this letter, my father was described as a person who showed the zeal, energy, tact, and ability that indicate the making of a good teacher. I am sure that my father missed the good life in Couva but knew that sometimes growth demands movement. He saw this as a fact of life.

On his appointment to the city school, he returned to the family residence in St. Joseph. His younger brother, Horace, whom he had taken with him to Couva in order to supervise his school studies, returned to St. Joseph as well. It is interesting to note that this is the only reference that my father made to his looking after his brother.

When my father assumed his duties at the new school, he was placed in charge of the fourth standard class, which was described by the principal as the *"Pons Assinorum,"* or the "bridge of asses" of the school. It seems that the habit of assigning the worst-behaved class of a school to a new teacher is an old test of endurance. I have seen it done many times in schools where I have taught. I called it baptism by fire.

As my father said, he took charge of the class and set to work doing his best. After a year of teaching this fourth standard class, the principal, Mr. Grosvenor, asked my father to correct some written work in English composition. He went through the work carefully, correcting errors of syntax, encircling words wrongly placed and showing where they should have been placed, and, where necessary, improving a sentence to render clear the idea or thought intended to be expressed.

A month or two later, my father was assigned the head class. As was customary, this class was always located on what was called the platform or stage of the school. It seems that all schools had this feature. The entire width of one end of the school was raised by about 4 feet. The area below was used for storage. This stage was used for concerts, plays, speeches by visitors, or whatever events were presented to the entire student body or to the parents.

The principal had a desk on one side of this stage, and the top class occupied the other side. This location gave the class a position of superiority and a place to which serious students could aspire. The students in this class were being groomed to write the college exhibition exam, where success assured them free secondary education.

The principal would sit at his desk and literally oversee the entire school. He had on his desk a little chrome bell. When the level of noise throughout the school got a bit too high, which it did very often, he would ring his bell once. It was his symbol of authority. At its sound, the entire school would fall silent. This necessary bit of equipment was known as a *silence bell.* When its objective had been achieved and quiet had lasted a few seconds, the principal would say in a stern voice, "Go on quietly."

It was a ritual that everyone got used to — even the principal, because sometimes he would forget to make his pronouncement, and the silence would continue for an uncomfortable length of time. Eventually, some brave teacher who was anxious to carry on his lesson would do just that, almost in a whisper. Soon the usual level of activity would resume, and all would be well.

Sometimes, however, when the noise had risen to an abnormally high level, the entire school would inexplicably become silent on its own accord. Students would look up at their teachers and at each other, seeking confirmation or perhaps clarification. Then a whisper would run through the school: "An angel is passing through." Soon normal activity would resume, throughout the school, till the next ping of the silence bell or perhaps the arrival of the next angel.

In addition to his regular classroom duties, my father was required to teach maths to the student teachers of the school and also to those of the Duke Street Girls E.C. School, which was located not too far away. This instruction was done during an early-morning session of the school. He also taught music and singing to the students of the school.

With respect to nature study, he got the boys to grow seedlings in seed boxes. The seedlings were then transferred into garden beds situated in a small area on the school premises. As the plants matured, students were excited to see the results of their hard work, especially lettuce and eggplants, growing in a city school garden. This would have been a rarity. Their enjoyment was shared by the teachers.

My father also showed great interest in the school soccer team and accompanied them to their matches against the other schools who were competing for the Football Cup competition. He mentioned nonchalantly that the Richmond St. Boys E.C. School team won the cup in the years 1924 to 1926. It is interesting to note that these years coincided with his interest in and support of the football team. He certainly enjoyed his chosen vocation.

* * *

During my father's five-year tenure at Richmond Street Boys Anglican School, he took the opportunity to form a chess group comprised only of teachers. They were E.B. Grosvenor, James Worrel, George Hyland, Gillis Cobham, himself, and a gentleman identified only as Mr. Palmer.

The teachers played tournaments among themselves and on one occasion, in order to sustain their interest in the game, they invited the chess masters of Trinidad to engage them in simultaneous displays. The first master to do so was Mr. Dunn, an executive of the Trinidad Government Railway. The second master was Mr. Campbell Williams, the Chess Editor of the *Trinidad Gazette* and Secretary of the Chess section of the Royal Victoria Institute. The last was the Hon. Dr. A. H. McShine, the Chairman of the Chess Section of the Royal Victoria Institute (RVI).

After each display, time was spent discussing the game and enjoying some light refreshments. During this period of relaxation following the last of the simultaneous displays, Dr. McShine asked Campbell Williams to reform the Chess Section of the RVI and to invite the members of the teachers' chess group to become members. My father noted in his memoirs that the RVI, which was built in 1892, had burnt down on 1 April 1920 but had by that time been rebuilt. (I have always admired this building. As a teenager I used to visit it often, since it housed the Trinidad Museum of History and Anthropology.) The Chess Section was duly reformed, and the members of the teachers' group who so desired became members. They were put into the C class, and they had to work their way up to the A class, the highest grade of players.

The teachers' chess group continued to be active and once played a tournament against the chess group of the Queen's Royal College (QRC), whose members included Dr. Bedell, Mr. Patten, the Scott brothers, who were sons of the Medical Officer of the Municipality of Port of Spain and, as my father put it, "a Stanford brother." The teachers' chess group was victorious by a score of three wins to two. My father played a drawn game against Dr. Bedell, which pleased my father immensely, much to the delight of Campbell Williams, seeing that Dr. Bedell was a top-ranking member of the Goodwood Chess Club.

* * *

When I read about Dr. Bedell, I recalled a somewhat amusing incident at QRC. He was a stern master in the science department who inspired fear by his mere presence. I was never in any of his classes, for which I was eternally grateful. He could make a student quiver at 20 paces. One lunch time, a bunch of us boys were hanging around the steps of the North Block, waiting for the bell to signify the end of the break.

Dr. Bedell approached with his usual measured and determined step and with a severe look in his eyes went up to a student who was wearing a QRC cap. Such apparel was permitted. However, the recognized design was one that was made up of alternating triangles of material in the official school colours, light blue and dark blue, blue being of course a royal colour. The student in question had somehow dared to wear a cap that, though of the authorised colours, was constructed of concentric circles of material. Atop his head, it looked very much like a horizontal bull's eye target.

Dr. Bedell approached the student and, with outstretched hand, lifted the cap off the boy's head. With a most disdainful look on his already serious face, Dr. Bedell walked off towards the office in the Main Block, keeping the cap literally at arm's length, with the surprised student and some of his closest mates following at a very respectful distance. The rest of us followed at an even safer distance.

At the office, Dr. Bedell calmly dropped the cap on the counter, turned around, and, almost bumping into the student who by this time was quite close, strode off towards the Science Block. I am not sure if the student in question ever wore that cap again.

* * *

While his work at school went on efficiently and apace, my father's chess activity was also improving swiftly, and at one Annual General Meeting he was raised from a class B player to a class A. At the end of the meeting, Dr. McShine congratulated him and decided to play two quick games, or "skittles," with my father. In the first one, the doctor surrendered only a pawn; in other words, he played as a class A player meeting a class B. In the second game, they played as two class A players.

My father highly regarded the doctor's gesture, but it took him some time to discover the real honour that was accorded him by the doctor that evening, which was, in my father's words, as follows: "Hereafter, I am able to say that the last game I played as a class B player was against Dr. A. H. McShine, a class A player; and as a class A player, the first class A player I confronted was Dr. A. H. McShine, President of the Chess Section of the Royal Victoria Institute." It was in effect a gracious welcoming gesture on the part of Dr. McShine.

Sometime after his promotion to the class A players, my father was listed among a team of players selected from the RVI Chess Section to meet a team of players from San Fernando, in the annual North-South Match. He travelled to and from the match together with Dr. McShine in his chauffeur-driven car.

When the match started, my father was set to play against Dr. Tothill, a strong player of the South, who played white. During the first four or five moves, which might well have been considered a normal opening, my father recognised that his opponent was working at setting a trap in the early stages of the game. He also noticed that two South visitors had their eyes on the board. He remembered in his reading that if a player set a trap during the opening stage of a game and it did not go in his favor, he was bound to lose the game.

My father, always the astute one, therefore turned aside from what he called "opening play" and engaged in "positional play," making some moves that seemed to have no sequential relation one to the other, while his opponent continued the setting of his trap. It happened, however, that an exchange of heavy pieces was followed by the smothered mating of the opponent's king by my father's knight at bishop seven, giving North a very early win. This was one of many games in which South was defeated.

On 31 January 1939, Dr. Alexander Alekhine, chess champion of the world, gave a simultaneous display against 40 Trinidadian players at the Royal Victoria Institute in Port of Spain. My father was one of the players selected to participate in this momentous event. In an event like this, the player who lasted the longest was deemed the best player of the group. My father was the second-to-last player to concede victory to the world champion. He lasted 12 minutes and 40 seconds. The winner lasted 5 seconds longer.

* * *

While still working steadfastly at school, my father pursued his evening study of music. In December 1923, he got a Certificate of Music from Trinity College of Music, London, in Junior Practical — Pianoforte. He had already received the London Junior Theory from the said Trinity College. He considered these achievements another important step in his life.

One day, in 1923 or perhaps a bit later, the Right Reverend Dr. A.A. Antsey, the Lord Bishop of Trinidad, paid a visit to the Richmond St. Boys E.C. School. He was in search of a few teachers who wanted to study, as he put it, "for a purpose." Mr. Grosvenor recommended my father as one, and he accepted the call.

On three afternoons during the week, my father went up to the home on Dundonald Street, where the bishop had established a hostel for teachers. There, along with other interested teachers, he joined student teachers who were working towards the Senior Cambridge Exam. This was the purpose the bishop had in mind. Apparently, my father had not totally given up on the idea of going abroad to study.

Before the end of their studies, all of the teachers who had accepted the Lord Bishop's call were appointed as head teachers of schools. I assume that the bishop's call was an attempt to find out how serious the teachers were about their profession. My father remained and took the exam. The results showed that he was rejected for not having obtained the required aggregate number of marks, a result of his not having taken enough subjects. However, he obtained a credit in English. Once again, he was foiled in his attempts to further his studies. He was then about 24 years old.

* * *

One evening in 1925, my father came home from school to find his mother deep in conversation with two carpenters. He was asked to join in discussing the demolition of the unfinished house in which they had been living and the construction of a new one.

Agreements were made, and plans were drawn up. With a capital of 300 dollars, the old building was demolished, and the debris, cleared away. They got as far as erecting a new framework set on concrete pillars about 4 feet high before the money ran out and construction was halted.

No indication was given as to where the family was living during this activity. I can only assume that some temporary accommodation had been provided. A businessman who noticed the halt in activity suggested to my father that he visit the Building and Loan Association in Port of Spain and discuss the situation, adding that they were certain to lend his mother the money to finish the house.

My father and grandmother followed the suggestion, and after solving some initial problems caused by the fact that my grandfather's will had not been properly probated, money was loaned and construction restarted.

An interesting aspect of this process was that the meeting at which the decision to loan the money was made was chaired by none other than Dr. A. H. McShine. In his notes, my father wrote that, following the meeting, the doctor said to him, "Walrond, this is a good thing you are doing for your mother."

Due process was followed, and an order to a hardware store was given to supply all the material. A note was sent to the Trinidad Co-Operative Bank to pay for the material and labour. This bank was closely associated with the Building and Loan Association. (I remember visiting this Association Building with my father when I was a young boy. It is located in a very elegant building in Port of Spain and was established in 1891.)

During the building of the house, Dr. McShine visited the site regularly to make sure all was in order. These visits were all part of the conditions of the loan. My father describes Dr. McShine as having become his guide and patron.

Chapter 14
My Father's Guide and
Patron, Dr. McShine

I have to confess that by the time I had reached this point in my story, my curiosity had gotten the better of me. I had come across the name of Dr. Arthur Hutton McShine several times. And yet I knew little about him. Yes, he was a successful doctor, he was a kind and generous man, and was always affable. My father had a special appreciation of his efforts to make life comfortable for himself and for my grandmother. He was also was very encouraging when it came to the game of chess, of which he was a master. In addition, he owned a car and employed a chauffeur. My father also considered him his guide and patron during the building of the house at Scott Street. This was all I knew.

I decided to do something about my lack of knowledge regarding Dr. McShine. Once again, the Internet provided copious information. One article I found is called "The McShines and rise of middle class" by Marion O'Callaghan, and is dated 28 December 2009. The other article is entitled "Arthur Hutton McShine: Trinidad and Tobago Icons Volume 2."

The story of Dr. McShine epitomizes the post-emancipation problems faced by the descendants of slaves. His educational achievements were pioneering accomplishments. He inspired and befriended not just my father but many others. Some of his descendants were my contemporaries in high school, the same one he attended. One was even a teacher of mine for a short while. Dr. McShine's life is still referred to from time to time, as are his achievements. I believe Dr. McShine's story is what my father would have liked his story to be.

* * *

Once again, we must travel back to a bygone era. In 1784, Trinidad was still a Spanish colony. This year saw the arrival in Puerto d'España of the last Spanish governor, Don José María Chacón. This was also the year in which the capital of the island was officially moved from San José to Puerto d'España. At the time, the new capital consisted of only three streets. But the population of the town was growing, and its physical expansion was taking on a life of its own.

In order to facilitate and organise this growth, one of the first things the new governor did was to divert a filthy stream of water that drained the St. Ann's Valley. Called the St. Ann's River, it flowed right through the center of the town, across what is now called Woodford Square, down what is now named Chacon Street and into the Gulf of Paria. The governor created a new course down the eastern edge of the town.

This stream, however, was a seasonal one, and for about half of the year, its bed was more dry than wet. This new course, since in reality it was no longer the St. Ann's River, became known as the Dry River. Before long, the area of the town on the far side of the new river became known as East Dry River. As time went on, more streets were added to the growing town of Puerto d'España, on the western side of the Dry River.

When Trinidad was surrendered to the British in 1797, Port of Spain began to take on a different look. Foremost among the changes were the names of the streets. A look at a present day map of Port of Spain, to give the town its new English name, would show that Park Street, one of the major east-west roadways, crosses the Dry River on the eastern side of the town.

The area of Port of Spain across this Park Street bridge was without doubt the poorest region of the city. Although many improvements have been made over several years, it is still an area that needs a lot of attention. It was here, in the East Dry River area of Port of Spain, that Arthur Hutton McShine was born on 2 December 1876. He was the fourth child of John and Caroline McShine. This couple were post-emancipation immigrants from the island of St. Vincent.

Nothing is recorded about John McShine, and Caroline became a single parent of four children. She looked after herself and her family by working as a domestic servant, or maid, in the households of wealthy families. Her workdays were long and tedious, often 12 or 13 hours. Holidays and Sundays made no difference to her schedule. Spending quality time with her children was not an option.

At the appropriate age, Arthur enrolled in the Eastern Boys' Government School. This primary school was one of the better ones from which students could win exhibitions or scholarships to secondary schools. Winning an exhibition meant that no fees had to be paid, and books were supplied as well. Endowed with a strong work ethic, a dogged determination to succeed, and an unfailing desire to make something of himself, Arthur won an exhibition in 1888 and elected to attend Queen's Royal College.

I must mention at this point that the McShine family was so poor that his mother could not afford to have the house in which they lived outfitted with electricity. Young Arthur was forced to do what many other students in similar positions did: He studied under the gas light of the streetlamp close to his house.

Spurred on by his initial success, Arthur McShine won an Island Scholarship in 1896. He elected to study medicine at the University of Edinburgh in Scotland. As soon as he had completed his premedical degrees, he returned to Trinidad and began to work at the Port of Spain General Hospital. In 1902, he went back to England and did post-graduate studies at the Moorfields Eye Hospital in London.

But he did not stay there long. He returned to the University of Edinburgh, and in 1903 he defended his thesis on glaucoma. He was successful in this endeavor and earned his medical degree. On his return to Trinidad, he became the island's first trained specialist in ophthalmology. He immediately opened a clinic on Frederick Street in Port of Spain. He also performed free surgical eye operations twice a week at the General Hospital.

It is interesting to note that the area in which the General Hospital is located is also on the east side of Port of Spain. The era after the 1797 British takeover of Trinidad saw an enormous amount of population growth, and along with this came even more physical expansion of the town. The south-flowing St. Ann's/Dry River still marked the eastern boundary of Port of Spain. The eastern end of Park Street stopped at the north-south running

Charlotte Street. This was formerly called St. Ann's street because it ran parallel to the river.

North of Park Street, the old St. Ann's Street led to the Orange Grove Barracks, where the British garrisoned their troops at the time of the takeover. This area of soldier barracks and orderly management afforded medical facilities and services not only to the soldiers but also to the general population of the town. It was the best-equipped place they could go to, and the area quickly became synonymous with medical treatment.

The St. Ann's river flowed to the east of the Barracks, so technically this area was inside the boundaries of Port of Spain. Thus it was that many years later, when the City of Port of Spain decided to establish a hospital, this site was chosen. The barracks became the Colonial Hospital and was the precursor to the General Hospital where Dr. Arthur McShine performed his weekly surgeries.

Dr. McShine's free clinics at the hospital were not his only effort at improving the health of his fellow citizens. He was also instrumental in establishing the Trinidad Association for the Prevention and Treatment of Tuberculosis. He became a member of the Council of the Medical Board of Trinidad for over 20 years. During this period, but at different times, he served as president and vice president of this organisation. He also represented Trinidad on the editorial panel of the *West Indian Medical Journal.*

Notwithstanding the duties involved in all these medical activities, the doctor found time to serve on the Board of Directors of the Trinidad Co-operative Bank for 32 years. He was a founding member of this bank, and for 28 of these 32 years he was the president. Under his directorship, this financial institution became known as the "Poor Man's Friend." It promoted the idea of "low-cost" housing in Trinidad. Dr. McShine was clearly interested in the welfare of his fellow citizens, especially in those who faced health and financial problems. No doubt he always remembered his roots in the East Dry River area where he was born and where he grew up.

In 1891, The Building and Loans Association was founded to facilitate low-cost housing in Trinidad. It was a very prosperous enterprise that benefitted all concerned. Dr. McShine was one of the leading members of this organisation.

The doctor was also a member of the Board of Industrial Training, which was founded in 1906. The Board was in charge of overseeing the training and eventual employment of apprentices. Headquartered at the Royal Victoria Institute, in Port of Spain, it spearheaded the introduction of the City and Guilds of London Institute exams for trainees. One of its early accomplishments was the establishment of a technical school in San Fernando. Many early mechanics, engineers, and craftsmen benefitted from the work of this organisation. My maternal great-grandfather, who was born and grew up in San Fernando, was one of its early graduates; his certificate, of which he was very proud, is dated 1908. He trained as a carpenter.

Dr. McShine also made the time and found the strength to become involved in the politics of the island. In 1914, Port of Spain decided to re-establish the City Council. Dr. McShine was among its first elected members. He remained a member for 14 years, and he was elected mayor in 1921. He served in this capacity for one year. Between 1920 and 1926, he was elected deputy mayor on three different occasions. Due primarily to his efforts as a councilman, the Laventille Hills were provided with a piped water system.

In addition to all these commitments, he served as an unofficial member of the Trinidad Legislative Council from 1921 to 1943, and he was appointed to the Executive Council from 1937 to 1943. When the good doctor finally did retire, King George VI of England decreed that Dr. Arthur Hutton McShine would retain his title of "Honourable." This title was certainly well-deserved.

Dr. McShine died on 4 August 1948. His legacy, however, lives on even to this day. At the top of the Laventille Hills, near the Forts Chacon and Picton, there is a McShine Reservoir. It was opened on 27 April 1922 and is part of the piped water system he helped establish for the area. In the Belmont area of Port of Spain, just across the St. Ann's River behind the General Hospital, is a street called McShine Terrace. On this street, you find a low cost housing development that was built through his efforts at the Trinidad Co-operative Bank.

The legacies of the Honourable Dr. Hutton Arthur McShine prove him to be a real Renaissance man. These roots were established and still remain in the East Dry River area of his no-doubt beloved Port of Spain.

The life and achievements of Dr. H. A. McShine are testimony to the power of education to the values of social and personal improvement. His life would have been an example and a model for many to follow or at least to aspire to. I am sure that my father drew great inspiration from Dr. McShine.

After reading about this man, I came to understand why he was the way he was — and why my father was drawn to him. Dr. McShine obviously never forgot his roots and was determined to do all he could to improve any unacceptable family situation.

Not many people have the ability to improve their own lives and to leave a meaningful legacy in the same physical setting as their roots. To some people, improvement always means movement. In the case of this man, improvement came full circle.

* * *

On a visit to Trinidad in 2013, I visited the area of East Dry River. I went looking for the reservoir that bears the McShine name. The streets in the area are so narrow and steep that my driver could not find the actual spot. When we asked for directions, we were pointed to two huge concrete reservoirs that were built to augment the one we were seeking. A resident did point out what he thought was the roof of the original one, though.

That was as close as we could get, so we went on to find Fort Picton. There I spoke with some workers and was saddened to discover that none of them knew who Dr. Arthur McShine was. I told them his story, and I believe they were impressed with his efforts.

Chapter 15
Princes Town and the
Caledonia E.C. School

My grandmother's house, which in a way Dr. McShine made possible, held many precious memories for me. I lived in this house with my parents and siblings from August of 1945 to 2 January 1947. We had a soursop tree, a tropical plum tree, and a breadfruit tree on the Scott Street side of the house. These fruit trees offered shade and sustenance to us all. There was also a small clump of sugar canes growing next to the house. Although as a family we lived there for a little less than two years and I was quite young at the time, I still recall living there.

Uppermost in my memory is the day I noticed a piece of sugar cane that had been placed on the top shelf of a cupboard to be out of my reach. I was a determined young chap, though, so I placed a chair beside the cupboard, climbed upon it, and reached up to grab my objective. Unfortunately, my left hand and one leg of the chair slipped into a hole in the wooden floor (a knot had fallen out and had not been repaired). The result of this incident was a broken elbow. My tender life — I was about 3 years old — now became one of bus trips to the general hospital in Port of Spain. I especially remember the bus rides to the hospital for physiotherapy.

I once reminded my mother about this incident and the first trip to the hospital. She told me this story. We got on the bus in Curepe and sat next to a lady who engaged my mother in conversation. When this total stranger was told what had happened, she promptly forsook her errands and accompanied us into Port of Spain and all the way to the hospital. She stayed with us until I was seen by a doctor and was attended to by nurses. When she was satisfied that all was well with my mother and me, this angel of mercy simply disappeared.

On another trip into Port of Spain with my mother — she tells me we were on our way to the market on George Street — we got off the train and started up Broadway towards Frederick Street. Somehow or other, as we crossed Marine Square, we both ended up sprawled on the road in the path of an approaching mule-drawn cart. I believe we had tripped on the tramcar rail lines. My mother had just sufficient time and enough presence of mind to push me out of the path of the oncoming animal and wheels. My guardian angel had come to the rescue once again. Shortly after this incident, my family moved back to Couva.

* * *

At this point, I must turn for a very brief moment to my father's diary to continue my story. He began his entries on Saturday, 2 December 1933, with this simple statement: "Residing at Manahambre Road, Princes Town."

It was not much — in fact, not even a sentence. As soon as I read the words Princes Town, memories began to flood my mind. Sometime in 1950, while we were living in Couva, Daddy took us on a drive. In those days, children were supposed to be seen and not heard, so queries like "Are we there yet?" and "Where are we going?" would have been completely out of the question. After what seemed to me a very long time, we arrived at Princes Town. When I first heard the name, it sounded like "Princess Town." Visions of a beautiful maiden vanished soon after we arrived there.

Either way, I was curious as to the reason for this strange name so I decided include in my story all I could about the history of the town.

The story of Princes Town began in 1687, when a call went out from the Spanish monarchs for missionaries to start converting the indigenous people of Trinidad to Christianity. In answer to this call, some Capuchin priests came to the island from Spain and set up a mission on the coastal area near San Fernando; they called it the Purísima Concepción de Naparima. (Naparima is the name of the area around San Fernando.)

The priests then went eastwards for 8 miles along a section of the Camino Real to its junction with the southern end of this road, which the Spanish government had built from Port of Spain. There they called together all the local Amerindians. The numbers justified the building of a church in the region. This was the only requirement for the establishment of a mission by the priests. This one they called La Misión de Savana Grande. The church sat atop a low hill that was surrounded by a large savannah of low rolling hills and plains that gave the mission its name. Another branch of this main Camino Real ran south to yet another mission, that of Siparia.

By the 1860s, Mission, as the town of Savana Grande was then called, was a very busy commercial centre. Sugar cane was an important crop in the area. There was a large sugar mill about 4 miles west. Other garden crops were grown for sale in the local markets as well. A tramway supplemented the road and the nearby Cipero River, and together these three modes facilitated the transport of sugar and other produce to the coastal shipping port and marketing area of San Fernando. By 1879, an Anglican church had also been established in Mission.

In 1880, the British training ship HMS Bacchante was on its return trip from Australia to England. Aboard as cadets were Prince George and Prince Albert, the two grandsons of Queen Victoria. The Bacchante made a stop in San Fernando, and a tour was arranged for the two teenage princes. They would visit the Devil's Woodyard, an area of mud volcanoes on the outskirts of the town of Mission. The two visitors rode the tram from San Fernando and then mounted two horses to complete their excursion. The tram ride was an adventure in itself, the carriage having jumped the wobbly and uneven tracks; it had to be lifted back on.

On their return to Mission later in the day, the Princes were asked to plant one small tree each on the grounds of the St. Stephen's Anglican Church. This act was to commemorate the first ever royal visit to Trinidad. These two Poui trees, one yellow and one pink, are still growing, presenting their beautiful blooms early in the year, to the everlasting delight of the citizens. The attraction of these trees is that the copious blooms come out in the spring (April and May) before the leaves show. When the blossoms start falling to the ground, the colourful display is even more beautiful. In honour of this royal visit and to commemorate the planting of the two trees, the town was renamed "Princes Town." I was able to take some pictures of the church and the two trees when I visited the area in October of 2013. This, then is the story of the naming of Princes Town.

My father drove through the town and after a while turned off the main road and proceeded down a rather narrow and winding one that went across beautiful rural country. Soon we turned on to an even narrower lane and went across a little bridge into a large clearing. On a not-too-distant little hill at the edge of this savannah stood an old building. My father seemed to know the area very well. The mystery was over. We were visiting the Caledonia E.C. School.

As I said earlier, this was in 1950. While we were driving along these country roads, I kept wondering why we were visiting the area. The answer was simple, and it was made clear in my father's memoirs.

* * *

In 1928, my father was appointed principal of the Caledonia E.C. School and lived in Princes Town. The story of his arrival there is revealing of his character and what I call good fortune but what others may want to refer to as being all-in-all spiritual. In any event, it is a very interesting tale.

Early in 1928, my father noticed that the head-teachership of the Caledonia E.C. School had become vacant. He was still teaching at the Richmond Street school as the assistant master or vice principal at the time. He wrote to the bishop and offered himself as a candidate for the vacant post and asked for an interview. His request was granted, and a date and time, set.

My father made sure he arrived a few minutes before the assigned time, entered the building, and made his way to what he referred to as "The Great Hall," where the bishop's office was located. Here is my father's description of what happened next:

> When I entered the hall, I saw him seated at his table at the far end and I began walking towards him. When I was about four or five feet from the table at which he was seated, he greeted me thus, "If I were you, when I get to that school I would change the atmosphere of the school if it were even by sticking up pictures on the wall." Believe it! That ended the interview.

The only glitch was that my father was still preparing to write the Senior Cambridge Exam, which was scheduled to take place at the end of July. Schools were still in session during this month, so my father asked that someone be appointed to act as principal in his place. The bishop agreed, and my father thanked him, said goodbye, and left.

My father ended this section of his memoirs with this statement: "When the time came, I sat the Senior Cambridge Exam together with the student teachers, among whom were Harry Joseph and Samuel Thornhill."

This was the last comment made by my father regarding his desires to pursue further studies. There was no mention of how well he did in the exam. I must say, though, that the two gentlemen he named here were life-long friends of my father, and they visited our home several times as we were growing up.

Once the appointment was secured, my father's next step was to familiarize himself with the area and with the school. This he did early in the month of August. He took the train to Princes Town and then a bus to the village of New Grant, located about 4 miles further east. He visited his cousin Percy Walrond and got information as to where to find the Caledonia E.C. School. He then borrowed his cousin's bicycle, rode back to Princes Town, and located the San Croix Road. (In 2013, I tried to find the school and asked for the location of the San Croix Road. No one knew what I was talking about.)

My father found it, though, as he was destined to. Here is his description of his journey of discovery and fulfilment:

> I turned on to this [San Croix] road and as I travelled along, the Spirit of God said to me, "Look carefully at every house you see along the road and find the one you consider suit-able for a school master to be living in. On your way back, knock at that home, reveal yourself and your appointment in the district to the residents, and ask whether they would kindly accept you in their home as a boarder and resident."

He travelled onward and entered Realise Road, and after about a mile onward, came to a few homes. At that point he made enquiries, and a resident told him to continue on, and he would come to a road on the right. He was told to turn onto that road, and the first building on the right hand side, about one hundred yards on, would be the school. He did as was suggested and not long after came to the school.

My father described the school in this way:

> The school was a little wooden building covered with galvanized iron sheets, standing on lands a little higher than the Cunjal Road. This road led downward from Realise Road, through a little forest then upwards across a little bridge to the school. To the north side of the school, there was shrub lands; to the west there was more shrub lands running down a slope; to the south, the road continued with one little house a short way off, and another house to the south-east of the school. To the east of the school, there was more shrub land descending downwards, and in the far distance there were tall immortelle trees which indicated the location of the Caledonia Cocoa Estate, owned by a Scottish gentleman named Mr. Kirkwood. Reflecting on the scene, the school, bereft of beauty, stood like a beacon on high ground, beckoning to children unseen to come to the temple of learning and be mentally uplifted.

My father then returned to Princes Town, but not before knocking on the door of the house he had selected as his place of residence. A gentleman answered, and my father explained his situation and asked if he could please be accepted as a boarder and lodger. As my father described it, the man was nonplussed and excused himself to discuss the matter with his wife. It took only a few minutes for them to accede to his request. Preliminary arrangements were made, and my father pedalled on to the residence of the church minister and presented himself as the new head teacher. He then continued on to his cousin's house. The next day he returned to St. Joseph.

Towards the end of August, my father made the final preparations to begin his new job. He bought a bicycle with a carrier at the back, a stout pith helmet with a wide brim for protection against the sun, and an umbrella to keep off the rain. He then went to Princes Town and took up residence at the home of the Massiahs.

My father recorded the first day of school that year as follows: "On the first Monday in September 1928 — I don't remember the day — I set out to take up my appointment at the school, well prepared to begin work in my new status as Head Master of a school."

The first activity at the school was making the acquaintance of the staff. There was only one other teacher, who was in charge of the infants' department. There was also one pupil teacher attached to the school. The first comment that my father made about his first school is that there were 50 children on roll. Forty of them were East Indians, no doubt grandchildren or children of immigrants. These were either of the Hindu or the Islamic faith.

Among the non-Indians, and I took that to mean Negro children, was one girl whose mother was the pupil teacher. However, soon after, they both moved San Fernando. Thirty-four years later, in June of 1961, I was appointed a junior clerk to the Office of the Senate in Port of Spain. I was introduced to the staff, and later on in the day, the Secretary to the Speaker of the House of Representatives came into the office. We were introduced to each other, and when she heard my name, she immediately asked if my father was ever the principal of the Caledonia E.C. School. When I said that he was, she proudly and happily informed me that she had been a pupil at that school for a short while when he was there; her name at the time had been Pearl Smith. Her husband was Dr. Harvey, who was a celebrated music instructor.

When I related this information to my father, he was very impressed with her progress "from low estate to greatness." There is no doubt in my mind that my father was a great believer in upward mobility.

It was not long before my father had established a working routine in his school. In his memoirs, he wrote the following:

> By this time I had settled down to work in the school, which was very pleasant and gave me much joy. I had to ride a bike to school and I made it possible to get there at 8 a.m. or a little past eight o'clock, early enough to let the children find me there on their arrival. On arrival, the children came to my table — those who came before the bell rang — and bade me good morning with a smile, drawing from me a "good morning with a smile." They taught me to smile.

This must have been a pivotal moment in my father's life and in his career as a teacher. I believe that it was around this point in his career that he finally gave up his dreams of becoming a doctor and reconciled himself to enjoying the vocation that he had embarked upon. I firmly believe that the happiness he enjoyed thereafter, despite all his previous successes and near misses, was instrumental in allowing him to become the person he was.

Here is his description of his daily routine for getting to school:

> I rode to and from school, and therefore had to study the rainfall system during the wet season. If a shower fell at six o'clock in the morning, another shower would fall at six o'clock in the evening. The next day a shower would fall half an hour earlier. During the rainy season I therefore left home at a time which would enable me to get to school on time or at a time which would enable me to reach a place of shelter before the shower started and shelter there and yet get to school on time, when the shower of rain stopped falling.

* * *

When the routines of the school were well-established — to the satisfaction of the students, staff, and administration — my father turned his attention to the game of cricket. The mere word evoked memories of a very important incident in my life. Cricket is a very popular game throughout the English-speaking countries of the world.

I could never understand the game and did not pay much attention to it. However, its existence and popularity in Trinidad did afford some advantages to high school students. Whenever there was an important tournament in town, all schools, especially those that had a strong English atmosphere about them, such as Queen's Royal College had, were given a half holiday so that those staff and students who wanted to could attend the game.

Once, when a very important series was being played in Port of Spain, my school was, indeed, given an afternoon off. Being a somewhat patriotic citizen, I decided that I would attend the match, which was being played at the dedicated cricket ground known as the Oval, located not far from my school.

At the cricket grounds, I paid for a ticket and literally inched my way into the mass of humanity, all of us bent on watching this event. I paid as much attention to the game as I could. I really tried to enjoy the activity. I clapped when everyone else did and shouted whatever and whenever everyone else did. Being somewhat diminutive in stature, I saw very little of the game. But I really tried.

Unfortunately, after about an hour, I was thoroughly bored and decided to go home. I exited the Oval and got into a taxi. As you can imagine, all radios were tuned in to the ongoing game. As soon as I had gotten into the taxi and it had moved off, there was a loud, almost incomprehensible outburst on the car radio. A riot had broken out in the Oval. The umpire had made a universally unpopular ruling, and the stands had erupted in a volley of missiles — mostly beer and pop bottles, along with cans (full and empty) and anything else that could be hurled onto the field. The game was called, as would be expected. It took two days to clean the cricket pitch and grounds before the game could continue.

I sat very silently in the taxi, thanking my lucky stars that I had decided to leave when I did. Two minutes later would have been two minutes too late. Needless to say, I have never even thought about going to a cricket match again.

Back in 1929 however, my father thought that it would be a great idea to introduce this peaceful, almost monotonous game to the quiet little country school of which he was the headmaster. Here in his own words is the process he followed:

> The work with respect to the syllabus of the curriculum being well organised, I began to speak to the boys about cricket. I requested them to bring to school any old cricket bats which they had at home. This they did, resulting in two old bats. The next step was a cricket pitch. There was none. But there was some uncultivated land on the far side of the road opposite to the school. On inquiring, I found that the owner was Mr. Sooknally, who lived on the San Croix Road, along which I travelled to and from school. One afternoon, on my way home, I stopped at his home and asked him to rent me a portion of his land opposite the school to make a cricket pitch for the school boys. He told

me, with much pleasure, to use as much as I would want, and to just give him a few shillings to pay the taxes at the end of the year.

The next step for my father was to approach some of the older boys in the village and ask them to come to the school on a Friday afternoon and help prepare the cricket pitch and then teach the children to play the game. They agreed, and as my father put it, "Cricket was on the way."

Caledonia C.C. Win School Cricket Tourney

Wed 9th August 1939

Sunday   Guardian   Correspondent
Princes Town.

THE final match in the Dr. Mahabir Inter-School Cricket Shield Competition was played on Wednesday at the Knolly's Recreation Ground between Caledonia E.C. School and Brothers' C.M. School.

Caledonia E.C. School won the game by 15 runs, and as a result, registered the first lien on the lovely trophy, emblematic of cricket supremacy among schools of the Princes Town district.

Occupying the crease first Caledonia E.C. were all dismissed for a total of 34 runs, 19 of which were contributed by F. Paul. He hit one six and two fours.

Brothers C.M. reached 19 runs, of which S. S. Ramdeen was responsible for 12.

An outstanding performance of the game was a brilliant catch by Peter of Caledonia E.C. School who, after running a considerable distance across the ground, caught out a batsman.

Bowling honours fell to Ashnool and F. Paul of Caledonia E.C. who respectively bagged six wickets for 10 and four for nine.

I can only imagine the great amount of happiness and pride my father experienced as, 10 years later, he cut and pasted in his book this newspaper report which erroneously referred to the school as the Caledonia C.C. School.

The mention of cricket brings to my mind one of my father's contemporaries of whom he had written on several occasions. The friend was Ben Sealey. He was born in St. Joseph on 12 August 1899. He and my father had both trained to be teachers at the same time. Ben, however, was an athlete, and I am not sure how long he remained in the teaching profession. As an accomplished cricketer, though, his career spanned the years 1924 to 1941. In 1933, he was selected to tour England with a West Indian team. His tour was a busy one, and he was successful both as a bowler and as a batsman.

He was a frequent visitor to our home, especially in the early and mid-'50s. By then, he was working for the Caroni Sugar Estate. He loved to drop in just around mealtimes. He was a jovial man and was always welcome to visit.

In 2013, I was able to contact his son Frank, who now lives in the family home in St. Joseph, and I obtained a picture of Ben. (By the way, Frank confessed that he, too, likes to drop in on his friends around mealtimes. As he put it, as long as he had a friend, he was not going to go hungry.)

* * *

At school, my father encouraged one of the more industrious girls to become a pupil teacher, the previous one having left. She accepted the challenge and passed the required exam. She lived with her mother in a single-parent home and was the eldest of three sisters. She was appreciative of the opportunity and was happy to receive at the end of every month a salary of three dollars, which, as my father said, "she was led to believe came from the school manager." My father certainly remembered the opportunity and encouragement he had received when he decided to become a teacher and passed it on as soon as he could.

The next step my father undertook was in regards to making the students of his school more aware of their homeland. He did this by organising a field trip to the Abbey of Mount St. Benedict. He wrote to the Abbot and permission was granted. Here is what he wrote in his memoirs:

> On the date appointed, the children, their parents and myself went off on our trip to the Abby of Mount St. Benedict on the southern slopes of the Northern Range of Trinidad. We were received by the Abbot and were all

conducted through the premises where all were permitted to go. Beyond this point, only the male visitors were conducted. We visited the library, a very large room with books on shelves on the four walls from the eaves to the floor. We also visited the woodwork center where timber from the mountainside was being converted by motor power into boards and scantling.

After a while, we came together outside the church and stood gazing at the surrounding landscape. The minds of the children must certainly have begun to wonder at the vastness of space. To the north of them was the mountain, towering steeply to great height. To the south, southeast and southwest a vast plain stretched out before them as far as their eyes could see. This vastness of space their little minds would at some time later compare with the closeness of the countryside where their little homes were located. We finally went into the church where we spent a short while silently, and then left on our return trip to Princes Town. We arrived there at about four p.m., driving the bus into the district in which the children and parents lived.

This description of my father's excursion to Mount St. Benedict reminded me very much of field trips I went on many years later when I was a pupil of the Couva E.C. School and my father was the head teacher. We went to the pitch lake in La Brea, to the Bermudez biscuit factory in Mount Lambert, to the bottle factory which was a part of the Carib Beer Brewing Company in Champ Fleurs, and to the Emperor Valley Zoo in Port of Spain. I thoroughly enjoyed these trips, and this probably influenced me to take students on so many trips to Europe later on.

My father remained headmaster of the Caledonia school for six years. He ended his memoirs with his description of his visit to Mount St. Benedict in 1932. In May of 1934 he was appointed headmaster of the Craignish E.C. School, located not far from Princes Town but further to the east and still in the parish of St. Stephen's.

I tried very much to get more information about the Caledonia school but had no success. One day, I came across this report on the establishment of the Lengua Islamic Primary School:

> Built in a rural area in Cunjal, just east of Princes Town, the Caledonia E.C. Primary school was the place for many of the children of the village to get their first taste of education. Nestled amongst the sugar cane fields, it was the only school for miles around. Children walked, most of them barefooted, through the tracks and dirt roads to get to school. Some of them with just a copy book rolled up and stuffed into one pocket, and their lunch, also rolled up in brown paper, pushed into the other pocket. Sadly, in 1951, a fire broke out in the school. After the smoke had subsided there was nothing left but cinders.

This accounted for the lack of information regarding the Caledonia E.C. School. The school was replaced by an Islamic Denominational School that was better able to serve the predominantly Muslim community. This information reminded me of the comment my father had made regarding the ethnic composition of the Caledonia school when he went there in 1928.

* * *

From his experience at Couva, my father knew that his position as the headmaster of the Caledonia E.C. School would entail a lot of work at the parish church of St. Stephen's in Princes Town. He immediately became involved in the Sunday School Program and was soon the organist and choir master at the church.

During my visit to Trinidad in October of 2013, I decided to walk in as many of my father's footsteps as possible. With this in mind, my hired driver and I visited Princes Town. Our first stop was at the St. Stephen's Anglican Church. I wanted to take some pictures of this building, but more than anything else, I wanted to see and photograph the organ which he had played there. Unfortunately, the church was closed. A stout chain secured two massive looking metal grills, which formed the doors to the building.

Through these wrought iron barricades I could see the darkened interior and some of the nearby pews. All else was barely distinguishable. I could hardly see the altar, and the organ was not in sight. I had to be content with pictures of the church and of the two poui trees and their accompanying plaques.

A cemetery was located in front of and to the right side of the church. I walked through and saw one headstone bearing the name Massiah. This was the name of the family who had granted room and board to my father when he first arrived in Princes Town in 1928. I did not, however, take a picture of the stone.

I wandered down a wide driveway from the church towards a building that seemed to be part of the compound. I was attracted by its open door. I entered a large rectangular room that was bare of furniture, except for a stack of folding chairs along the back wall. It was obviously a dance hall as well. I heard voices coming from a room at the far end of this hall, so I ventured down. I stepped gingerly into the room where three ladies were seated at desks. After introducing myself, I asked if I could be allowed into the church.

Unfortunately, the ladies were not in any way connected to the church. The building was a community hall, and they were just some of the employees. I chatted a while with them, but they could offer no information about the Caledonia E.C. School or even where it could be found. I asked about the San Croix Road and drew a blank there as well. Because I knew that it was a main road, I persisted, even spelling out the name. S-A-N C-R-O-I-X. The lights went on. "Oh! You mean the Saint Cross Road!"

I would have never guessed at that pronunciation. However, it all made sense. The problem was that, true to the religious, political, and linguistic background of Trinidad, the name of the road is made up of *San*, the Spanish word for "saint," and *Croix*, the French word for "cross." In a typically diplomatic and Trinidadian solution to pronouncing what was in fact a manufactured Spanish/French term, the English translation of each word was adopted. The name San Croix, if properly translated, would mean Holy Cross, recalling the religious origins of the town as a Catholic mission.

Once they knew what I was speaking about, each of them gave me — or rather, tried to give me — her own directions to find this road. I got mentally lost trying to make sense of three different sets of directions and gave up. I then asked where the church office was, hoping to get some more tangible information from someone there. Those directions to this building were a bit easier to understand, and my driver and I set off. We still managed to almost get lost, but eventually found the building.

I was greeted by the lone occupant of an office that reminded me of my own — shelves overcrowded with books and material, desks and tables stacked with papers and binders. I felt at home. The young lady sat before a computer, so things looked promising. Her youth was against me, however. The young lady had absolutely no information about a Caledonia E.C. School. She offered to phone someone and enquire. I accepted this proposal, and she dialed a number.

The gentleman she spoke with did remember going to the Caledonia E.C. School as a very young boy to play a soccer match. But he could not remember where the school was. (Perhaps he should have played cricket.) I mentioned the fact that my father used to play the organ at the church and I would have liked to take some pictures of it. She did not have the keys and could not leave her post in any case. She promised to ask the organist if some pictures could be taken, which she would e-mail to me. I thought that was a great idea, and we exchanged addresses. I left the office somewhat crestfallen. Needless to say, I am still waiting for pictures to arrive. I did send her a reminder, but still nothing has resulted.

It was getting late, and we still had to drive to San Fernando, so we decided to leave Princes Town. We drove through the town for the last time. It was much larger than I had anticipated. Princes Town is hilly. It is situated on the wide crest of a low hill. Parked cars clogged its main and side streets. Delivery trucks blocked the sidewalks, forcing pedestrians to vie for space with crawling vehicles. The many side streets leading off the main street, some downhill and some uphill, made the town appear mysterious, for they all disappeared round corners.

Schools had just been let out, and many young children and their parents were heading home. Older students, laughing and chattering loudly, walked lazily to their homes or to bus stations. Different school uniforms were on display: Plaid skirts of different colours for the girls, with white blouses and school ties; the boys wore khaki trousers and white or blue shirts, also with the school ties. I was reminded of my days at Queen's Royal College, for I, too, wore the school uniform and tie.

We crawled along with the traffic and soon came to a signpost indicating Manahambre Road. I knew from my maps that San Fernando was 8 miles away. We turned westwards and headed out of the downtown Princes Town area. We had entered the town through another, more northern road. The phenomenon of side streets that went either downhill or uphill continued, but the traffic on Manahambre Road was certainly diminished. There were still many business places on both sides of this road: shops and stores, cafés and bars, the odd gas station and automobile repair shop. Every now and again, we would see a crowd of people, mostly men, who had gathered simply to pass the time of day. In Trinidad, this is called *liming*.

As we progressed, the business places gave way to more and more family residences. We were now clearly on the outskirts of Princes Town. Manahambre Road turned and twisted, rose and fell as it followed the contour of the land.

Now and again we would pass an unusually large family house. It would most often be multicoloured with several sometimes conflicting rooflines, as though built in stages as money became available or the family was extended. Bright blues and greens, reds and yellows were the favourite colours. Another preferred feature were massive columns, not unlike those of Greek architecture.

Some homes were built to look either like Islamic mosques or Hindu temples, and indeed may even have been exactly that. (I have been into East Indian houses where prayer rooms were incorporated into their design and structure, in one case just beside the indoor swimming pool.) These buildings were always beautiful to look at. They were made to appear even more attractive by the fact that they were offset by more humble homes beside them. But perhaps one day, these smaller homes, too, would evolve into rival palaces.

It was not long before all houses gave way to rolling hills and verdant valleys. We were now crossing the Naparima Plain. This entire area was once home to many small sugar plantations owned by indentured immigrants who had served their indentureship and were then granted tracts of land, as had been promised to them.

Our road continued its tortuous way across the beautiful countryside. But the plains were now no longer covered with sugar cane plants. The land was overgrown with whatever took root. Nature seemed to have reclaimed the land. Only once in a long while could I discern any sign of formal agriculture on these once heavily cultivated shallow valleys and low hillsides.

As we drove along, I could not help visualising my father as he made this same journey so many times, going back and forth between Princes Town and San Fernando and sometimes eventually to his home in St. Joseph. In his time, he would have seen these same fields planted with sugar cane and would have witnessed the activities of burning, reaping, and transporting the canes to the nearby factory as the months and years went by. His experiences would have been far different and more varied than mine were on this single journey from Princes Town to San Fernando. But on we went.

Then suddenly, around one bend and up a long gentle slope, I saw in the distance signs that we were approaching the once prosperous village of Ste. Madeleine. Located halfway between Princes Town and San Fernando, this village grew up beside a sugar factory.

We will join Ste. Madeleine's history just after the emancipation of slaves in 1838. At that point, the village was organised around a simple sugar estate owned by Marie Madeleine. It has been described as the only Caribbean plantation owned and operated by a woman.

The roads that led to and from her estate were not very well maintained. In the rainy season, June to December, they became veritable slipways. Marie Madeleine conducted her business with what she considered the courage of a saint, so she called her plantation Sainte Madeleine.

What saved her operation was that it was situated on the Cipero, a river which emptied its waters into the Gulf of Paria at San Fernando, the shipping port for sugar and other goods from the south of Trinidad. This river, then much wider and deeper than it is now, became her highway to the sea. And so she prospered.

Greater success was to befall the estate known as Ste. Madeleine after 1872. At this time, the Colonial Company, which already owned many of the surrounding estates, acquired the Ste. Madeleine operation. This company immediately erected a state-of-the-art sugar manufacturing plant. It was the largest and most modern factory in all the sugar-producing countries. This operation now became known as Usine Ste. Madeleine (*usine* being the French word for factory). It was not long before the village and the factory shared the same name.

Elsewhere in Trinidad, another rival company was also on the move. In 1937, Tate and Lyle, a British Company, acquired Caroni Sugar Estates, which included operations in the Waterloo and in the Brechin Castle areas of Couva. The entire operation was called Caroni (1937). In 1960, Caroni (1937) bought the Usine Ste. Madeleine company. Ten years later, the Trinidad government bought out Caroni (1937), and five years after that, Caroni (1975) was created.

In 2003, Caroni (1975) was shut down, and sugar manufacturing in Trinidad drew to an abrupt close. Forty-four thousand workers lost their jobs overnight. At the same time, more than 75 million acres of fertile land became available for other uses. Most of the land was given over to housing. In Couva, for example, the area just behind the house where I grew up became a housing development, complete with a modern government school, occupying a large area of the former sugar cane fields.

As we drove along the Manahambre Road, we looked for and found an area where we could stop safely for a while. I got out of the car and looked for a spot from which I could take some pictures. What I had spied from the top of the distant hill, and what I was now looking at, were the rusting remains of the Usine Ste. Madeline sugar manufacturing plant. This once-regal residence of King Sugar was now a rapidly fading shadow of its former self. And yet I could still imagine the ghosts of workers milling about the plant.

I could not see all the buildings or the whole property — it was too large. It was all behind locked gates, I was sure. I was viewing it from a little rise along the Manahambre Road. Bushes and brambles, palm trees and banana trees framed what was left and hid most of the compound from sight. It was an epitaph to an industry that had its roots in the aspirations of Christopher Columbus. The sugar industry, which started in Hispaniola in 1498, died, as far as Trinidad was concerned, in 2003.

My driver and I finished our journey to San Fernando. There I took some pictures of St. Paul's Church and, in it, the organ at which my father practised. The attendant there said that the instrument was so old that whenever it needed repairs, the church had to fly someone down from England to do the job.

We then returned to Port of Spain. Although I did not get to walk in all my father's footsteps, I was happy with what I had accomplished. Perhaps on another visit I would be more successful.

Chapter 16
Tying My Memories to
My Father's Diary

Fortunately for me and my story, although my father's memoirs ended in 1932, he kept a diary starting in 1933. The entries in this diary are sporadic at best. They cover only seven years from Saturday, 2 December 1933, to Sunday, 17 March 1940, and they can be easily divided into two distinct periods:

- **1933–1935:** The entries from December 1933 to 1 January 1935 are significant in that they chronicle the end of his teaching career in the southern part of Trinidad. He had moved to Princes Town in 1928. While there, he further strengthened both the educational and spiritual foundations of his vocation as a head teacher.

- **1937–1940:** In March of 1936, my father was transferred back to Couva and appointed head teacher of the E.C. School there. This school was the new one for which funds were being raised during his first stay in Couva. His diary entries began again on Saturday 7 August 1937 and ended on Sunday 17 March 1940. These entries cover 37 months and deal primarily with his domestic life.

In spite of the brevity of the diary, there can be no doubt that the entries represent what was of supreme importance to my father. He was certainly a busy person, and his descriptions portray a side of his life that would have remained unknown if he had not taken the time to record these events, actions, and reactions. His closeness to the Anglican Church is also further defined.

The entries also serve another purpose. Some of them reminded me of events that happened after I was born and to which I was witness. I was reminded of people whom I came to know as time went on. Other entries caused me to stop, to think, and to react. Such is the nature of human memory. I would like to share with you some of these entries and the effect they had on me.

* * *

Mon 4 Dec 1933 I took a day's leave and went over to St. Joseph and then to Tunapuna where I paid the water rates on our house at Scott Street, St. Joseph. I drew house rent on the said property and then called to see Mr. M.A. Ghany, who happened to be away from home. I however met his daughter who had just returned from England about two months earlier. She gave the impression of being very English in speech and in ways.

Mr. Ghany was a neighbour of my father. He lived on the same northern side of the Eastern Main Road but on the eastern side of Scott Street in the Curepe area of St. Joseph. He was a businessman of some kind. His house was a very large one. In fact, I suspect it used to be the plantation house of the Santa Margarita Estate, from which my grandfather had leased the lot on which his house was built.

As a young child living in my grandmother's house, I used to gaze at Mr. Ghany's house and wonder what the inside was like. The outside was interesting enough. Two stories high, when all others around it were single storied, it presented an imposing presence on the extensive and carefully manicured grounds. The lawn at the front of the house, for it was set well back from the main road, was dotted with fruit trees, notably mango and citrus. I don't know what the rear of the house looked like. A high bushy fence hid it from view. The large windows of the upper storey were covered with shutters, of the kind called *jalousies* in Trinidad. All in all, it was a picturesque house.

In 1957, our family moved from Couva to the Champ Fleurs area of St. Joseph. We attended the St. Savior's Anglican Church, which was close to the junction of the Eastern Main Road and the Southern Main Road that led to Couva, San Fernando, and all points south. This junction is not far from Scott Street.

In 1960, when I was in my final year at Queen's Royal College, a new priest was sent to St. Savior's Church. This was a two-church parish, with two priests who alternated with the other church in Mount Lambert, an area west of St. Joseph. This new priest was a relatively young man, and I believe he came from Guyana. Shortly after he took up his duties, he found out that I was interested in languages and that I was good at French.

As a matter of fact, the previous year, when I had my first try at the Senior Cambridge Exam, my French oral exam was conducted by Mr. de Verteuil, who was connected with the *Alliance Française* in Port of Spain. Apparently, I did quite well in this oral exam, and Mr. de Verteuil was so impressed that he made special reference of my ability to my teacher. He in turn described this satisfaction to the whole class. Upon this disclosure, I was dubbed "Mr. De Verteuil's son." (Fortunately, this new name did not last very long.)

This new priest, whose name I have forgotten, asked if I would tutor him in French, because he too was interested. I hesitated at first but then relented and agreed. I was even further elated when I found out that he lived in an apartment in Mr. Ghany's. Here was my chance — a dream come true. On the evening my tutoring started, I rode my bicycle to the house and went in. It was a small apartment, to be sure, but at least I got to see part of the inside of the large house. Mr. Ghany had died and the house had been converted into apartments. What a shame.

What a shame, too, that when my father found out about my foray into the teaching business, even though it was as a paid tutor, he told me to stop and to concentrate on my own studies. He said he would discuss the matter with the priest, which he did. I was preparing to rewrite the comprehensive Senior Cambridge Exam.

In a sense, I was glad I did not have to continue. I did concentrate on my studies and was able to upgrade my certificate from the Second Division I had received the first year to a First Division on my second try. All the boys in this my last year at QRC were "repeaters" of the exam. We had all received either second- or third-class certificates the previous year. I must say, with pride, that only one other student from this class was upgraded on the second try.

With my tutoring experience cut short, I went back to looking longingly at the large "Ghany" house. Eventually the house was bulldozed, and the area was converted into a shopping mall. I sometimes go there when I am in Trinidad. Visits there serve to refresh and maintain my memories of the area.

* * *

Sat 23 Dec 1933 I went to San Fernando where I spent the night with Randolph Hart. It was a very pleasant time. Next morning his mother and sister called on him on their return from church. I was introduced to them both and in a little while Randolph and I accompanied them to their home at Mon Repos [a small residential area on the out-skirts of San Fernando], where I spent a few hours. On the whole, we were all indeed very happy.

When I read the name Mon Repos, I remembered an incident that took place sometime in the mid-1950s or perhaps even a bit later. One night, our family was returning from San Fernando to Couva. Just outside San Fernando is the Mon Repos roundabout. While negotiating this phenomenon, another vehicle clipped our car — just barely, you understand. But it was the first time anything like that had ever happened to us.

Not far, within walking distance of the roundabout, was the Mon Repos Police Station. Daddy decided to report the "accident" to the police. He had switched on his turn signal light, but the other car hit us anyway. My father thought he had cause to complain. An hour or more was spent going back and forth to the police station.

By the time it was over, we were all even more tired. I don't believe anything ever came of the incident. I guess the message here is one that I have often heard my father repeat: "Look after the pennies, and the pounds will look after themselves."

* * *

Fri 14th Dec 1934 Rode to North Trace Gov't. School with Mr. I. Jones where we attended a School Concert and Dance. Enjoyed the Ribbon Drill item of the concert best of all. On the whole, I spent a fine time. Goodwill Flyers Dr. A. Forsythe and Mr. A. Anderson crashed at Woodbrook, Trinidad W.I.

When I read this, my mind began to wander. For some reason, because it was totally unrelated to the rest of the entry, the last sentence reminded me of a phrase that my father used to say whenever (which was often) he heard us children arguing among ourselves. He used to say, "Personal self-esteem." If our reactive faces showed lack of comprehension, he would expand a bit and say, "Always have personal self-esteem." And if further elaboration were needed, "Always show personal self-esteem." It was up to us to figure out the rest.

I eventually realized he was challenging us to think about what was going on and to remedy the situation. To me, his sentence about Forsythe and Anderson was such a challenge: "If you don't know who these man are, find out." So I did.

Alfred Anderson was born on 9 February 1907 in Bryn Mawr, Pennsylvania. He developed an abiding interest in airplanes and in the science of flight when he was a 6-year-old lad living with his grandmother in Stanton, Virginia. At the age of 13, he applied to the Aviation School at the Drexel Institute but was turned down because he was black. A few years later, he applied to join the army in order to become a pilot. He was turned away for the same reason.

In 1929, he used his savings and borrowed funds to buy a used plane and taught himself to fly. He earned his private pilot's license that same year. In 1932, he earned a commercial pilot's license. He was the first black American to be granted such a license. At the time, he was working as a chauffeur.

When his employer found out about the pilot's license, she fired him. She was upset about his patently obvious ambitions of upward mobility. She is said to have suggested that he allow his pilot's license to take care of him. The rest of his story shows that he did just that. As a result of this setback, however, he went to ground. In fact, he went somewhat underground. He became a ditch digger for the local Works Progress Administration.

His plight came to the attention of Dr. Albert Forsythe, who lived in Nassau. He too was a lover of planes and flight. And he had money. He went in search of Anderson and formed an alliance with him. They decided to go on goodwill tours to encourage black Americans to get involved in aviation. The press dubbed them "The Goodwill Flyers."

Their first venture was a transcontinental flight from Atlantic City, New Jersey, to Los Angles, California, and back. This was in 1933, and their flight was the first round trip made by black Americans. Their equipment, other than the plane — a Fairchild 24 Monoplane they called "The Pride of Atlantic City" — was minimal. It consisted of a compass and an altimeter. Some reports claimed they also had some roadmaps. This first flight went a long way to change the racist attitudes that permeated the aviation industry at the time. A few schools began admitting black students. Slowly but surely, these two aviators were achieving their objective.

In November of 1933, the now famous duo added another accomplishment. They became the first black Americans to fly across the international border between the United States and Canada. They flew to Montreal. In 1934, they planned and began a Pan American Goodwill Tour (the prefix *pan* means "all.") Their planned flight would take them to Nassau, in the Bahamas, to the Virgin islands, down through the West Indies, and on to South America. They used a new Lambert Monocoupe plane, which they christened "The Booker T. Washington" at a ceremony held at the Tuskegee Institute in Alabama. (I remember reading about Booker T. Washington when I was about 10 or 11 years old. I especially remember the part of the story explaining that the *T* stood for Taliaferro, a name that his mother liked.)

Their first stop, in the Bahamas, was a real experience. It was the first time that a plane, any plane, was going to land in the Bahamas. There were no landing strips, but there were many roads. And it was dark. The noise of the approaching plane drew a large crowd. The aviators made a few passes over the heads of the delighted observers. They finally realised that they had to get out of the way so the plane could land. All was resolved when the cars formed a pair of parallel lines and illuminated a "landing strip" along a straight stretch of road for the tired flyers.

Dr. Forsythe and Anderson island-hopped to Jamaica, Cuba, the Dominican Republic, Grenada, and down to Trinidad. They used racetracks as landing fields after the incident in the Bahamas. When they arrived in Trinidad, they discovered to their dismay that there were trees in the middle of the racetrack, which itself was in a developing residential area of Port of Spain. Anderson had to land in the middle of a nearby street.

Anderson's apprehension was extreme when the moment of departure arrived. Reports indicate that when he tried to take off again from Taylor Street, in Woodbrook, on Friday 14 December, a wing clipped some of the nearby trees. Although no one was injured, damage to the aircraft was severe enough to put an end to the tour. Fortunately, the accident occurred at or close enough to the projected end of the mission. The worldwide attention attracted by this tour did much to advance the interest in aviation of the black community everywhere.

On their return to the United States, the duo did other goodwill tours within continental America. In 1940, Anderson was hired by Howard University in Washington, DC, as a flight instructor. Also in 1940, Tuskegee Institute in Alabama hired him as chief primary flight instructor. It was there that he acquired the title "Chief."

At Tuskegee, Anderson developed a pilot training program for the school. This institute was one of six in America that participated in the Civilian Pilot Training Program designed to provide pilots for wartime emergency. At the time, Anderson was still the only black person to have a commercial pilot's license in America. He was instrumental in creating the famous Tuskegee Airmen of World War II.

Charles Alfred "Chief" Anderson died in 1996, after a protracted fight with cancer. He was, and still is, an inspiration, not only to black Americans who want to become pilots but also to anyone who sets out to accomplish something in his or her life.

Dr. Forsythe was also always mindful of the fact that blacks could be just as successful as anyone else once they put their minds to the task at hand. On one occasion in the Caribbean, he and Anderson were flying over a ship. Dr. Forsythe asked Anderson to fly close to the boat — close enough, he said, so they could "see that we are two black men flying this plane."

The story of the Goodwill Flyers who crashed in Woodbrook in 1934 clarified why my father entered the fact in his diary. It was important to him, and he made sure that it became part of his legacy. I am sure that he had followed the exploits of the Goodwill Flyers in the newspapers, and no doubt he thought highly of the personal self-esteem demonstrated by these two men.

* * *

Sat 15 Dec 1934 Posted letter and Christmas greetings to my friend Daniel Darius Haynes, Settlement Officer of Punta Gorda, British Honduras [Now known as Belize].

As children, we enjoyed looking at the family photo albums. In one of these albums, three pictures always intrigued me — especially the one of a coconut tree with side shoots. I had never seen coconut trees with side shoots before.

I rediscovered these pictures during my short visit to Trinidad in October of 2013. When I did, I noticed the name D.D. Haynes at the bottom of one. I recognised this name from my father's diary. Curiosity got the better of me.

The Internet revealed that Daniel Darius Haynes was born in Guyana. He was an instructor who pioneered rice production in the Toledo district of British Honduras, Belize, in the 1930s. I have no idea how and when my father met Mr. Haynes, but I bet it would have been a very interesting story.

(I did some more research into the phenomenon of side shoots on coconut trees. I found out that the roots of palm trees grow from stem or trunk tissue and not from other roots. The root initiation zone of a palm can sometimes work its way up the trunk of a tree. Although arrested when exposed to a dry environment, root initials in these zones can at times resume growth in a moist environment. Mystery solved!)

* * *

Fri 28 Dec 1934 Went to Port of Spain. Stopped at Ralph and after took car and called to see Miss Oxley , her sister and the Mapps. all of whom reside at 8 Meyler Street, Belmont. Here I was introduced to a certain Mr. Gilkes, teacher at Pamphilian High School. The Mapps and the Oxleys were all well. In fact, to me, Doris looked charming and I felt I loved her more than I ever did before. She cast

a matron- like atmosphere around her. I was very happy in
the company of the home. I left about 10:30 and returned
to St. Joseph.

My father's mention of the Pamphilian High School in his diary entry
brought back a lot of memories about my uncle Horace.

In January of 1915, as Joshua lay dying, Mathilda asked him who would
look after little Horace. Joshua responded by pointing to Daddy who was
14 years old at the time. Randolph nodded in acceptance and silent promise
was made to his father that he would take care of his two year old brother.
The next mention of this younger brother was in 1923, when my father was
appointed Assistant Master at the Richmond Street E.C. School and moved
back to St. Joseph. In his memoirs, my father mentions carrying with him
his younger brother "whom I had taken with me to Couva in order to supervise his studies at school." Horace would have been about 10 years old at the
time.

The last mention of Horace Walrond came in the form of a progress
report from the Pamphylian High School. It is dated 1927, which would
make him about 13 years old at the time.

We came to know Uncle Knolly, as we all called him, much later on, in
the 1950s. By then he was working in the southern part of the island for an
oil company called the United British Oilfields of Trinidad, more familiarly
known as UBOT. He lived at the whim of the company, sometimes in Point
Fortin and at other times in Penal.

As he worked, he studied to become a pharmacist. It was hard work,
but he was determined. Perhaps his high school motto, *Nihil Sine Labore*
("nothing without hard work"), guided him. He eventually did succeed.
He later moved away from the oilfield environment and opened his own
drugstore on the Eastern Main Road, in the Mount Lambert area, between
Champ Fleurs and San Juan.

* * *

Tues 1 Jan 1935 Arrived home at about 1 am from Service
accompanied by Frank, Louvina and Agnes. Wished
Mother a happy and prosperous New Year. Afterwards

went with Frank to his home and from there, to one Toby, a friend of his. Here was a very pleasant fellow who seemed satisfied both with himself and the world. He presented in his impressions of religion a touch of those things which arouse a sense of Africanism. At his gate, on the inner side, a candle burned flickerlessly as if in defiance of the New Year's breeze, and way back in his inner yard there was a small and slightly raised platform of earth on which was set an image like object before which burned a few candles. Inside, his sitting room was small, neat, clean and cozy. Against one of the walls was a small but beautiful Victrola, which discoursed sweet music while small talk and a few drinks went round. While thus engaged a chap whom I knew and who hailed from Caroni came up. He was a smart remarkable chap from the fact that though a Negro, the profile of his head presented a most exact likeness of the head of a North or South American Indian.

I still wonder who these two men were.

Chapter 17
My Mother's Family
A Bicultural Experience

The following entry is probably the most significant one in my father's brief diary:

> **1937** This was a most auspicious year in my life, it being the year in which I was joined in Holy Wedlock to Miss Floris Daphne Lee Young, eldest child of Mr. and Mrs. James Lee Young of Spring Village, Couva.

> **Sat 7 Aug** Spent the greater part of the day at Spring Village at the home of my fiancée assisting her in decorating her home. This was the eve of our wedding day.

These entries marked an important turning point in my father's life. A family was started the next year. Four years later I was born, and , I suppose, that was the real start of my story.

In March of 1996, on a short visit to my parents, I was relaxing on the veranda when my father came out to join me. As he approached, he asked me, "Did I ever tell you how your mother and I met?"

"No," I answered, "you haven't."

"Well, sit down and let me tell you." This was his story, word for word, as far as I can remember:

When I was a young man, I taught for a while at the Richmond Street Boys E.C. School. One day, the Head Teacher said to me, "Walrond, I want you to teach a special class of students. They are preparing to write the Government Exhibition Exam." So I was assigned this special class. The class consisted mostly, but not entirely, of some Chinese children. I was so impressed by their eagerness to learn, their willingness to apply themselves, and their general industriousness that I said to myself, "I should marry a Chinese girl one day."

Well, time went by, and I was assigned to different schools in other parts of Trinidad. In March of 1936, I was appointed head teacher of the Couva E.C. School. As the head teacher, I was expected to be a lay minister of the Church, as well as the organist and choir master of the church. You see, the minister of the Anglican Church was also the manager of the school.

Part of my job was to be at the organ well before the Sunday service was due to begin. I sat with my back to the congregation, and I had to keep turning around to see when the priest would give me the signal to begin playing the processional hymn.

One Sunday, as I sat at the organ, I heard a voice say to me, "Walrond, get up and go to the back of the church." At first I ignored the voice, but it kept repeating, "Walrond, go to the back of the church." Finally, I got up and started to make my way to the back of the church. I noticed that the priest and acolytes were in their position, waiting for me to begin playing. I got the oddest look from the minister as I made my way towards the back of the church. When I got to the side entrance of the church, there was a young lady struggling to lift her bicycle up the stairs and into the entrance hall of the church. I gave her a hand and quickly returned to my post at the organ.

After the service, I made some discreet enquiries as to who that young lady was. I was informed that she was the daughter of a shopkeeper and lived along the Balmain Road, about three and a half miles from Isaac Junction. The next Sunday, after the service, I got dressed, got on my bicycle, and rode along the Balmain Road and knocked on the side door of a shop. The proprietor's name was listed on the outer wall of the building, so I knew that I was at the correct place.

The door was opened by a short bespectacled Chinese gentleman. I presented myself as Mr. Randolph Walrond, headmaster of the Couva E.C. School, and requested his permission to court his daughter. He looked at me, asked me to come in, closed the door, took me to the foot of some stairs, and said, "Look, she's upstairs. Go nah [Why don't you go ahead?]." So I did.

I think I thanked my father for telling me the story. I am not sure what he replied, because I was making mental note of what he said, since I knew that it would bear repeating. As soon as I could, I wrote down the story of how my father met my mother.

As a child, I could never understand why my mother's siblings — and there were nine of them — all called my father Hello. I finally got the courage to question my mother. She explained that when my father came to visit, her youngest brothers, a set of twins, would peek out from behind chairs and other items of furniture and say, "Hello." My father would respond by saying, "Hello." They would repeat the same greeting. The game was afoot. In a short time, he became Hello, and the name stayed with him. This explanation solved another mystery.

* * *

The following letter also filled in a blank that I did not even know was there. I am grateful to my father for having kept it for so many years.

Spring Village
Couva
4th September 1936

Mr Randolph Walrond
Pascall St
Couva

Dear Mr Waldrond

We have consulted our daughter Floris, respecting the communication with which you favoured us, and the result is that we are perfectly satisfied, and you have therefore our consent to pay your addresses to her.

It may not be out of place here to tell you how devoted we are to her, and with what tenderness and care she has been reared, while she has been to us a most dutiful and affectionate daughter and we believe will make a good wife.

I desire also that the time be fixed within 18 months, as of

Yours truly
Mr & Mrs James Lee Young

As children growing up, my siblings and I spent a lot of time at our grandparents' house in Balmain. My mother was the eldest of ten children. She had six brothers, then one sister, and then two more brothers — twins. As time went on, her six older brothers got married and had children of their own. There were always more and more cousins to meet at the house in Balmain.

* * *

My mother's father, James Lee Young, came from Canton, China. The date of his arrival is unknown. He established himself in the village of Balmain, where he and my grandmother ran their country shop.

He also operated a chocolate factory. The area around Balmain is noted for the high quality of its cocoa beans. He bought beans from the growers, roasted them, and then ground them into a paste, which he passed through a machine that turned out three parallel strings of chocolate, about half an inch in diameter, somewhat like a pasta machine. He would cut these tubular lengths of chocolate paste into 4-inch-long segments and then let them dry. These he would stack, package, label, and sell. The amazing thing about this factory was that the equipment he used was homemade wherever possible.

He was also a budding engineer. He used an old Morris car engine mounted on large wooden blocks to run his grinders and mills, all connected via overhead belts and pulleys. I used to enjoy just standing around and watching these spinning wheels and listening to the cough and sputter of the old car engine.

My mother's great-grandfather was John Chow. He was among the first Chinese immigrants to arrive in Trinidad aboard the Clarendon in April 1853. On his arrival, he was either assigned or chose the name Martin. It was customary in those days for immigrants to change their names, especially if their intention was to be businessmen.

He did in fact become a businessman, owning a small fleet of fishing boats. He soon became a Christian and married Margaret Augustus. She was the daughter of Scottish missionaries and was a teacher by profession. I believe that she may have come from the Scottish town of Kinghorn, because this was the name she chose for her second son.

Her first child, John Edwin Martin Jr., was born on 27 December 1867. On 14 December 1892, he married Florence Mathilda Callendar, who was born in Barbados and was a descendant of slaves. John was a builder and carpenter by profession, and he was proud of his certificate from the Trinidad and Tobago Board of Industrial Training. It was dated 3 June 1908. He built the family home, which was always decorated with Chinese paintings and pictures. We visited this house quite often.

By virtue of the fact that Mathilda Callendar was from the island of Barbados and was born of slaves, all the descendants of John Edwin Martin were also linked to the "Africanism" of my immediate ancestors. Her provenance therefore strengthened the link between Barbados and Trinidad as far as my heritage is concerned.

John Edwin's and Mathilda's second child, one of 12, was Alma Beatrice Martin. She married James Lee Young, and together they set up their business in the village of Balmain.

Agnes Martin, another daughter of John and Margaret Chow Martin, married Henry Akan, who is believed to have come from Canton as well. He is known to have visited China on three different occasions, and on one of his trips, in 1922, he took his son, Henry Gaston Jr., with him. Henry Jr. remained in China, married, and raised a family there. (His is another case of what I have called reverse immigration. I wonder how many cousins I have still living in China.)

* * *

Growing up with my Chinese relatives was important to me. The whole experience taught me that although the world was filled with people of different races and skin tones, we were all people. Even among my own siblings, given the diversity of our ethnic origins, our skin tones were not all identical, especially when we were first born.

As I grew up, my life's experiences began to change from a bicultural one to a multicultural one. I had already learned that there are many different types of people and that they all should be accepted as they were. I learned, for example, that, in addition to the members of my Chinese family, there were East Indian people, and that some of these were Muslims and others were Hindus.

Out of nine children, I was the fourth from the top. When I was about 4, we moved into a house on Edgar Street in Couva. Edgar Street is a secondary road that runs parallel to the principal Southern Main Road but one block to the south. The school at which my father taught was located on the Southern Main Road, about halfway between the police station and St. Andrew's Junction, where the Anglican church was located.

As I have said, this school was in effect the new school for which funds were being raised in 1920 when my father first worked in this town as a vice principal. Directly across the main road from the school lived an elderly and very gentle East Indian man. His name was Sankha Bissessar. We all called him Mr. Sankha. His property extended from the main road, across Edgar Street to the trace that separated it from the cane fields. He therefore owned two lots. The house in which we lived and where the last three of my siblings were born was situated beside Mr. Sankha's back lot.

What was very noteworthy of Mr. Sankha's property was that both lots were divided into two equal sections by a pathway that led all the way down the middle from the Southern Main Road to the very end of his Edgar Street lot. Before we moved into the house, my father obtained permission from this kind gentleman for us children to use this pathway to access the school and so save us the extra walk all around the block. The school was located directly across the main road from his property. He agreed, and so a very friendly relationship was established.

On the left side of Mr. Sankha's front lot, as you faced it, was a very beautiful but small house in which his mother and two sisters lived. On the other side of this lot was another building. The front part of this structure, which was set about 15 feet from the main road, housed a bicycle repair shop operated by Mr. Sankha. Behind the shop was a small room where he slept. Next to this was the family kitchen and washroom areas.

The dividing pathway continued on past a small fenced-off garden area and chicken run. The central path extended all the way back to Edgar Street and continued to the rear lot, which was also divided down the middle by a path. This second lot was entirely given over to a garden, where vegetables and other essential ground provisions were grown. There were pigeon peas, cassava, corn, sweet potatoes, and I can't remember what else . . . oh yes! There was also a guava tree.

As my family grew in number and we children grew in size, we would play together in the front yard of the house. A tall hibiscus hedge separated us from Edgar Street, except where a gap and a bridge allowed our car access to the garage. One day, a lady was going by and noticed my father, who was busy doing something under the hood of his car, and us, who were playing in the yard. She stopped and looked at us for short while, and then in a loud but cheery voice, she said, "Mr. Walrond! All these and those are thine?" Then she walked on, laughing loudly.

My father answered with a wide grin on his face that we were indeed all his. From that day on, the lady in question, whom my father knew but we did not, became known as "Miss All These and Those Are Thine" — undoubtedly a long name but not one soon forgotten.

As I grew up, I spent a lot of time in Mr. Sankha's bicycle repair shop, chatting with him, and looking intently at whatever he was doing, learning a lot as the days went by. I believe he grew tired of all my questions, because he used to threaten to send me, a mere child, off to the Korean War, which was being waged at the time.

As I said, I spent a lot of time there, and by the time I inherited my elder brother's bicycle in the late '50s, I was able to maintain it in perfect working order. I remember that one August vacation, as a challenge and to ease my boredom, I took apart the bicycle completely; repainted the frame and fenders a bright red; changed all the bearings, pins, nuts, and bolts; and reassembled it. I remember how simply and effectively the handle post was attached to the frame. I had always wondered how it was done.

Between Mr. Sankha's bicycle shop, the mango and coconut trees, and the cane fields and all the pleasure I derived from them, I was truly sorry when the time came and we moved away.

* * *

I have to return for a moment to the diary entry of 7 August 1937. In it, my father mentions helping to decorate the home of his future wife.

Many years later, the home was decorated a second time in honour of the wedding of my mother's only sister. This would have probably been in the mid or late '50s. No one I spoke to could remember the exact year, and sad to say, my aunt has now passed away.

I believe I was about 11 years old at the time, and I was a guest at the wedding — not at the church but certainly at the reception. The home was a two-storey building, with my grandparents' country shop taking up the front section of the lower floor. Behind this was a large dining area with the longest table I ever saw. There were some chairs, but mostly we sat on long benches. If these were not enough, extra boards were placed on the ends of the benches for the smaller, lighter children to sit on. There was always room for everyone, and on Sundays and special occasions, there were always a lot of guests. My grandfather's chocolate factory was located adjacent to the dining area.

One of the most special occasions was 10 October each year. This is the birthday of my grandfather, James, my mother, Floris, and her twin brothers, Claude and Selwyn. It was always a happy occasion for us all. This was especially so as the years went by and as the number of cousins grew. My grandparents also had a pig and poultry farm and a considerable vegetable garden on the property, so the food was always fresh and delicious, cooked Chinese style, of course. All in all, this was a happy time for the Lee Young and Walrond families.

With regards to my aunt's wedding, I don't remember many details about the decorations. There were Chinese lanterns and lots of coloured streamers hanging from windows and door frames. What I do remember, however, is that at some point during the celebrations, my grandfather called my mother into the shop and, pointing upwards, drew her attention to the fact that the flooring beams were showing significant signs of stress due to the large number of guests on the upper floor. The guests were therefore encouraged to adjourn to the lower level.

Many years later, on a return visit to my grandparents, I discovered that the entire upper floor had been removed and new living quarters had been built on the lower level. The idea of downsizing took on new meaning. It was a sad day for me, because I had really loved that house. A cousin of mine bought it and still lives a farmer's life there.

* * *

Here are a couple of other interesting entries from the second part of my father's diary.

> **Tues 8 Feb 1938** Made cream [ice cream] at home. Sent some to the Henry's at his pharmacy. Mrs. Henry called at about 5:00 p.m. Was at home when I arrived from school. Chinka [Floris's brother], Floris and I had cream together. Some little while after Floris broke a glass. After tea we paid a visit to the Buyans. Soon after we arrived at his home, Bryan left for Carapichaima. Immediately on returning home, Ahing [Floris] broke the lampshade. We had a glass of stout and lemonade together and afterwards sat down, she to read the papers and I to complete the writing of

some questions for my class at school. At about 9:45 p.m. Floris turned in to bed and within a few minutes she broke a utensil. A peculiar breaking influence seemed to have been lurking around in her.

Sun 18 Sep 1938 Our first born, a son, was baptised today. He was named Wilbur Alexander. His God-parents were Miss Dorothy Alleyne [cousin], Miss Naomi Martin [great aunt], Leslie Pershing Lee Young [uncle] and Frank Leopold Walrond [uncle]. Guests present were the Misses Inez and Naomi Martin, the Misses Enid and Dorothy Alleyne, the Misses E. Gill, Myra Walrond [sister] Mrs. C. Patrick, Mrs. Cole, Mr. and Mrs. Frank Walrond, Mr. Patrick, Mr. L. Henry, Horace Walrond, James Austin, Mammie and Pappie [Floris' parents, James and Alma Lee Young], John Carrington [brother-in-law]. Regretfully absent was my mother.

Reading the names of the guests at my brother's christening reminded me of another wedding I attended as a young boy. This would have been around 1952, and I was about 10 years old, if that. The groom was Mr. Carlton Alleyne, and he was my godfather. I really wanted to go to this wedding, and I was allowed to attend.

I am not sure, but I believe the ceremony was held at the St. Margaret's Church in Claxton Bay. It was a rainy day, and the churchyard was quite muddy. The reception was held at the bride's parents' house located on the beautiful Caura Valley Road, which branched off the Eastern Main Road just past Tunapuna. I remember when our car turned onto this road, a member of the bride's family was stationed at the corner and giving directions to the house.

Although I was excited to be at the wedding, I was almost totally ignored, which was fine with me. I enjoyed the food, though, especially the devilled eggs. They were delicious. That was the first time I ever ate them, and they are still a favorite of mine.

My godfather, Carlton, was the last child and only son of Aubrey Alleyne. Carlton's sisters were Enid, Dorothy, and Edna.

Aubrey was a cousin of my father, Randolph. Aubrey's mother, Gertrude, and my father's mother, Mathilda, were sisters and were among the early immigrants from Barbados. Their parents were Joseph and Mary Chandler.

I remember visiting Aubrey Alleyne as a young child. He lived in a town called Fyzabad, located in the oil-rich area of southern Trinidad. At the time, he ran a small dry goods store.

He was a very generous uncle. On one visit, he gave us some toys. Mine was a small mouth organ. I think I drove my parents mad with it. Thank heavens it was not a drum!

* * *

My father was not one for telling stories about himself. As a matter of fact, the one about how he met my mother was one of only two I can think of. This other one is perhaps just as interesting in that it deals with what I call moving on in life. The incident took place while he was principal of the Couva E.C. School.

He had been thinking of becoming a school inspector and at some point must have mentioned it to the gentleman who held that post for the region that included my father's school. One day, just before the school was due to be adjourned for lunch, the inspector arrived at the school, and in his always-authoritative voice — I knew this man — said to my father, "Walrond, I want you to come with me."

My father literally dropped what he was doing and got into the inspector's car, and they drove off. My father became more and more perplexed as they went along, heading off into part of the major sugar cane growing area near the school. Soon, however, the car came to a stop and, surrounded by waving sugar cane plants, the incumbent school inspector ate his lunch. Not a word was spoken as my father, the aspiring school inspector, sat and watched in silent bewilderment.

His lunch over, the inspector started his car, turned it around, returned to the school and deposited my astonished father and drove off. My father was sure that there was a message attached to this bizarre behavior but just could not figure it out. It was, as my father put it, a few days later that the message became clear.

The inspector wanted to demonstrate to my father, whose offspring numbered nine at the time, that being a school inspector was a lonely job that took the incumbent miles away from his family and was perhaps a job that my father should not aspire to. My father got the message, and no more was said about the subject.

This next incident can be best described as a lesson without words. Yet my father communicated it as eloquently as always.

The house on Edgar Street in which we lived was small, but it did have three bedrooms. On a high shelf in what was called the girls' bedroom, there were two violin cases, each holding its own instrument. One violin was old and in a mostly fallen-apart state. The other was in a starting-to-fall-apart state.

I knew the violins were there because I liked to explore forbidden territory. In the case with the better violin, there was also a tuner. It consisted of four metal chambers about 1.5 inches long set via valves to four different notes. Blowing through one end produced a sound like a car horn. I loved to play with it, but of course only when my parents were out of the house.

One day my father took down the better of the two violins and began to repair it. Bits and pieces had fallen off here and there. The bow was unstrung, and the violin had no strings either. However, as the days turned into weeks, my father worked on the instrument. He would mix a little white powder with water — it smelled terrible — and glue back just one piece at a time. A clamp would secure it until such time as the glue had done its job.

As these repairs went on, I hung around my father, watching carefully what he was doing. I remember the little piece he told me was a bridge. Of course, I did not know the function of that beautifully but intricately carved piece of wood till much later.

Soon the bow sprouted horsehair and the violin itself was equipped with catgut and steel strings. Satisfied that all was in order, my father began to tune the violin. This took a long while. My father was very particular about this. Each string had to be tormented individually until my father was satisfied. I can still hear the sound of the tuner followed by the plucking of the strings and the accompanying squealing of the pegs as they picked up the stress of the strings. After what seemed to me to be a very long while, he looked satisfied.

Then, to my utter amazement, my father tucked the violin beneath his chin and gently but deftly began to play that violin like it was an old friend, which I suppose it really was. I had no idea that he could repair a violin, let alone play one so well. That day I learnt the true meaning of this activity: Make new friends, but keep the old; one is silver, the other gold.

Chapter 18
Land

In contemplating the vast amount of information I acquired throughout my research, I came to the conclusion that there was another constant that linked all the families who bore the name of Waleran or Walrond. This thread was the role of real estate in the lives of these men. Owning landed property was an important factor to them all.

To give you a clear perspective of this, I must revisit the story of Waleran Venator. You will remember that shortly after 1066, he was granted extensive lands and estates by his benefactor, William the Conqueror. These properties were located in the south of England, and more than 500 years later and after more than 20 generations, Humphrey Walrond inherited his father's estates in 1620.

Because of his participation in the English Civil War on the side of the king, Humphrey Walrond was held hostage, and his estates were seized by Parliament. Legal procedures ensued, and he was eventually fined and released from prison, whereupon he regained ownership of his property. In 1650, the Commission of Compounding with Delinquents discovered that he had sold his estates and gone to Barbados, where he purchased two sugar plantations.

Not one to learn from experience, Humphrey Walrond continued his political endeavors, still on the side of the king. The Barbadian theatre of the English Civil War was just as unfavorable to the well-being of Humphrey as the home front had been. In time, he was banished from Barbados, and his plantations, seized. By 1668, his whereabouts were unknown. I found no mention of his name in relation to any of the plantations that existed or that still exist. His name seems to have been expunged from all records.

Yet his name still exists on the maps of Barbados. On the western boundary of the Parish of Christ Church, near the eastern Parish of St. Philip's, lies a village named Walronds. I am not sure whether the village is in Christ Church or in neighbouring St. Philip's. However, it must be remembered that one of Humphrey's estates was in the Parish of St. Philip's.

The name Walrond is also associated with an abandoned tomb in the Parish of Christ Church. In the 18th century, a descendant of Humphrey built a tomb which was later sold to the Chase family. This tomb is famous because lead coffins placed in it were wont to wander around behind sealed doors. Perhaps the Walrond name has nothing to do with these peripatetic coffins. The tomb has remained empty for over 150 years now. I visited it once and took some pictures.

The name Walrond also lives on in the large numbers of African Barbadians who carry his name. As I have related, when emancipation came in 1834, many slaves migrated to Trinidad and Guyana. Among the Walronds who moved to Trinidad were brothers Joshua and Charlie. Let us take a look at how real estate impacted the life of these two men. This will best be done by looking at some of the many documents left behind by my father, Randolph.

Port of Spain
28th July 1914

Received from Mr Joshua Walrond the sum of One dollar and forty-four cents for preparing a copy of his deed of lease of lands at St Augustine Estate for ... (Exhibit ... 1914) ...

As you can see, Joshua Walrond leased the land on which he lived and on which his widow Mathilda lived until her death in 1957. In his memoirs, Randolph describes the building of a house starting in 1925.

The following information pertains to a later date and was taken from notes my father made. It refers to the house his mother had had built on Scott Street in Curepe:

> Joshua's daughter, Agatha, was the last of his children to live there. When she died on November 14th 1965, the residence started to depreciate rapidly. By 1978, the wing which housed the kitchen, pantry, bathroom and toilet had disappeared. The breadfruit tree had fallen on these rooms. The premises were left with only one tap in the yard to supply running water. Thereafter the house became unfit for human habitation. It was apparent, though, that someone or some people were squatting there.

The final destinies of both the house and the breadfruit tree, which I am sure had provided some sustenance, were thus fulfilled at the same moment in time.

Sometime between 31 July and 13 August 1987, while on a visit to Trinidad, I took some pictures of the house. It was still in a derelict state. Believing it to be abandoned, I climbed over some rubble and tried to enter it by the rear door, which had fallen off its hinges. I was mistaken, though, for I had awakened someone, and so I beat a hasty retreat.

Shortly after my return to Canada, I learned that the house had burned down. This was 62 years after it was built. The property lease was close to its end, and the land reverted to the government.

I will now turn to Charles Walrond and his experiences with real estate. Consider the following documents:

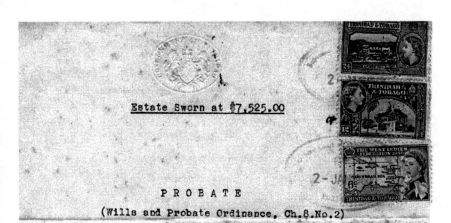

Estate Sworn at $7,525.00

P R O B A T E

(Wills and Probate Ordinance, Ch.8.No.2)

———

IN THE SUPREME COURT OF TRINIDAD AND TOBAGO

In the Estate of

CHARLES WALROND

late of the village of Curepe, in the Ward of Tacarigua,
in the Island of Trinidad, proprietor, deceased.

———

No.L680/59

The annexed Will of CHARLES WALROND who died at
No.69 Eastern Main Road, Curepe aforesaid, on the 8th
day of June, 1959, was proved in the Supreme Court of
Trinidad and Tobago on the 9th. day of November, 1959,
by RANDOLPH OSRIC WALROND of Champs Fleurs, in the
Ward of St.Anne, in the Island of Trinidad aforesaid,
the sole executor therein named.

Dated this 9th. day of November, 1959.

Eric J.A. McCarthy
Registrar.

This is the last will and testament of me, Charles
Walrond of the town of St Joseph in the Ward of Tacarigua
in the County of St George East in the Island of Trinidad.
I declare this to be my last will and testamentary
deposition heretofore made by me.

I name and appoint my nephew, Randolph Osric
Walrond Executor of this will.

I declare that I am seized and possessed of all
and singular that parcel of land comprising one lot more
or less situate at the town of St Joseph with a galvanized
building standing thereon at the corner of Francis Street
and Eastern Main Road. Also five (5) acres 1 rood 28
perches of land more or less situate at Mon Plaiser
Village in the Ward of Cunipia in the County of Caroni.
Also a Burial lot at Lapeyrouse Cemetary Port of Spain
situate at Second Street.

I give and devise the lot of land and the house
situate at St Joseph to my wife Angilina Walrond and my
nephew Randolph Osric Walrond: to my wife for her life
and after her death her vested interest in the property
to go to my nephew Randolph Osric Walrond.

I also give and bequeath the said parcel of
land comprising 5 acres 1 rood 28 perches situate at
Cunipia to the following persons as hereunder detailed:
To my wife Angilina Walrond half acre, to my nephew
Horace Eton Walrond half acre, to my son Michael Walrond
half acre, to my niece Myra Walrond quarter acre, to my
niece Mrs Olga Carrington quarter acre, to my niece Mrs
D. Cole quarter acre, and the remaining portion to my
nephew Randolph Osric Walrond. If at any time the above
mentioned parties are desirous of getting their half or
quarter share respectively the same is to be given to

them at the back of the said five acre one rood twenty

eight perches block.

I also give and bequeath the Burial Allotment

situate at Second Street Lapeyrouse Cemetary to my

nephew Randolph Osric Walrond. In witness whereof I

have set my hands to this my last will and testament.

In the presence of each of us)
and who in our presence and in)
the presence of each of us set)   Charles Walrond
his hands this 19th day of April,)
1958)

In witness whereof

Vernon Scott
  Head Teacher
    Tacarigua E.C. School

Ivan B.J. Rouse
  Head Teacher
    Tacarigua Orphanage E.C. School

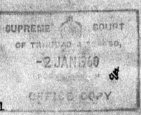

A.C. Clarke
Commissioner of Affidavits.

TRINIDAD AND TOBAGO

IN THE SUPREME COURT

IN the Estate of Charles Walrond
late of the Village of Curepe in
the Island of Trinidad, Proprietor,
deceased.

NATURE, EXTENT AND ESTIMATED GROSS VALUE of the Estate
of the deceased referred to in the application for
probate.

(Irrespective of debts and charges)

Description of Property		Value
Cash in hand	Nil	
Cash in bank	Nil	
Furniture	Nil	
Shares	Nil	
Policies of Insurance	Nil	
Mortgages	Nil	
Property (if any) situate abroad	Nil	

Any other property:

(1) All and Singular one lot of land situate
at corner of Francis Street and Eastern
Main Road Curepe in the Town of St.Joseph
in the Island of Trinidad with a building thereon valued at $5,500.00 $5,500.00

(2) Five acres 1 rood 28 perches situate
at Mont Plaisir Cunupia Caroni valued
at $2,000.00

(3) Burial lot.   25.00

Total $7,525.00

Dated this 13th day of July 1959.

Randolph Walrond
Applicant.

To the Registrar of the Supreme Court.

Statement Re valuation of the properties
of the Late Charled Walrond.

I the undersigned General House & Commission Agent Reg No 391-D
of Cor Clifford & Jackson Streets Curepe,with around eight years
experience in valuating Etc,hereby submit my valuation of the
properties of the Late Charles Walrond of Curepe,comprises of as
follows.

House & Land

One tapa house 24 x35 on 1 lot land free hold

    close gallary

    small dressing room

    dining room

    drawing room

    2 bed rooms

    kitchen attached 15 x 12 on concrete pillars covered with

    galvernize,situated at the cor E.M.R. & Francis street

    Curepe at $5.500

Lands at Waren Village.
----

  5 acres)-# 1½ acres planted in canes by 2 tenants

     1 ½ acres empty land with a 2 Room house

  at $400 per acre $2.000

Total value of both properties

      House & Land $5.500

      Lands $2.000

The word tapa should read tapia. Tapia is a material similar to adobe.

As this will portrays, Charles Walrond died in possession of three pieces
of real estate. It also shows that when he died on 8 June 1959, he left the
major portion of the land in Cunupia to his nephew, Randolph Walrond,
my father. The rest he left to other members of his family. It took five years
to probate the will. Finally, Randolph was able to turn his attention to his
"mini estate."

I was able to use some notes that my father left in order to trace the development of his inheritance, which was made up of the house and land where his aunt had lived and the acreage in Cunupia.

Starting in April of 1964, he engaged a gentleman to live on the property in Cunupia and to plant coconut and citrus trees. The plan was to sell the produce and at least cover the taxes on the land. This first contract was terminated in 1971, and in May of 1972, another person was hired to collect the nuts and fruit. However, this second employee had his own ideas, and early in 1973 it was discovered that he had started to occupy more land than he was supposed to. In other words, he had started to squat on part of the land.

In June of that same year, my father started to develop the property into lots. He sold the property in Curepe and used the proceeds to improve the land in Cunupia. He hired a topographical survey company to survey and divide the land into housing lots. For reasons unknown, this took a few years to accomplish.

In June of 1982, the Water and Sewage Authority carried out percolation tests, and in December of 1983, the Engineering firm of Lee Young and Partners was hired to take over and oversee the development of the lands. (If this name sounds familiar, you are not mistaken. This firm is headed by Selwyn, one of my mother's twin brothers. He and his son, who is also his partner, are engineers with Ph.D. degrees in their field.)

By April of 1986 work, was almost completed, and the lots went on sale. My father was 86 years old by this time. He was asked to name one of the streets after himself. He was reluctant to do so at first but finally agreed. However, with his usual modesty, he used his middle name, by which hardly anybody knew him. Osric Drive in Cunupia is part of his legacy.

Chapter 19
My Father's Books, Magazines, and Other Papers

My story now takes on a more personal note. While I was in the process of organising some papers, I came across a notebook in which I had recorded some notes about a journey I made to Trinidad at the end of August 1991.

The purpose of this one-week stay was to spend some time with my parents. Daddy had been in the hospital for the previous week and had returned home the day before I arrived. He was resting comfortably when I arrived at the house at about 3:00 in the morning.

He was looking as well as could be expected, considering what was ailing him. As the days went by, for the week I was there, he got visibly better and felt much improved. Anyone who visited him was good for about one hour of conversation.

I had a few chats with him about my children André and Larissa, about Beth, about myself and other things in general. We also talked about his life story, which was always very interesting. His memory, though slow at times, was always lucid. As we spoke, I would often forget that he was over 90 years old.

Mammy, as usual, was a moving tower of strength, always ready, willing, and able to do anything for anyone. For example, I thought my laundry from the flight down was safely out of sight, hidden behind my flight bag at the foot of my bed. I had intended to do some washing the next day. However, next morning, when I got out of bed and looked out the window,

I saw my mother, hanging my laundry on the line to dry. She had beaten me to it. She did get frustrated at times, though, especially when she felt that she was being called upon to do more than three things at once.

Besides spending time with my parents, I was able to do several things that I had always wanted to accomplish. The first thing I did was to I visit my old high school, Queen's Royal College. While there, I asked the secretary to pull out my old academic records for me to look at. I had graduated in 1960. I could not help laughing to myself when I read the comments by some of my masters regarding my (lack of) work habits, achievement, and so on. To this day, I can't quite figure out whether I became a high school teacher because of the teachers I had at QRC or in spite of them — or because of or in spite of myself. I am convinced, though, that if I had had better math and science teachers during my early years at this school, my life would most likely have gone in another direction.

I also visited Stollmeyer's Castle, also known as Killarney, a Scottish baronial style mansion facing the Queen's Park Savannah in Port of Spain and located not far from my high school. I had always admired its exterior and longed to see the inside. Although it was in a severe state of disrepair and was being renovated at the time of my visit, I still enjoyed touring the building. I was able to climb the stairs within the tall, circular tower until a loud creak in the steps caused me to beat a hasty retreat. It was just as well, though, because at that same moment, I looked up and noticed a giant nest of vicious wasps dangerously close to my head.

Finally, on this visit, I was able to pay a visit to the Maracas Waterfall, located in the mountains above the old capital of St. Joseph. Although the site is not very far from my family home as the crow flies, this visit entailed a lengthy hike through some of the hills and mountains of the Northern Range. But it was worth it. I had read and heard so much about this waterfall that I simply had to go. Many years later, I took my wife and grown-up children to see it.

When I left Trinidad on 27 August 1991, I went to Barbados. There I visited the archives and looked through the ancient registers of births, deaths, and marriages, looking for information about my grandfather Joshua and his brother Charlie. It was a fruitless visit from that point of view, because I had no dates or locations to guide me.

I was quite frustrated when I returned to Nanaimo, on Vancouver Island, and carefully looked through the papers I had brought back with me, which were photocopies of some documents that my father had stored away. There I found a letter from Uncle Charlie to my father in which he gave his complete date of birth. If I had had that information while in Barbados, I would have fared much better. I later inherited these and other papers, and they became the basis of a large part of this book.

On my return to Canada, visions of hot and sunny weather, white sandy beaches, tropical foods, and suntanned bodies haunted me for several days. How I managed to concentrate on teaching, at least for a while, I will never know.

Two years after my visit, in 1993, the following letter arrived in Nanaimo addressed to my son.

Palm Drive
Champs Fleurs
St Joseph
Trinidad W.I.
Mon 19th July '93

Dear Andre.
It is a pleasure getting
letters and cards from you on special
days and speaking to you on the
phone. To-day, however I decide to write
you a letter because sending you a letter
and getting one from you would be
like chatting one with the other.

As you know, I went through the serious
spell of my illness during my life in
the years '91 and '92 and I got through
by the grace of God except for a
defect at the lower part of my back
near my buttock due to RADIO-THERAPY
which I received and which has to be
taken care off of. Except for that I
think I can say I am doing well.

We are now in the Hurricane
months July August and September.
A few days ago we had a freek
storm along the southern slope of
the northern Range from Champs Fleurs
to Chaguaramas and much damage
was done to some Buildings and a few
trees were blown down. The lower floor
of Tatil building was damaged in
its lower floor – this building is in
Maraval Road in Port of Spain.

Now tell me something about yourself. You should now be a well grown lad far removed from the little chap I used to see when last I was in ~~Nanaim~~ Nanaimo.

I love the Hi! Grandpa! Card you and Narissa sent me. The words are full of Truth and truth and beauty go hand in hand.

The drawing at the front shows that I am still a happy old soul.

Well André! My age and health do not permit me now to travel or I would have come once again to see the folk at your end. I however do hope to see Vancouver and the folk over there once again.

My regards to all the family at your end.

I am
youre ever
Grandpa.

The illness that my father referred to was prostate cancer. We had all followed his treatment and recovery by telephone calls. The letter, though, shows the strength with which he had coped with his medical problems. When he died in 1996, although he may have died with residues of cancer, he did not die from it.

In January of 2010, I had to confront the same demon that my father had faced in 1991. It was suspected that I had prostate cancer, and a diagnosis confirmed it. I have to say that I derived a lot of courage and hope from the cool and collected way in which my father had dealt with his illness. I, too, took things one step at a time. I had surgery in September of that year. When people asked me how I was doing, it was actually easy for me to reply, "Fine." I could not and did not complain.

A year or two before, I had watched a good friend of mine, a fellow teacher, die a slow and painful death from this "curable" disease and was determined to do all I could to avoid such a fate.

* * *

Just when I thought I had looked at all the papers that my father had left, I came across the cover of a copy of *The Illustrated London News*. Some readers will recognise this as one of the most popular British news magazines around. This particular cover was dated late October 1948. I wondered what my father would be doing with such a publication and, above all, where he would have gotten it. I turned the sheet over, and the mystery was solved. On the reverse side was a picture that brought back a flood of more memories.

The house we lived in on Edgar Street, from 1945 to the end of 1956, had a 6- or 7-foot high hibiscus hedge in front of it. There was a gap in this fence that gave access to the house via a bridge over a shallow drain that ran beside the street. I remember climbing in among the branches at one end of the hedge and pretending that I was the driver of a train and that the rest of the fence was my locomotive and carriages. I would rock from side to side, and soon the entire fence would sway in much the same fashion as a train rolling along an uneven track. It was fun.

One day some workmen arrived at the house and chopped about 10 feet off the other end of the fence and dug up the roots. Then they built a bridge over the drain. Soon another workman arrived and built a shed beside the house. I watched every move he made. When the shed was finished, he climbed a ladder and cut away about 6 or 7 inches off the top of each of the outer posts along the long side of the newly built shed. The roof he had built fell, and lo and behold, it had a definite slope to it. The top of the shed was covered with galvanized sheeting.

Then he cut the top and bottom off some oil drums and split the resulting cylinder open. With much hammering, he flattened what used to be drums into sheets of metal. These became one long and one short side of the shed. The wall of the house formed the other long wall of the shed, and a pair of wooden gates enclosed the new shed.

A few days later, my father went into Port of Spain and returned with a brand-new 1949 Hillman Minx Saloon. It was a picture of this car that I saw on the cover of the *Illustrated London News*.

Ours was a lovely blue in colour, and we were all happy. A few weeks later, the car had to be taken back to the dealership to be repainted. Apparently, the blue paint used was of a post-war inferior quality. When it was returned, the car was black.

We soon got used to the new colour. There were August holiday trips to the beach at Los Iros on the south coast of Trinidad and Sunday drives to here and there. We took one early-morning trip to Piarco Airport to see some Australian Air Force Canberra jet bombers that were on a world tour. I remember them swooping over the tarmac in silence, their thunderous roar and exhaust following behind. What fun!

When the car was about two years old, my father took it back to the dealership to have the engine "decarbonised." He was gone all day. When he returned, the car ran as though it were new again. A year or two later, my father decarbonised the engine himself. I watched him and helped him, mostly by handing him the tools he needed. When I asked him how he learned to do what looked to me like a major job, he answered that he had watched the mechanics do it at the dealership before.

He had a definite routine to follow. First he drained the radiator and removed it. Next, all the parts of the engine up to and including the cylinder head came off. Decarbonising meant removing all the carbon from the underside of the cylinder head and from the tops of the pistons and around the valves. Thereafter, we performed the operation every year or two. By the time I was 12 or so, I could do most of the easy parts job myself.

Apparently, my father was also a mechanic.

Sometime around 1960, my father sold the 1948 car and bought a 1959 model Hillman. It, too, was black. This was the car I drove until I left for Canada in 1964.

* * *

The year 1956 was an exciting one for the family. Plans had been drawn up, and discussions were held. My parents were going to have a new house built. My father had bought the property, and all was set.

The lot was situated in a sub-division called Champ Fleurs, located in the southern foothills of the Northern Range of mountains, near the town of St. Joseph, a short distance from where he was born. The site was named after a former sugar plantation.

When we, the children, finally got to see the site, the house was almost finished. The area was beautiful, and the mountain scenery behind the house was magnificent. We could hardly wait for moving day. It came soon enough, just after Christmas of 1956.

The house had the required three bedrooms as well as a nicely appointed kitchen with a fridge — we had never had a fridge before — and a special kerosene stove with built-in oven. The stove was special because through a special process, the kerosene was converted into a gas, which was then used for cooking. We also had electricity. The house we had lived in at Couva, although it had running water, had no electricity. For the first time in ten years, we also now had an indoor toilet.

The house itself was built on 8-foot-high pillars at the front and about 6- or 7-foot pillars at the back, for as I said, it was located on the foothills of the northern mountain range. Years later, the area below the house was converted into a garage and extra rooms.

It was not the biggest house on the street, but it was not the smallest either. What was big was the family that moved into it: There were 11 of us altogether. It was going to be a new and different life for us.

This was the year that I started going to school by train. In addition to classmates, I now had train mates. Life was getting better, and so were my marks at high school. I finally came to understand what it meant to be a student.

It was also the year in which I came to realize that Latin, French, and Spanish were all associated languages, and my study of them took on a new significance. And it was the year that I decided I wanted to become a language teacher. I never changed that decision, and it led to a career I thoroughly enjoyed.

Moving into that new house was a life-changing experience for me. I lived in that house until the end of August 1964, when I moved to Montreal to begin my studies in French and Spanish, the first step towards my profession as a teacher.

* * *

One of the most perplexing bits of paper that my father left was this folded half sheet on which he had written these three pieces of poetic literature. One bit had been written, amended, and then rewritten. They were puzzling to me because I could not fathom the reason why he wrote the lines. I first came upon them in 1991.

The lines are beautiful, packed with emotion and yet mysterious. I thought about them for a long time but could come to no conclusion as to the motive for their creation.

In 2013, I visited my relatives in Trinidad. Mammy had just turned 95 and was doing as well as can be expected. She was frail but mentally alert. Her speech was a bit slurred at times, but one could still speak with her.

One day I went downstairs into what used to be my father's study and started looking through his bookshelf. He had quite a collection of books. Among them, I came across several that he had without doubt greatly treasured.

One was a diary he had kept about his visit to Vancouver in 1968, the year he came up to Canada for my graduation from McGill University. Another was the copy of Jane Austen's book *Sense and Sensibility* that was given to him on 5 December 1933 by the rector of St. Stephen's Church in Princes Town. It is a beautiful blue leather-bound copy. He also had a copy of *Pride and Prejudice* — another novel written by Jane Austen — appropriately inscribed with his name. This book was bound in red leather. Both of these volumes came in matching cases. They, however, showed their age and would probably not stand another reading.

Another book I discovered was a copy of Virgil's *Aeneid: Book VI,* edited by T. Page, M.A. The copy is inscribed with my father's name and address and is dated Tuesday, 8 November 1927. This book, except for the introduction, which is in English, is completely in Latin. It was copyrighted in 1888, and the last date of issue was 1922. I suspect that he bought this book in this latter year and used it either for personal enrichment or while he was studying for the Senior Cambridge Exams. Throughout the text there are highlights and notes in my father's handwriting. What I found interesting about finding this book is that it explained why he was able to help me when I was struggling with Latin in 1955, my first year of high school. Thus was the answer to another curiosity brought to light.

The last book I discovered was a copy of *Enoch Arden,* by Lord Tennyson. My father bought this book on 29 February 1932, when he was living on Manahambre Road in Princes Town. This book, too, was well-read and annotated by my father. This poem ranks as one of the best — if not the best — written by Alfred, Lord Tennyson.

Enoch Arden relates the story of the three children: Enoch Arden, son of a sailor; Philip Ray, only son of the village miller; and a pretty girl named Annie Lee. They grow up playing together on the village beach. Enoch prospers, and before he is 21, he owns his own boat and has married Annie.

They have two children, a daughter and a son. Then tragedy strikes Enoch in the form of a fall from a mast and a broken limb. A third child, a sickly son, is born while Enoch lies at home recovering. Enoch loses his business while recuperating.

A former captain hears of Enoch's plight and offers him a job that requires him to leave home. He accepts the offer because he has no other options. He sells his boat and uses the proceeds to establish Annie as a shopkeeper, converting the front room of his house into a place of business. Before he leaves, Enoch kisses his wife and the two oldest children, but because the sick son lies asleep, Enoch cuts a lock of the child's hair and keeps it with him. The child eventually dies.

With Enoch gone, Annie is heartbroken. She is no good at running a shop, and she would perish if not for the silent and steadfast help and support of Philip Ray, who has become a very successful miller. Ten years go by with no word from Enoch. Then Philip asks Annie to be his wife. It takes another two years before Annie agrees and becomes Philip's wife.

Enoch, in the meantime, has been shipwrecked on a tropical island. At length, a passing ship takes him off, and he finds his way back to England and makes a cautious entry into the village in which he grew up. He is greatly changed in appearance and is able to rent a small house and remain undiscovered, which is his desire.

One evening, he creeps up to the Ray house and, through the undraped window, silently watches the happiness and comfort in which Annie and her family live. Enoch creeps away and, kneeling on the ground, promises himself that he will never let Annie know that he has returned and that he has seen her.

He knows his death was close at hand and beseeches his landlady that after he has died, she should give the lock of his son's hair to Annie. After Enoch dies, his story is voiced about the village, and he is given the most lavish funeral the village had ever seen.

After I read the poem, I realized that it could have been the inspiration for these lines that my father had written:

> Bright, calm, sweet self-possessing stars,
>
> High up in the horizon set,
>
> To light and cheer the toilsome way of man,
>
> To raise his manhood up to higher plane

And cause him to present as offering poor

All that is great in him

With a sunny heart, a mind which is always cheerful and hopeful and sympathetic, age has little in common.

The mightiest force in the world is the silent power of love.

Slowly but surely, I was finding out more and more of my father. What an interesting though private life he had led — private as far as we, his children, were concerned. Although he had formed a constant and even dominating part of our existence, still he was like a sphinx in other ways. I have to admit that in his pre-family days, he led a dynamic life, always giving whenever and whatever he could to others around him.

* * *

Sometime before he retired in 1959, my father was transferred to the Curepe E.C. School as headmaster. This school, also known as St. Joseph E.C. School, is located not far from the house on Scott Street. In 1994, this school celebrated its 50th anniversary. The foundation stone had been laid on 13 June 1944, the day on which my father celebrated his 45th birthday.

Chapter 20
Saying Goodbye

One of the most interesting comments I ever heard Daddy make was that he was ready to go on up to the big classroom in the sky. This was during a visit I made with my family to Trinidad in the spring of 1996.

The comment was interesting not just because it told me that he was quite prepared to meet the end of his life but also that he still thought of himself as a teacher. Somehow I felt sorry for Saint Peter. I knew, however, that Daddy was truly satisfied with the way his life had turned out. No doubt he felt that he had accomplished all he set out to do and perhaps even more. I began to wonder, though, what other people thought about him.

I am happy to say that I do not believe that there is only one yardstick that can be used to determine the measure of a man. The human being is a complex entity, and we have been admonished to judge not, lest we be judged. Yet we are allowed to formulate opinions.

Perhaps the preceding recognition, which was accorded Randolph Walrond by the staff of the last school of which he was headmaster, can be used as one measure. This school, as I said before, was also the one at which he began his teaching career as a monitor.

I also offer the following letter written by a former elementary school student of my father. It is dated 28 February 1975. By then, my father had been retired for 15 years. The [. . .] symbol indicates words I could not decipher. The original letter follows.

At Home

Lengua Cunjal Road

28/2/75

To: Mr R. O. Walrond,

X Head Master,

Caledonia E. C. School

Dear sir,

This with great pleasure. I am sending you these few lines hoping that you are enjoying the best of health. I spoke to Mr. Ali at Texaco, Point à Pierre and he told me that you are still working. I was glad to speak to you on the phone. But I could not reach you at the church the morning you told Ali that you will be at Princes Town. Sir, I would be very glad to see you at my house, to spend a day with me. And we will go around by some of the old boys of our school.

I cannot forget you for your good work you have done to my education. I cannot pay you. But it's necessary for my life. I am now employed by the Victoria County Council, Princess Town, as Road Supervisor in the Ward of Moruga. I did not write you at the [. . . time?] for the [. . .] house was not too well. But now I will be very glad (for you) to send me a few lines to say what day you can come at me, Cunjal Road. Sir, I will always say that if you did not push me with some education I will not be able to do my office work. I will be on the Roads and Traces cleaning.

Thanks to you I cannot forget you. Sir, this page is insufficient to say all I have to tell you. I am very glad to know that you can still drive a motor car to Princes Town, so a little more to see me — four and a half miles more. St Croix, Realize Road then to Cunjal Rd. A new [. . .] school is being erected by [. . .] Still you can find me, Baboolal Maraj, very easy.

Hoping these few lines reach you and send me an early reply also a date and send me an early reply.

Baboolal Maraj

At Home
Rougoa Cunjal Road.
28/2/75.

To Mr R.O. Walrond.
X Ha Master
Caledonia E.C.I School.
Dear Sir,
                This with great plea-
I am sending you these few lines hoping that you are Enjoying
the Best of Health. I spoke to Mr Ali at Irvos Point a lum
and he told me that you are still working I was glad to
Speak to you on the Phone, But I could not reach you at the
Church on the morning you told Ali that you will be at
Princes Town. Sir I wanted be very glad to see you at my
home to spend a day with me. and we will go around
By some of the old Boys of Our School I cannot forget
you for your Good work you have done to me Education
I cannot Pay you But its a *necessary* memory for my life I am
now Employed By the Victoria County Council Princes Town
as Road Supervisor in the ward of Moruga. I did not miss
you at the time for the *Warden's* Madam home was not to well Bu
now I will be very glad to send me a few lines to say
what day you can Come (at me *in the*) Cunjal Road. Sir Sir
will always say that if you did *not spend* your good time
to Push me with Some Education I will not to able to do
my office work I will Be on the Road + Gruss Clean give
        Thanks to you I cannot forget you Sir This page is in
Sufficient to say all I have to tell you. I am very glad
to know that you can still Drive a motor Car to Princes
Town as a little more to see me 4ts miles more, St Croix
Realign Road. then to Cunjal Rd a new (muslim) School is
Been Erect By (Roeveraayo Boroola) All you can find
Babonlal *Mstaj* my boy.
                        Hoping these few lines reach you
+ My address   And send me an Early reply
        To Mr Babonlal.

This letter speaks for itself.

E. C. SCHOOL

ST. JOSEPH

6th. July 1928.

RANDOLPH WALROND ESQ.

Head Teacher, Caledonia E.C. School.

Dear Sir,

We, the teachers and pupils of the above named school feel it our bounden duty to offer to you our sincere congratulation on your selection by His Lordship The Bishop as Head Teacher of the Caledonin E.C. School.

It is a source of joy to us as your connection with us has been for a very long period.

First, as pupil and pupil-teacher; then, as Assistant-teacher and acting Head-teacher.

You have always acquitted yourself admirably, and your activity, especially during the few past months in which you endeavoured to bring about success for the school in its different branches of work, partic-ularly in handicraft will always be remembered by us.

We wish you God speed in your new sphere of labour and we ask you to accept the accompanying present as a token of our high regard and esteem for your work, and we shall evermore pray that you may be blessed with health and prosperity to continue the good work you have so nobly begun with us.

We are on behalf

of the School

* * *

The following is an address made by my brother Owen at Daddy's funeral on 5 August 1996:

> On Saturday July 27th, our dear Daddy passed away at the age of 97 years. I always remembered him as a strict old man. This was because when I came to be, Daddy was 50 years old, and in my eyes 50 seemed so old. However, in my adult eyes, 50 is still young.
>
> Daddy was an educator all his life. His young wife, our mother, and all us nine children were his special pupils. I truly believe that Daddy was a very good father to us and a very good husband to our mother. In training, educating, and guiding us, he treated us equally with the same amount of effort and with the same method. We were all familiar with the strap. I always remember the day Daddy disciplined me with the strap in front of the entire Couva E.C. School. What an embarrassment!
>
> He did the right things right; he made the wrong things right. In our house, he was the King, and what he said, you did. He dispensed very good values, and he lived those values, which I still uphold today and pass on to my three children. It's hard to do that these days, but, like you, Daddy, I will not give up doing it. I held a lot of respect for Daddy. He demanded it and got it. Even in my adult life, he lectured me on bringing up my children, and with the greatest respect, I listened and acknowledged what he said.
>
> Daddy was a very cautious and caring father. He wanted to know exactly who our friends were, and where we were going, and for how long. He cared about each of us. I am extremely happy that he was a father that took us places when we were in our young years through teenage years: Carnival; the beach; trade fairs; visiting the many family, friends, and relatives; and all the many more places we all went together. I am even more grateful that there were times when he and Ian and I went out alone to sports functions,

cycling races, scouting functions. I will cherish these many moments forever, and so he will always be in my heart. I loved my Daddy and still do, even though I may not have said it but showed it all the time.

I am grateful to see so many of you here today, and this family thanks you all for joining us in the celebration. Daddy is gone from us, but he hasn't been taken away from us. His soul is resting with the Lord. Mammy, my sisters and brothers, and your families and all the relatives and friends here present and away, I assure you that Daddy, in his death, still continues to teach us about life.

I thank the Lord for this beautiful celebration, and I believe we will see him again. Daddy, may you rest in peace. Amen.

The following poem was written by his granddaughter Larissa Walrond. It was submitted for inclusion in the program for the Celebration of Life of Randolph Walrond. Larissa was 15 years old at the time.

Hurt and alone,
On the edge of tears,
I'd go to the edge of the earth,
Just to calm your fears.

A love that no one heard,
To the edges you have flown.
A love that no one feared,
Dies once it is grown.

In the hardships you have prospered,
In the sadness you have smiled.
Together fighting nothing else
But the protection of your pride.

A marriage lasting always,
The partnership went on,
Children born. Things lost
On holidays, never found.

A celebration of a life,
Lasting through the years,
Coming to an end,
And bringing back our tears.

Your children will always miss you,
The grand ones and the greats.
The memory of your triumphs,
Shall yet decide our fates.

I still remember sitting in the cathedral, waiting for the service to begin and watching friends and family fill the pews. As I looked around, my eyes hazy from the deep emotion of the moment, I saw the pews slowly fill to capacity. By the time the minister came out of the vestry, there were virtually no seats left. And still there were people coming in.

The service was lovely, and when it was over I joined friends and family members and followed the casket out. When I got to the doors, imagine my surprise when I saw that there were about 40 or so more persons for whom there had been no room inside.

Among the faces, I noticed one gentleman who took me back at least 40 years. He was one of the teachers at my father's school in Couva, and he was my teacher in about 1954. I don't know if he recognised me at all.

Another face I recognised was none other than Ronald Ramcharan, a high school classmate. He smiled encouragingly at me, and I smiled back in recognition. I helped place the casket into the waiting hearse, and as I looked at the crowd, I could not help thinking about one of the lines in the 23rd Psalm: "Surely my father's cup runneth over."

At the cemetery, after the interment of the casket, flowers and wreaths were placed over the grave. They reached a height of over 2.5 feet. I had never before seen so many flowers all in one place.

* * *

Regarding the question of the measure of a man, I can only say that with regards to my father, I have my own answer. I hope that these few expressions of the esteem in which he was held by those who knew him will help you to form your own opinion of R. O. Walrond.

After Daddy's death, Mammy soldiered on. She looked after the home and kept it neat and tidy. A few years later, she made arrangements to have the rusting roof removed and replaced with a more modern one. She supervised this operation while still living in the house. After this, the living room louvre windows were removed and replaced with regular windows.

Every Christmas, she organized a garden party for the children of the neighborhood. At the end of the event, each child left with a bag of delicacies. When her age no longer allowed her to continue this activity, a gentleman two doors down the street continued the tradition.

As time went on, my mother became a bit wobbly in the legs. By age ninety-five, and still counting, she carried on with, as she herself put it, "No complaints." She was ever thankful that all her children did what they could to make her life as pleasant as possible. When she could no longer walk, my brother Ian came to live with her and did all the cooking. A sister, Alma, came on weekends to keep the house tidy and to cook Sunday dinner. Another sister, Lystra, did the shopping. All three of them looked after her creature comforts as well. Mammy recognized that we could not all be there all the time, but was happy that we kept in touch.

Her main hope at that time of her life was that we, as a family, would continue the be a family. She had seen too many families destroyed by squabbles that seemed so pointless. She herself had once been estranged from her only sister for reasons unknown to her. One day Mammy went over to her sister's house and visited for a while. The breach was healed. Such was our mother. A family must be a family forever.

Her death on 31 May 2015 was a very peaceful one. Her last words were to my sister Alma as she was being put to bed for the evening. With her hands across her breast, she asked Alma to "Pray for them." Then she went to sleep.

May she rest in peace.

Part IV: Appendixes

Appendix A: Pictures

31 Aug 1964   On Mount Royal 1965   On Mc Gill Campus

With BCFS personnel in Strathcona Park, BC, 1965
In the Cartography Lab, Mc Gill

At Fort Ware, Finlay River, BC
In a wetsuit and in the small row boat,
Queen Charlotte Islands, Haida Gwaii Summer 1968

Brian Logan and I

Beth and my 1969 Mustang

The two tree crushers

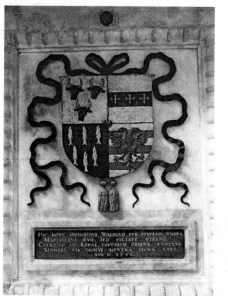

Monument to a Humphrey Walrond at St. Mary's Church, Ilminster, ca 1580
The Walrond Coat of Arms

Seine fishing in Trinidad
Sugar cane fields: Stages of harvesting

Burning a sugar cane field before harvesting

Map of the Caribbean

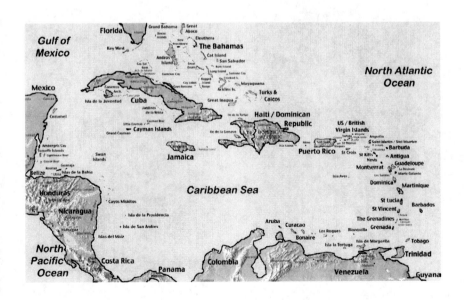

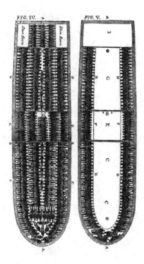

Decks of a slave ship

Ligon's early map of Barbados

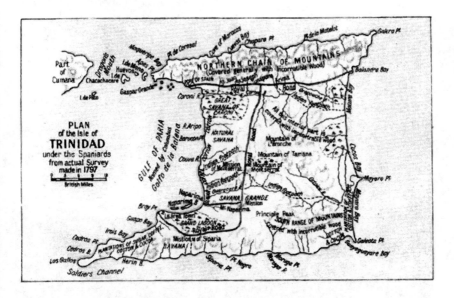

Trinidad, showing the Camino Real and Towns

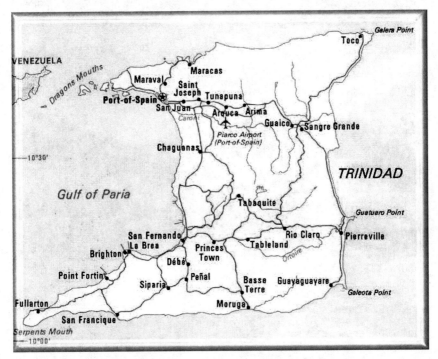

Friends, Schools, Churches
and Buildings

Christopher Patrick
Ben Sealey
Hutton A. McShine

Errol Patrick
St. Clair Jones
Richmond Street Boys E.C. School

Curepe (St. Joseph) E.C. School
Couva E.C. School

St. Sndrew's Anglican Church, Couva
St. Stephen's Anglican Church, Princes Town

Royal Victoria Institute
T'dad Building and Loan
23 Palm Drive, Champ Fleurs

Queen's Royal College, Port of Spain
Mount St. Benedict, Trinidad

Yellow Poui Tree
Osric Drive, Cunupia
The House on Edgar Street, Couva

The House at Scott Street, St. Joseph
The Co-operative Bank, Port of Spain

Walrond Family Members

Mathilda Walrond
Frank Walrond
Frank, Charles, and Randolph Walrond
Daniel Darius Haynes

Four Pictures of Randolph Walrond through the Years

Martin Family Members

John Chow Martin
Margaret Augustus Martin
Issa Martin
Agnes Martin and Henry Akan

Agnes Akan and her daughters
Henry Akan Jr.
John Edwin Martin
Florence Mathilda Martin at eternal rest

Amla Beatrice Martin
James Lee Young
James Lee Young
Floris Lee Young with some of her aunts

Floris Lee Young and her bicycle 1935
Randolph Walrond and PC 3076 at Champ Fleurs, 1957

Floris with Wilbur, Kermitt, Alma and Lawrence ca 1945
The only picture of the Randolph and Floris Walrond Family

The Walrond Violin. It was given to Owen,
who left it to his daughter Vanessa.

Family Crests

Martin Family

These icons portray the founding of the John Chow Martin family.

The yellow five-pointed star represents the Chinese ancestry of John Chow Martin, because this pentacle is also found on the Chinese flag. The prow of a boat, superimposed on the star, symbolises the chosen vocation of John. He was the proud owner of a small fleet of fishing boats.

The white diagonal cross on a blue background is a Scottish Saltire or Cross of St. Andrew. It represents the Scottish ancestry of Margaret Augustus. The open book represents her vocation as a teacher. The red background of these first icons represent the bloodline of our ancestry.

The two crosses, one superimposed on the other, symbolise the Christian union in marriage of John Chow and Margaret Augustus. The crosses also remind us that Margaret was the daughter of Scottish missionaries.

The five stars in the chevron represent the five children of our founding ancestors. The golden background of the chevron represents the respect with which we hold this first line of John's and Margaret's descendants.

The two palm trees on a green background represent the two-island nation of Trinidad and Tobago, the homeland of the Martin family.

The globe, superimposed on a blue background, represents the global community that we, the descendants of John and Margaret, have become. The four colours of the segments of the globe represent the multinational, multiracial, multireligious and multitalented nature of the families which now make up our global clan.

The words of the motto come from the mission statement that has been established for us. The red colour of the outer circle reminds us of the blood that binds the many branches of the Martin family.

Walrond Family

These icons portray the founding of some branches of the "Afro" Walrond families.

The three bulls' heads represent the name Walrond. They are adapted from the oldest identified crest used by this ancient English family. The head on the left represents the future. The head on the right represents the past. The center head represents the present. In this way, honour is paid to the past, present, and future generations of all those who are connected with the name Walrond.

The blue trident represents the island of Barbados. It was to this Caribbean island that the name Walrond was first introduced. The two Negro heads, one male and one female, represent the influx of Africans to this island.

The chain that surrounds the trident and the two human heads represent the slavery that was endured by these, our first African ancestors. At some point during the period of slavery, the name was transferred to slaves, thereby establishing the first families of "Afro" Walronds.

The island of Barbados and the slave population were both supported for centuries by the sugar cane industry, represented by the sugar cone.

The break in the chain represents the moment of emancipation of the slaves and the start of migration from Barbados to other Caribbean countries. Joshua and Charles Walrond migrated to Trinidad, which is represented by the hummingbird. Sam Walrond migrated to Guyana, which is represented by the Canje pheasant. The hummingbird and the Canje pheasant are the national birds of the respective countries.

The motto, *Labor Omnia Vincit,* translates as "labour conquers all things."

Appendix B: The Legacy of Randolph Walrond

The following documents and notes left behind by my father represent a record of some of the people and things that he held dear. To me, they reveal a side of him that I would not have otherwise known.

These papers have now become a tangible part of the legacy left behind by my father. But they transcend the boundaries of mere family. They present a window into the life of a man who gave his all. We can see the respect and tenderness which he showed to others come back to him. They also show the trials of just being alive and of making an effort to get ahead at a time when turmoil was rampant in other parts of the world. Growing up during the First World War and earning a living throughout the Second World War must have been a challenge. The Depression that overwhelmed the world in the 1930s must have been felt in Trinidad. Yet these worldwide trials were never once mentioned.

One memory of the Second World War that I have is based on the fact that my father was a member of the Air Raid Patrols that went out at night, asking people to extinguish their lights. The arms of the German war machine did extend to the Caribbean area. The American army bases that were established on the island were all geared toward protecting the nearby Panama Canal.

The other memory I have is of my mother almost constantly knitting socks. Yet I could never see any socks lying about the house. One day I asked her why she was knitting so many socks. She replied that they were for the

British soldiers who were fighting in the war. I thought that was such a noble thing to be doing. Later on, I saw a very small silver medal and asked her what it was for. She said it was from the Queen of England for all the socks she had knitted. I wonder where that medal is now.

Through these documents we get a firsthand look at how things were done in the good old days. The informality of things like recommendations or testimonials surprised me but is understandable.

I will, however, leave it to the reader to form a personal opinion of the times portrayed by these bits of "evidence of lives lived." I am able to comment on only a few of these documents. To me, they represent a large part of my memories of my father.

* * *

This is the birth certificate of Horace Eaton Walrond, younger brother of Randolph. Randolph is listed as the "Informant" and would have been about 14 years old at the time. Somehow, the name Horace became Norris. Horace was 2 years old when their father Joshua died, and Randolph promised to look after his education. Horace eventually became a druggist.

372

A.

DUPLICATE OF MARRIAGE REGISTER.

When Married	Names and Surnames of Parties	Age.	Condition.	Profession.	Residence at time of Marriage.	Place of Marriage.	Signature of Parties.	Signatures of Officiating for District Registrar Witnesses
Dec. 15th 1894	Charles Walrond	full	Bachelor	Police Constable (Carpenter)	Police Barracks Port of Spain.	Wesleyan Church Tranquillity Port of Spain.	C. Walrond	W.R. ...
	Julia Stoute	full	Spinster	Servant	Woodbrook		Ju Stout	

I, William Knaggs First Clerk & the Registrar-General of the Colony of Trinidad and Tobago, do Certify that the above Entry is a True and Correct Entry in the Duplicate Marriage Register, Recorded in the Registrar-General's Office as Number 33 Vol. 2 Folio 72 for the Year One thousand eight Hundred + ninety four

In Witness whereof I have hereunto set my hand and Seal of Office this 21 ...
day of November in the year of Our Lord One Thousand Nine and Thirty three

---

B N°. 101082   061665

TRINIDAD AND TOBAGO   DEATH IN THE Ward of St Joseph.

No.	When Dead	Name and Surname	Sex	Age	Rank and Profession and Country of Birth	Cause of Death	Signature, Description and Residence of Informant	When Registered	Signature Registrar
213	Fifth October 1935	Julia Waldron	female	74 yrs	Barbados	Chr cardio vascular Renal Disease cert by Dr G.E. Tracey M.D.	Frances Alleyne Tailor Jackson Street St Ally	Fifth October 1935.	Valentine G...

I, Prisella Ragoonanansingh Registrar General of Trinidad and Tobago, do certify that the above is a true and correct Copy of the Entry Number 213 ...
entered at Page 163 Register of Deaths for the Year 19 35

AUTHORISED BY

In Witness whereof I have hereunto set my Hand and ...
this 2nd day of October
Our Lord, One Thousand, Nine Hundred and Eighty ...

TRINIDAD & TOBAGO $2   - 2 OCT 1987

OFFICER AUTHORISED BY

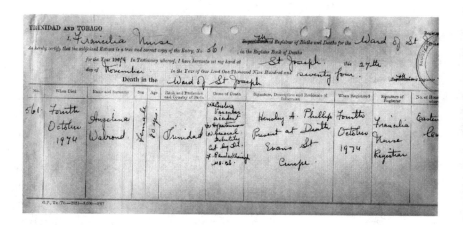

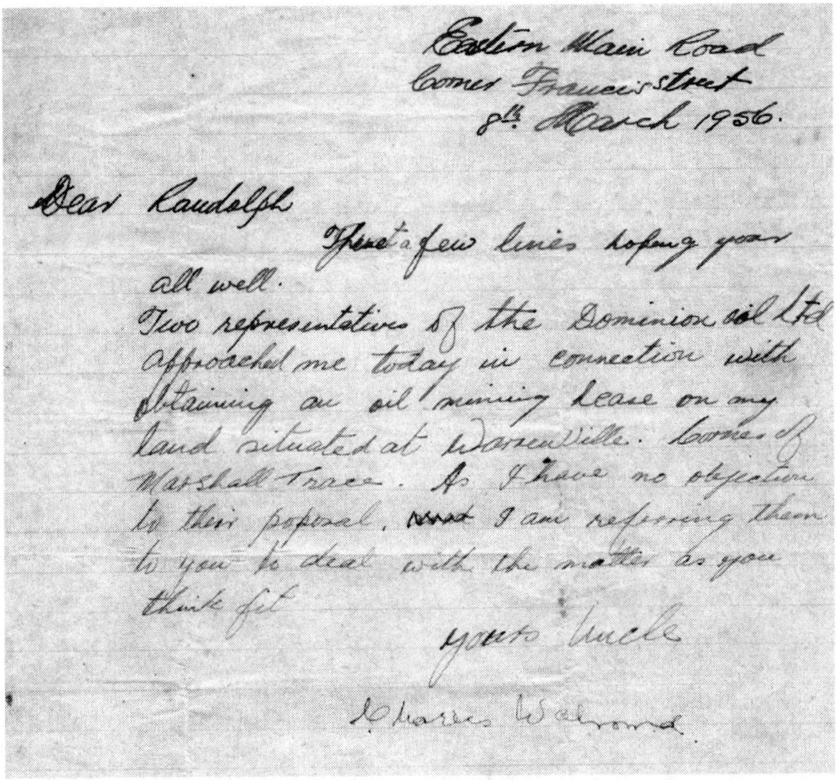

Eastern Main Road
Corner Frances Street
8th March 1956.

Dear Randolph

Just a few lines hoping you all well.

Two representatives of the Dominion Oil Ltd approached me today in connection with obtaining an oil mining lease on my land situated at Warrenville. Corner of Marshall Trace. As I have no objection to their proposal, I am referring them to you to deal with the matter as you think fit

yours Uncle

Charles Welmond

CHARLES WALDRON,
Corner of Francis Street and
Eastern Main Road,
St. Joseph,
In the Ward of Tacarigua,
In the Island of Trinidad.

        Further to a Deed of Option for Oil Mining Lease dated the 15th day of March 1956, registered as No.6395 of 1956 and made between yourself of the One Part and DOMINION OIL LIMITED, a Company incorporated in the State of Nevada United States of America, with its principal office at 206 North Virginia Street, in the City of Reno, Nevada, and having a place of business at No. 29 St. Vincent Street, in the City of Port of Spain, in the Island of Trinidad, we hereby give you notice that we do not intend to exercise our option to take an Oil Mining Lease pursuant to the provisions in the said Deed of Option.

        Dated the 27th day of January 1958

DOMINION OIL LIMITED

Per......................

For a short period of time between 1956 and 1958, there was a mild interest in searching for oil on the lands at Marshal Trace, Cunupia.

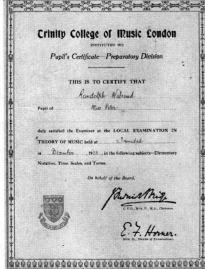

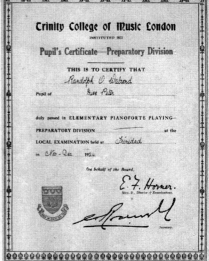

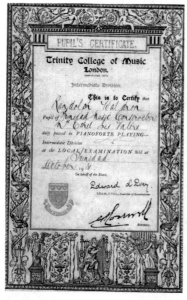

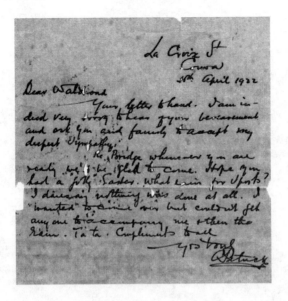

La Croix Street,

Couva

26th April, 1922

Dear Walrond,

Your letter to hand. I am indeed very sorry to hear of your bereavement and ask you and your family to accept my deepest sympathy.

Re Bridge, whenever you are ready, we'll be glad to come. Hope you had a jolly Easter. What rain for sports? I daresay nothing was done at all. I intended to come over, but couldn't get anyone to accompany me and then the rain. Ta ta! Compliments to all.

Yours truly,

C. Patrick.

[The bereavement being referred to is that of Nora Walrond, a younger sister of my father.]

Scott Street
St Joseph
1st March 1926

Dear Cyril

It was with great surprise and sorrow I read
of your Mother's death. I was sorry I could not be present
at the funeral but I can assure you that though absent
on that occasion I was, not nevertheless, among the sympa
thisers in spirit.

From past experience I am fully aware of the fact
that it is very hard for you to overcome the grief caused
by the ever unwelcome incident. In fact one rather feel
some solace in the act of bearing such a grief, and I hope
you would have the courage necessary for bearing it.

Yet God is not unkind: He has afforded us a physician
sincere — Time — and I hope you would yield to his gentle
hand and be healed of an affected heart.

I will not intrud on the parts already cured by dwelling
lengthtly   on the subject; I therefore join your kind
friends in tendering my condolence and wishing you
all that make for your future happiness.

Give my compliments to Mrs Richardson and tell to her
I hope she is enjoying health at Claxton Bay.

Yours truly
R Ozzafurat

Scott Street,

St. Joseph,

1st March 1926

Dear Cyril,

It was with great surprise and sorrow I read of your mother's death. I was sorry I could not be present at the funeral, but I can assure that though absent on that occasion, I was nevertheless present among the sympathisers in spirit.

From past experience I am fully aware of the fact that it is very hard for you to overcome the grief caused by the ever unwelcome incident. In fact, one rather feels some solace in the act of bearing such a grief, and I hope you would have the courage necessary for bearing it. Yet God is not unkind. He has afforded us a physician sincere — Time — and I hope you would yield to his gentle hand and be healed of an affected heart. I will not tread on the parts already cured by dwelling lengthily on the subject. I therefore join your kind friends in tendering my condolence and wishing you all that make for your future happiness. Give my compliments to Mrs. Richardson and tell her I hope she is enjoying health at Claxton Bay.

Yours truly

R.O. Walrond

Louvain
Poppy Day '26

My dear Walrond

Your very kind & encouraging letter to h____ and should have been answered be____ but I have been ill with fever a_____ not do so. Very many thanks for the ____ sentiments expressed therein.

It was my determination to succeed this year and thank God I've done so. My d_____ comes off in the 23rd inst and am _____ to put in a concert for the 18th _____ which I hope you'll attend. _____ the _____ will be a sad ____ and Parish in particular & the diocese in general. I will be losing a personal friend, I can't say more than that.

I thought I'd have seen you in Port y on Saturday but didn't! School is so so, I'm not strong & there is so much to be done in the next few weeks. Ta ta. Respects to your home

Yrs truly
_____

Couva,

Poppy Day, 1926

My Dear Walrond,

Your very kind and encouraging letter to hand, and should have been answered before, but I have been ill with fever and could not do so. Very many thanks for the sincere sentiments expressed therein. It was my determination to succeed this year and Thank God I've done so. My inspection comes off on the 23rd inst and I am trying to put on a concert for the 10th of December which I hope you will attend.

Yes, the rector's going will be a sad loss to the parish in particular, to the diocese in general. I will be losing a personal friend. I can't say more than that.

I thought I'd have seen you in Port on Sunday, but didn't. School is so so. I'm not strong and there is so much to be done in the next few weeks. Ta ta.

Respects to your home,

Yours Truly,

C. Patrick

E.C. School St. Joseph,

11th. October, 1927

His Lordship, Members of the Board of Control of Anglican Schools, Trinidad

Gentlemen,

It is my greatest pleasure to have to recommend Mr. Randolph Walrond, an old pupil and Teacher of the above named school, now Assistant Teacher of Richmond Street E.C. School.

I have the honour to recommend him in the best interests of Education in our schools. He is one of tried good habits, highly industrious and ambitious. Whatever is good he tries to be associated with and I am sure as far as my experience goes of country schools, he will be eminently useful if given a chance as Head Teacher.

As far as his educational capacity stands, he was second to none in his examinations at my school and as far as I can remember, in his III Class Certificate Examination under my tuition he took six Distinctions which at the time were the most in the Island.

His high moral temperament — which I have proved in all my work with him — will do the church and school incalculable amount of good wherever he is placed.

He is an ardent student and I am sure this will go a long way in aiding him in his work generally.

I shall be very grateful on behalf of our school if I hear Mr. Randolph Walrond is appointed to the post of Head Teacher of the Tableland E.C. School.

Thanking you in anticipation,

Yours obediently, Allan Lisle Henwood, Head Teacher, E.C. School, St. Joseph

Couva

11.10.27

My dear Walrond

Yours of 9th inst to hand. I've heard nothing about the Vacancy as yet, but I've written to ascertain all about it.

I really do not know when Revd Boodle will be back but the acting manager is Mr. H. R. Wood, New Grant, St Julien P.O Via Princestown, apply to him right away and be on the safe side.

In the meantime see whether you can get an interview with his Lordship play your case before him and if you think it necessary ask him to refer some re your ability etc. I shall only be too glad to help you.

I'm passing your way on the 22nd inst I hope between 11.40 & 12.15 p.m and will give you a look up.

Hope all your people are well

Yours in haste
Patrick

P.S
As soon as I get news from the South I'll let you know
P.

Couva 11th October 1927

My Dear Walrond,

Yours of the 8th inst. to hand. I've heard nothing of the vacancy as yet, but I've written to ascertain all about it.

I really do not know when Revd. Boodle will be back but the Acting manager is Mr. H. R. Wood, New Grant, St. Julien Post Office, via Princes Town. Apply to him right away and be on the safe side. In the meantime, see whether you can get an interview with His Lordship and lay your case before him and if you think it necessary ask him to refer to me re your ability etc. I shall only be too glad to help you. I am passing your way on the 22nd inst. I hope between 11:30 and 12:15 PM and will give you a look up. Hope all your people are well.

Yours in haste,

C. Patrick

As soon as I get news from the faith, I will let you know.

CP

E. C. School,

Couva,

14th October,

To whom it may concern,

This is to certify that Mr. Randolph Walrond was an Assistant Teacher of the above named school for a few years. During that time he showed that zeal, energy, tact and ability which indicate the making of a good teacher. Gentlemanly by nature, and religiously inclined, he should make a very capable Head Teacher and give satisfaction to his employer. It gives me great pleasure to give him this testimonial.

C. Patrick.

Head Teacher

Richmond St E.C. Boys' School
11th ~~Octbr~~ Port of Spain
11th October, 1927

His Lordship ~~and member of the board of~~ the Bishop of Trinidad, Council of the said School
of Trinidad

My Lord Gentlemen.
Gentlemen

Having heard of the appointment of Mr Hinds of the Table-land E.C. School to the Head Teachership of the Del'aford E.C. School, Tobago, I humbly beg to offer you my services as Head Teacher of the vacant school — Tableland E.C.

I am twenty seven years of age and ~~began~~ my teaching ~~career twelve years during the~~ have obtained the following qualifications:—

Second Class Teachers Certificate March 1921

Two Second class Pupil Teacher's Certificate in Rel Knowledge. 1917 1918

Third Class Assistant Teacher's Certificate in Rel Knowledge Nov 1919

Certificate in Proficiency in Physical Training Oct 1919

"   "   "   , Hygiene   Aug 1919

Certificates from of Music from The Trinity College of Music London:— Junior Theory   Dec 1924

Junior Practical   Dec 1925.

I have served as Pupil Teacher at the St Joseph E.C. School; as First Assistant at the Leonora E.C, and am serving now as First Assistant of the Richmond St Sch E.C. School.

association with
my service at

From these Schools I have gained much experience not only in method of teaching but also in the controling of a school. I enclose herewith testimonials from the various managers and Head teachers under whom I have worked. Trusting to receive your favourable reply. Should I be favoured with the appointment I shall endeavour to accomplish to the advantage of the school all that is required of me

I am, Gentlemen
Your humble servant
R O Walrond

Richmond Street Boys E.C. School

Port of Spain

11th October 1927

His Lordship the Bishop of Trinidad and Members of the Board of Control of the Anglican Schools of Trinidad

Gentlemen,

Having heard of the appointment of Mr. Hinds of the Tableland E.C. School to the Head Teachership of the Delaford E.C. School, Tobago, I humbly beg to offer you my services as Head Teacher of the vacant school, Tableland E. C. I am 27 years of age, and my teaching career extends over twelve years, and I have obtained the following qualifications:

Second Class Teaching Certificate, March 1921

Two Second Class Pupil Teacher's Certificates in Religious Knowledge. 1919 1918

Third Class Assistant Teacher's Certificate in Religious Knowledge, November 1919

Certificate in Proficiency in Physical Training, October 1919

Certificate in Proficiency in Hygiene, August 1919

Certificates of Music from Trinity College of Music, London:

Junior Theory December 1924

Junior Practical December 1925

I have served as Pupil teacher at the St Joseph E.C. School, as First Assistant at the Couva E.C. School and am now serving as First Assistant of the Richmond St. E. C. School.

From my service at and my association with these schools, I have gained much experience not only in Method of Teaching, but also in the controlling of a school.

I enclose herewith testimonials from the various managers and teachers under whom I have worked.

Trusting to receive a favourable reply,

I am, Gentlemen,

Your humble servant, R.O. Walrond

The above letter is one which may not have been mailed. No mention of a reply is made

18 Park St. Port of Spain.

22nd May 1928

Mr R O Walrond

Scot St. S fargh.

Dear Sir,

1. I have the honour to inform you of your appointment, with the approval of the Director of Education and of the E.C. Appointments Committee to the post of Head Teacher of Caledonia E.C. School; said appointment to date from July 1st 1928

2. The Director is pleased to approve of leave being granted to you for the month of June; but such leave will be under the half-pay regulation.

3. Mr Lawrence James, assistant Teacher of Craigpark E.C. school will act at Caledonia E.C. school, until you are able to take up the appointment in person.

Yours faithfully,

M E Doorly.

Sec. Appointments Committee

18 Park Street,

Port of Spain,

22nd May, 1928

Mr. R. O. Walrond,

Scott Street,

St. Joseph

Dear Sir,

1. I have the honour to inform you of your appointment, with the approval of the Director of Education and of the E.C. Appointment Committee, to the post of Head Teacher of Caledonia E. C. School; your appointment to date from July 1st, 1928.

2. The Director is pleased to approve of leave being granted to you for the month of June, but such leave will be under half-pay regulation.

3. Mr Lawrence James, Assistant Teacher of Craignish E. C. School will act at Caledonia E. C. School until you are able to take up the appointment in person.

Yours faithfully,

M. E. Doorly,

Sec. Appointments Committee

19th May 1929

Dear Randolph,

How! How? Old thing! Playing plenty chess, I see. I am glad that Mr. Hill got a warm reception but is so satisfied with the display that he is willing to play again. By now I guess the tournament is through. What about Delaford? Did you worry? I did not hear anything on Saturday and I do not think any appointment has yet been made. Some poor teacher here is always getting into trouble. Perhaps we do not take our calling seriously enough. Now McNish needs an Asst. Mistress. Two fellows got dismissed last month from other schools — all for "sowing seed." It is expected that Asst. Teachers will have to go soon. If you see Mr. Stoer's Report on the work of the school? Mr. John would know him. He is Beckles at Parlatuvier. Here is as dull as usual, so there is nothing to write. Give my love to the girls. My best wishes to the boys and a good kick — (a specially sound one in the soft parts for Baggy) — to each of the members of the staff.

Yours ever,

Dolly.

[Parlatuvier is a town in Tobago]

The Rectory
Princes Town
6th Nov. 1931.

To whom it may concern,

I have known Mr R. O. Walrond for the past
2 years. As the Head Teacher of the
Caledonia E.C. School he is doing splendid
work. The School has greatly increased in
the average attendance since he assumed
the Head Teachership. He is organist
and choir Master of St Stephen's Church and
also on the Vestry of the Parish. I have
always found him to be energetic, and
reliable; with the interest of the children,
School and Parish at heart. He is
deserving of promotion and I am sure
that he will give satisfaction for whom
soever he is working.

P. H. Dowlen
Rector & Manager

The Rectory,

Princes Town,

6th November 1931

To whom it may concern,

I have known Mr. R. O. Walrond for the past 2 years. As the Head Teacher of the Caledonia E. C. School he is doing splendid work. The school has greatly increased in the average attendance since he assumed the Head Teachership. He is Organist and Choir Master of St. Stephen's Church, and also on the Vestry of the Parish. I have always found him to be energetic and reliable, with the interest of the children, school and parish at heart. He is deserving of promotion and I am sure that he will give satisfaction for whomever he is working.

F. H. Dowlen

Rector and Manager

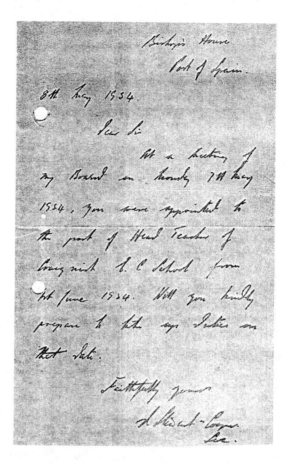

Bishop's House,

Port of Spain,

8th May, 1934

Dear Sir,

At a meeting of my Board on Monday 7th May 1934, you were appointed to the post of Head Teacher of Craignish E. C. School from 1st June 1934. Will you kindly prepare to take up duties on that date.

M. Stewart-Cooper,

Sec.

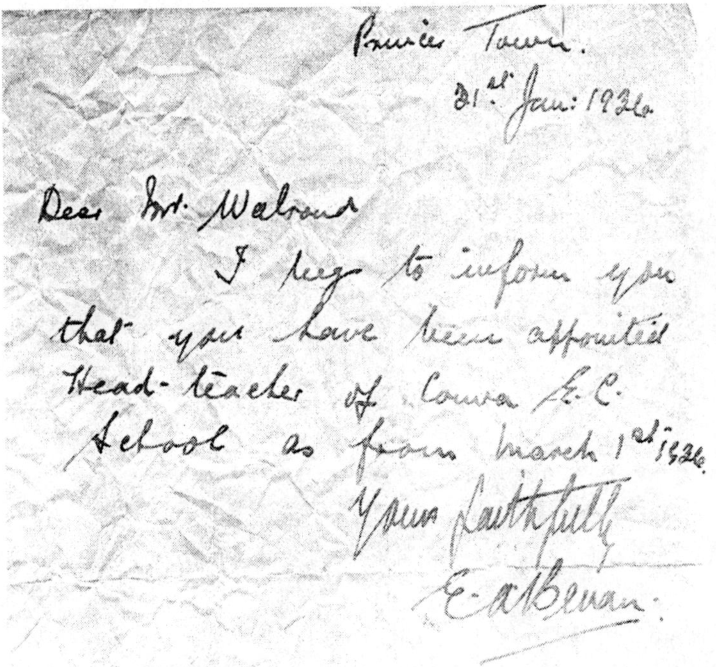

Princes Town.
21st Jan: 1936.

Dear Mr. Walrond
I beg to inform you that you have been appointed Head-teacher of Couva E.C. School as from March 1st 1936.

Yours faithfully
E. A. Bevan.

Princes Town,

21st Jan. 1936

Dear Mr. Walrond,

I beg to inform you that you have been appointed Head Teacher of Couva E. C. School as from March 1st, 1936.

Yours faithfully,

E. A. Bevan

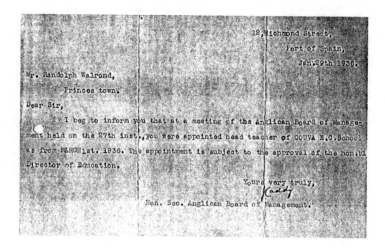

12 Richmond Street,

Port of Spain,

Jan 29th 1936

Mr Randolph Walrond,

Princes Town

Dear Sir,

I beg to inform you that at a meeting of the Anglican Board of Management held on the 27th inst., you were appointed Head Teacher of Couva E. C. School as from March 1st 1936. The appointment is subject to the approval of the honourable Director of Education.

Yours very truly,

J. Caddy

Hon. Sec. Anglican Board of Management.

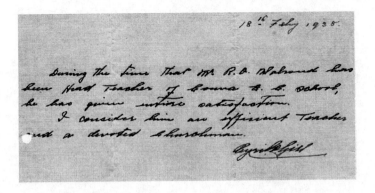

The Rectory,

Couva,

18th July 1938

During the time that Mr. R. O. Walrond has been Head Teacher of Couva E. C. School, he has given entire satisfaction. I consider him an efficient Teacher and a devoted Churchman.

Cyril O. Gill

8th Oct 1939.

Dear Mr. Walrond,

The state of the weather this afternoon is against my attempting to go out. It looks very much as if hardly anyone will be out. However, should it improve as to allow you to go please say evensong for the faithful "Four" who are likely to be present.

I did the rounds this morning despite aches in the head.

Many Thanks,

Yrs faithfully,

Cyril O. Gill

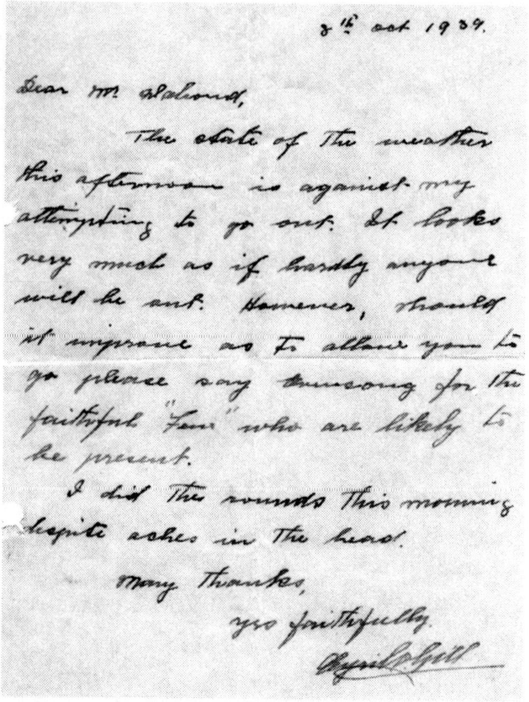

The Rectory,

Couva

8th October, 1939

Dear Mr. Walrond,

The state of the weather this afternoon is against my attempting to go out. It looks very much as if hardly anyone will be out. However, should it improve as to allow you to go, please say evensong for the faithful "Four" who are likely to be present. I did this morning despite aches in the head.

Many thanks,

Yours faithfully,

Cyrill O. Gill

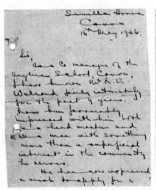

Sevilla House,

Couva,

16th May, 1946

Sir,

As a Co. Manager of the Anglican School, Couva, I have known Mr. R. O. Walrond fairly intimately for the past 9 years. I have been favourably impressed with him both as a Head Master and as a man with something more than a superficial interest in the community he serves.

He has now expressed a wish to apply for a transfer to an Anglican School in the north. While I would be sorry to see him depart, I sympathise with the desire to be employed nearer to his home.

In giving him this testimonial, I do so with a sense of gratitude for valuable help I have had from him both during the time when the Win the War Association was active here and as a fellow member of the committee of the local branch of the Child Welfare League.

Yours faithfully,

Wm. H. Gilbert, Attorney,

Caroni Limited

No..3 95.4/46.

Department of Education,
Trinidad, B.W.I.
31st August, 1946.

From: The Acting Director of Education

To: Mr. R.O. Walrond, Head Teacher,
E.C. School, Couva.

I have much pleasure in informing you that, with
the consent of the Anglican Board of Management, I have promoted you to be a Grade I Head Teacher, as from 1st September,
1946.

Acting Director of Education.

Department of Education

Trinidad, B. W. I.

31st. August, 1946

From: The Acting Director of Education

To: Mr. R. O. Walrond, Head teacher,

E. C. School, Couva

I have much pleasure in informing you that, with the consent of the Anglican Board of management, I have promoted you to be a Grade 1 Head teacher as from September 1st, 1946.

Rawl Ramkeesoon,

for Acting Director of Education

Education Department.
Oct. 3rd, 1946.

Dear....Sir...... ;

    I have to inform you that approval has been given for the creation of a Supernumerary Group of Grade 1 Head Teachers with effect from January 1st, 1946, and that you have been promoted thereto as from that date.

    A voucher for arrears due you has been passed for payment, payable at the usual pay-office.

Yours faithfully,

Director of Education.

R. Walrond, Esq.,
   Couva E.C. School.

Education Department,

Oct. 3rd. 1946

Dear Sir,

I have to inform you that approval has been given for the creation of a Supernumerary Group of Grade 1 Head Teachers with effect from January 1st 1946 and that you have been promoted thereto as from that date.

A voucher for arrears due has been passed for payment, payable at the usual pay-office.

Yours faithfully,

Director of Education

* * *

The following pages contain receipts for items and services purchased. They relate mostly to the construction of the house at Scott Street, St. Joseph. My father seems to have kept every single receipt relative to the construction of this house. The fragile state of most of them precludes my examining them fully, though doing so would have been very informative.

Received from R.O. Walrond the Sum of Six Dollars
($6.00) for making a concrete bridge and drained
Walked at a house at the corner of Scott St and Eastern Main Rd

Ernest . Wade

1st October 1927
St Joseph

Credited by **ALSTON & CO. LTD.**
BUILDERS AND CONTRACTORS
Lumber, Hardware and Saw Mill Department
33 MARINE SQUARE   32 SOUTH QUAY

11913
RECEIVED

ALSTON & CO, LTD.
LUMBER DEPT.

$5.00

PORT-OF-SPAIN.

Mrs Matilda Walrond

Trinidad Building & Loan Association

Nov 2   1932

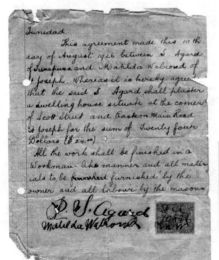

Trinidad

This agreement made this 10th
day of August 1926 between S. Agard
of Tunapuna and Matilda Walrond of
Joseph Whereas it is hereby agreed
that the said S. Agard shall plaster
a dwelling house situate at the corner
of Scott Street and Eastern Main Road
St Joseph for the sum of Twenty four
Dollars ($24.00)
All the work shall be finished in a
Workman- like manner and all materials to be furnished by the
owner and all labour by the masons

P. S. Agard
Matilda Walrond

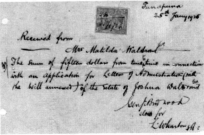

Tunapuna
25th Jany 1926

Received from
Mrs Matilda Walrond
The sum of fifteen dollars from time to time in connection
with an application for Letters of Administration with
the will annexed of the estate of Joshua Walrond

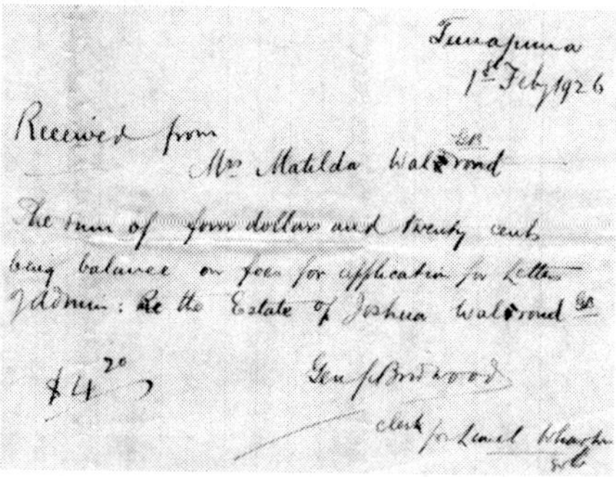

Tunapuna
1st Feby 1926

Received from
Mrs Matilda Walrond Sr.

The sum of four dollars and twenty cents
being balance on fees for application for Letters
of Admin: Re the Estate of Joshua Walrond Sr.

$4.20

Geo. [illegible]wood
Clerk for Lionel Whagh... [illegible]

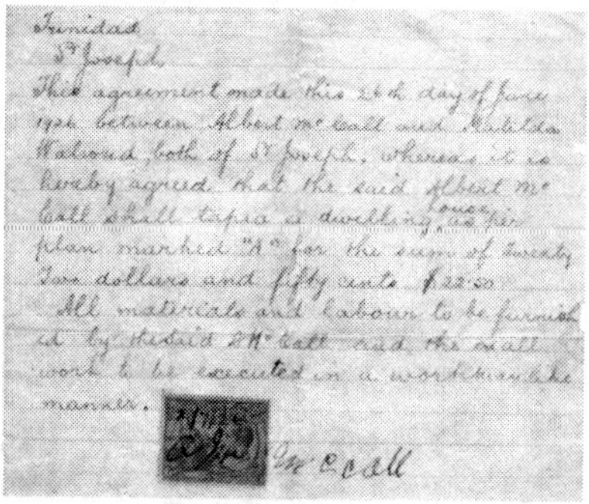

Trinidad
St Joseph
This agreement made this 26th day of June
1926 between Albert McCall and Matilda
Walrond, both of St Joseph, whereas it is
hereby agreed that the said Albert Mc
Call shall [illegible] a dwelling house as per
plan marked "A" for the sum of twenty
two dollars and fifty cents $22.50
All materials and labour to be furnish
ed by the said A McCall and the [illegible]
work to be executed in a workmanlike
manner.

A McCall

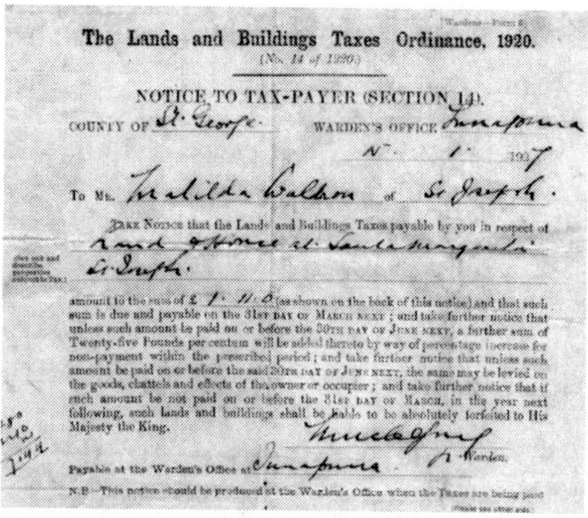

(Wardens—Form 8)

The Lands and Buildings Taxes Ordinance, 1920.
(No. 14 of 1920.)

NOTICE TO TAX-PAYER (SECTION 14).

COUNTY OF St. George WARDEN'S OFFICE Tunapuna
Nov 1 1927

To Mr. Matilda Walrond of St Joseph.

Take Notice that the Lands and Buildings Taxes payable by you in respect of
Land & House at Santa Margarita
St Joseph.

amount to the sum of £ 1. 11. 0 (as shown on the back of this notice) and that such sum is due and payable on the 31st day of March next; and take further notice that unless such amount be paid on or before the 30th day of June next, a further sum of Twenty-five Pounds per centum will be added thereto by way of percentage increase for non-payment within the prescribed period; and take further notice that unless such amount be paid on or before the said 30th day of June next, the same may be levied on the goods, chattels and effects of the owner or occupier; and take further notice that if such amount be not paid on or before the 31st day of March, in the year next following, such lands and buildings shall be liable to be absolutely forfeited to His Majesty the King.

[illegible]
for Warden.

Payable at the Warden's Office at Tunapuna

N.B.—This notice should be produced at the Warden's Office when the Taxes are being paid

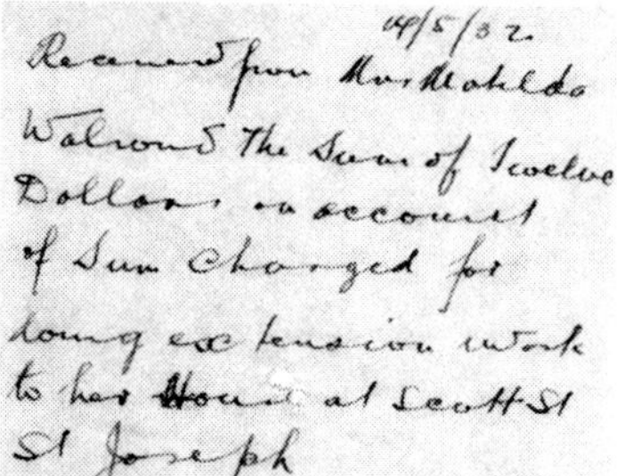

09/5/32.
Received from Mrs Matilda
Walrond The Sum of Twelve
Dollars on account
of Sum Charged for
doing extension work
to her House at Scott St
St Joseph

S. W. Broadhill

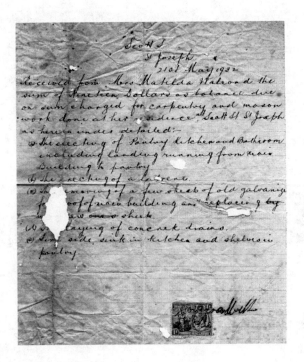

Scott Street, St Joseph

21st. May 1932

Received from Mrs. Matilda Walrond the sum of nineteen dollars as balance due on sum charged for carpentry and mason work done on her residence at Scott Street, St Joseph as herein under detailed:

a) The erecting of pantry, kitchen and bathroom including landing running from main building to pantry.

b) The erecting of a latrine.

c) The removing of a few sheets of old galvanize from the roof of main building and replacing with new sheets.

d) The laying of concrete drains on the side, sink in kitchen, shelves in pantry.

$19.00

Scott Street
51 Joseph
14th May 32

Received from Mrs Matilda
Walrond the sum of Nineteen Dollars ($19.00) as
balance due for painting work done at her
cottage at the corner of
Scott Street and Eastern
Main Rd St Joseph

James A. Brown

Painter

LUMBER DEPT.
TELEPHONE 471
PORT-OF-SPAIN
TRINIDAD, B.W.I.   192

BOUGHT OF THE
Trinidad Trading Company, Limited
INCORPORATED IN TRINIDAD B.W.I.

249 5

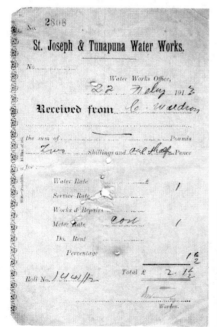

No. 2808

St. Joseph & Tunapuna Water Works.

No.

Water Works Office,
22 Febuy 1913

Received from C. Warden

the sum of   Pounds
Two   Shillings and   Pence

for

Water Rate   1
Service Rate
Works & Repairs
Meter Rate   Cost   1
Do. Rent
Percentage   1

Roll No. 1441/2   Total £   2.1

Warden.

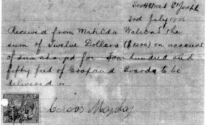

Scott Street St Joseph
3rd July 19

Received from Matilda Walrond the
sum of Twelve Dollars ($12.00) on account
of sum charged for four hundred and
fifty feet of Crapaud boards to be
delivered

Caius Mayday

330

Cyp is a type of local wood used for making furniture. I believe it is a type of cyprus (*cypre* in French).

THE T'DAD CONCRETE PRODUCTS Co.

1 – 5 – 1937

Received from Mr. R. O. Walrond

the Sum of Three Dollars sixty

Cents for $\frac{60}{100}$ Dollars

6 12" Concrete Flower Pots.

$ 3 60

C. BERMENT & Co., Ltd.

HIGH STREET. 410

PRINCES TOWN 1/5 193 5

Received from Mr. R. O. Walrond

the sum of Three Dollars and Cents

with thanks.

C. BERMENT

These two receipts are for the rental of a house in Couva when he was first appointed head teacher. There are altogether three years' worth of rent receipts.

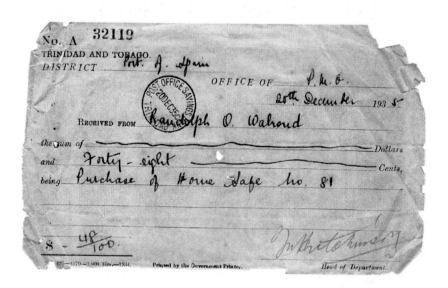

The Annual Empire Sports Day put on by the staff and students of the Couva E. C. School was legendary.

Please note the name S. Lee Young at the bottom of the left column. This is Selwyn Lee Young, my father's brother-in-law and one of the twins who named him Hello. Selwyn is also head of the engineering firm of Lee Young and Partners, which did the work for the Cunupia lands.

There must have been a dozen receipts like this one. Each was for the same amount: $1.00.

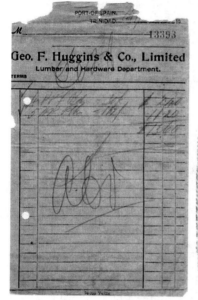

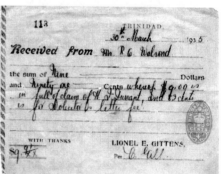

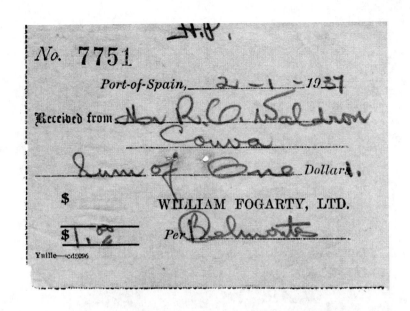

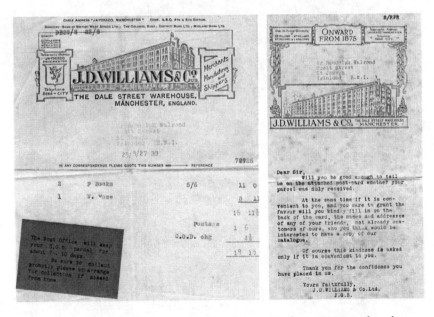

J. Peertamsingh ran a taxi service in Couva. As far as I remember, he was the one who used to drive us to Los Iros Bay, on the south coast of Trinidad for our August holidays before my father bought his car.

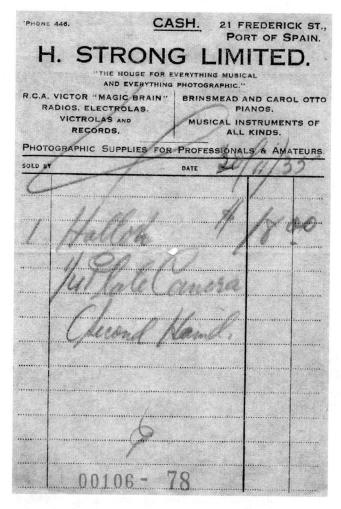

This is the receipt for the camera that Randolph bought. It was still around in 1964, although not usable.

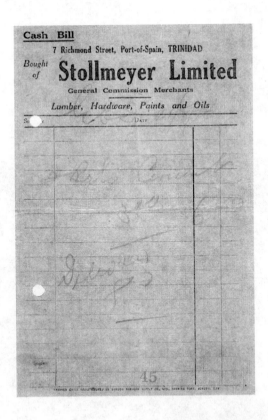

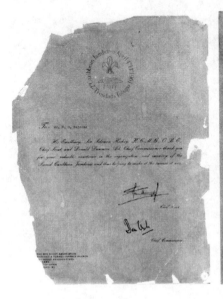

In this 1961 picture, Randolph Walrond is receiving his above awards for scouting from the Governor General, Sir Solomon Hochoy. I can still remember the occasion. My father was humbly proud of the award. He simply tucked it away with his other papers.

Note the scouts' traditional left handshake.

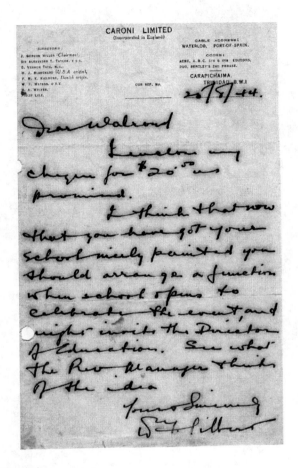

Dear Walrond.

I enclose my cheque for $20.00 as promised.

I think that now that you have got your school nicely painted you should arrange a function when school opens to celebrate the event and might invite the Director of Education. See what the Rev. Manager thinks of the idea,

Yours sincerely,

W. Gilbert

[Mr. Gilbert was the co-manager of the Couva E.C. School.]

Chess Notes

Richmond St. E C School
1st October 1926

Dear Sir

This is to inform you that the Hon Dr A H McShine has consented to play us the Simultaneous Chess Match on the 27th Inst.

At our last meeting it was decided that each member subscribe the sum of 2/- in order to provide refreshment for the occasion. I shall be much obliged if you will tender same by bearer.

Yours truly
R O Walrond

Names	Amt	Names	Amt
Mr J Licorish	48/pd	R O Walrond	48/pd
J Worrell	48/pd		
WB Jordan	24/pd		
Mr D Chevalier	48/pd		
G Cobham	Sick		
W Buckles	48/pd		
G Highland	48/pd		
H Simmons			
P De Peza	24/pd		
C Rumford	Regret		
E B Gervens	48/pd		

K. O. Walrond
Hon. Sec. T.S.C.

Queens Royal College
P.O.S.
30th May 1927

Dear Sir,

I am in receipt of your letter of even date. I regret to say that the 4th June, the day for the return chess match with us, suggested by you is not acceptable to most of our players. Mr Potter and myself have previous engagements and since the date will fall with a long week-end for us, I expect we should have difficulty in getting together a team capable of giving your players a decent game.

Perhaps, we could fix upon a date convenient both to members of your club and to those of ours in a little talk over the telephone? You could ring up, if you would be so good, 215 and talk to either Mr Dalton (my newly appointed assistant) or myself. Meanwhile I will find out from our members when they can play.

Thanking you for your letter and sincerely hoping that we shall meet in the very near future.

I remain
Yours faithfully
B. J. Bedell

R.O. Walrond. Esq,

Queen's Royal College

Hon. Sec. T.C.C.

P.O.S.

Dear Sir,

I am in receipt of your letter of even date. I regret to say that the 4th June, the day for the return match with us, suggested by you is not acceptable to most of our players. Mr. Patten and myself have previous engagements and since the date will fall into a long week-end for us, I suggest we should have difficulty in getting together a team capable of giving your players a decent game.

Perhaps we could fix upon a date consistent both to members of your club and to those of ours in a little talk over the phone? You could ring up, if you would be so good, 215 and talk to either Mr. Boldon (my newly appointed secretary) or myself.

Meanwhile, I will find out from our members when they can play.

Thank you for your letter and sincerely hoping that we should meet in the very near future,

I remain

Yours faithfully,

B.J.Bedell

Please note the second to last name on the list of players in the following newspaper clipping.

Alekhine Displays Chess Wizardry

Tuesday 31st January 1929

Zaltzman Snatches Game From Master

DR. ALEXANDER ALEKHINE, chess champion of the world, gave his first simultaneous display against forty Trinidad players on Tuesday evening at the Marie Louise Hall, Royal Victoria Institute.

His Excellency the Acting Governor, Capt. John Huggins graced the exhibition with his presence, and a large gathering of spectators, embracing a few of the officials, and many chess players and friends were also in attendance.

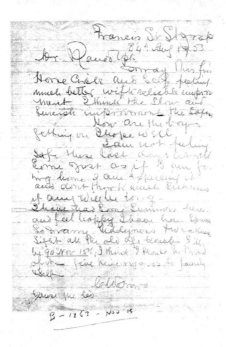

Francis Street, St Joseph,

24 August 1953

[. . .] Randolph

[. . .] This from home circle and self.

Feeling much better with reliable improvement. I think the slow and surest improvement the safest.

How are the boys getting on? I hope well. I am not feeling safe these last days at all.

Some just as if I am going home. I am expecting it and don't think much sickness if any will be long.

I have had some [. . .] here and feel happy.

I have been [. . .] so many giddiness [. . .] sight all the old age troubles.

I'll be 90 November 15th. I think I should be proud of it. Give kind regards to the family and self.

C. Walrond

In spite of his premonitions, Uncle Charlie did not die until 8 June 1959. As he said, he was almost 90 when he wrote this letter. This accounts for the trouble I had deciphering his writing. His life would have been a full and exciting one, I am sure. I feel very happy to have known him even if only slightly. His legacy was nonetheless very important to his descendants.

Appendix C: The Chronology of Randolph Walrond

Date			
Year	Month	Day	Life Events
1899	June	13	Born at King Street, St. Joseph, Trinidad
1903			Enrolled at St. Joseph E.C. School Enrolled at St. Joseph Government School Enrolled at Tunapuna E.C. School Enrolled at Richmond Street E. C. School to Fifth Standard
1911			Death of Grandfather Joseph Chandler
1914			Encouraged to take up teaching Attended the Contaste Commercial School Typewriting and Bookkeeping
1915	January		Death of father Joshua Walrond
1917			Passed the Pupil Teachers Examination in Religious Subjects Class II
1919	August	14	Awarded the Department of Education Certificate of Proficiency in Hygiene
	October	24	Awarded the Department of Education Certificate of Proficiency in Physical Training

Date			
Year	Month	Day	Life Events
	November	15	Awarded the Diocese of Trinidad Certificate in Religious Knowledge Qualified to become Assistant Master of a large school Worked as a pupil teacher at St. Joseph E.C. School with a salary of nine/ten dollars a month
1920	November	1	Began as Assistant Master at Couva E.C. School with Mr. Christopher Patrick as Head Teacher. Mr. Patrick sought out Randolph and offered him this job.
1923			Appointed Assistant Master at Richmond Street Boys E.C. School Randolph had attended this school up to the Fifth Standard.
	December		Awarded the Trinity College of Music Certificate in Theory of Music Founded the Teachers' Chess Group Awarded Certificate of Music from Trinity College of Music, Junior Practical
1924	March		Awarded the Department of Education Certificate, Second Class
	December		Awarded the Trinity College of Music Certificate in Elementary Pianoforte Playing
1925			Began building the new house at Scott Street, St. Joseph

Date			
Year	Month	Day	Life Events
1926	July	10	First Deed of Mortgage on new house $750.00
1928	May	22	Appointed Head master of Caledonia E.C. School
	September	1	Began as Headmaster of Caledonia E.C. School
1931	October		Awarded the Trinity College of Music Certificate in Intermediate Pianoforte Playing Awarded the Trinity College of Music Certificate in Rudiments of Music
1933	December	2	Residing at Manahambre Road, Princes Town
1934	May		Appointed Head master of Craignish E.C. School
1935			Residing at Princes Town
1936	March	1	Appointed Head Teacher of Couva E.C. School
1937	August	8	Married to Floris Daphne Lee Young
1938	April	20	Bought material to build screens for dividing Couva E. C. School into classrooms
	July	28	Birth of first child, a son
1940	January	27	Birth of second child, a son
1945	August		Moved into house at Scott Street, St. Joseph with family
1946	September	1	Promoted to Grade I Head Teacher
1947	January	2	Moved back to Couva with family
1957	January		Moved family into new house at 23 Palm Drive, Champ Fleurs, St. Joseph

Date			
Year	*Month*	*Day*	*Life Events*
1957 (c)			Transferred to St. Joseph E. C. School as Head teacher
1959			Retired from teaching
	June	8	Inherited lands at Cunupia on the death of his Uncle Charlie
1961	March	20	Received an Award for Scouting
1964	April	25	Began agricultural development of lands at Marshal Trace, Cunupia Working as Credit Manager for Sterling Service Battoo Brothers car dealership
1973	June	25	Began development of lands at Cunupia into lots for sale Started with a topographic survey
1974	July		Posed with his entire family for the only such photograph
1986	April	3	Start of construction work on the development of lands at Cunupia
1987	August	25	Celebrated his 50th wedding anniversary
1996	July	27	Death of Randolph Walrond

Appendix D: The Kings and Queens of England from William the Conqueror to Charles I

The Normans

1066–1087: William I

1087–1100: William II

1100–1135: Henry I

1135–1154: Stephen I

The Plantagenets

1154–1189: Henry II

1189–1199: Richard I

1199–1216: John I

1216–1272: Henry III

1272–1307: Edward I

1307–1327: Edward II

1327–1377: Edward III

1377–1399: Richard II

The Houses of Lancaster and York

1399–1413: Henry IV

1413–1422: Henry V

1422–1461: Henry VI

The Houses of Lancaster and York (cont.)

1461–1470: Edward IV

1470–1471: Henry VI

1471–1483: Edward IV

1483: Edward V

1483–1485: Richard III

The Tudors

1485–1509: Henry VII

1509–1547: Henry VIII

1547–1553: Edward VI

1553: Lady Jane Grey

1553–1558: Mary I

1558–1603: Elizabeth I

The Stuarts

1603–1625: James I

1625–1649: Charles I

Appendix E: The Lineage of Waleran Venator

1. Waleran Venator

    The descendants of Waleran Venator are numerous.

2. Robert de Bradfelle

3. Richard de Bradfelle

4. Richard de Bradfelle

    This Richard came from the parish of Uffculme in Devon, England. He lived during the reign of King Stephen (1135–1154).

5. Richard de Bradfelle

    This Richard de Bradfelle was also of Uffculme. He lived during the reign of King Richard I (1189–1199). This old Devonshire family was called, at different times, de Waleran, Wallerende, Walleronde and Walrond. The family was seated at Bradfelle at the time of Henry II (1154–1189)

6. Richard Walrond

7. William Walrond

8. John Walrond was alive in 1267

9. John Walrond m. Joan Nefford

    John Walrond lived during the reign of Edward II (1307–1327)

10. William Walrond m. Jean (Minell)

    Samuel William Walrond lived during the reign of Edward III (1327–1377).

11. William Walrond m. Julian Mellior

12. William Walrond m. Alice Ufflet

13. John Walrond m. Gennet Gilbert

    John was alive in 1465

14-1. John Walrond of Bradfield

  He was alive in 1491

14 -2.   William Walrond of Bovey

  He was alive in 1489. This William was the ancestors of the Walronds of Bovey.

15. John Walrond

16 -1.   Humphrey Walrond of Bradfield m. Eleanor Ogan

16 -2.   Osmond Walrond of Dulford, Devon

  He was the ancestors of the Walronds of Dulford.

17. Henry Walrond of Bradfield m. Eleanor Whitings

18. Humphrey Walrond of Bradfield

19. Humphrey Walrond m. Mary Willoughby, who died 17 April 1586

20. William Walrond of Bradfield m. Mary

  Sandford, who died 19 July 1627

Note: At this point, although there is a lot of information, there are not enough cross references such as dates. This is complicated by the custom of naming the sons after ancestors. Reliability improves a few years later with Humphrey Walrond of Sea.

1. Humphrey Walrond of Sea m. Elizabeth Brokehampton
2. Henry Walrond of Sea m. Elizabeth Devenish
3. Humphrey Walrond of Sea, d. Feb 17 1621, m. Elizabeth Coles
4. Humphrey Walrond of Sea, b. c1600, m. Grace Seaman

   1. George Walrond

   2. Humphrey Walrond

   3. Lt. Gen. Henry Walrond

   4. John Walrond

   5. Col. Thomas Walrond

   6. Edward Walrond

   7. Grace Walrond

   8. Bridget Walrond

   9. Anne Walrond

   10. ... Walrond

Appendix F: The Lineage of the Martin, Chandler and Walrond Families

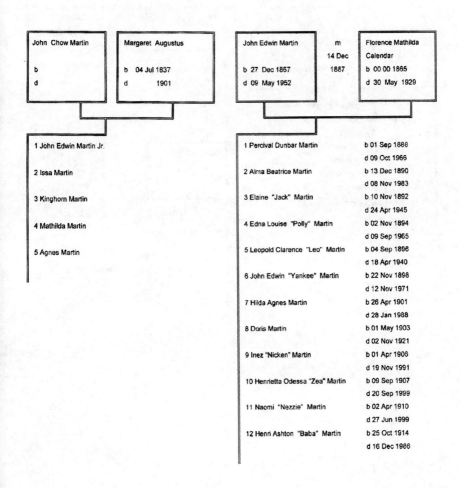

John Chow Martin	Margaret Augustus		John Edwin Martin	m	Florence Mathilda
				14 Dec	Calendar
b	b 04 Jul 1837		b 27 Dec 1867	1887	b 00 00 1865
d	d 1901		d 09 May 1952		d 30 May 1929

1 John Edwin Martin Jr.

2 Issa Martin

3 Kinghorn Martin

4 Mathilda Martin

5 Agnes Martin

1 Percival Dunbar Martin   b 01 Sep 1888 / d 09 Oct 1966

2 Alma Beatrice Martin   b 13 Dec 1890 / d 08 Nov 1983

3 Elaine "Jack" Martin   b 10 Nov 1892 / d 24 Apr 1945

4 Edna Louise "Polly" Martin   b 02 Nov 1894 / d 09 Sep 1965

5 Leopold Clarence "Leo" Martin   b 04 Sep 1896 / d 18 Apr 1940

6 John Edwin "Yankee" Martin   b 22 Nov 1898 / d 12 Nov 1971

7 Hilda Agnes Martin   b 26 Apr 1901 / d 28 Jan 1988

8 Doris Martin   b 01 May 1903 / d 02 Nov 1921

9 Inez "Nicken" Martin   b 01 Apr 1906 / d 19 Nov 1991

10 Henrietta Odessa "Zea" Martin   b 09 Sep 1907 / d 20 Sep 1999

11 Naomi "Nezzie" Martin   b 02 Apr 1910 / d 27 Jun 1999

12 Henri Ashton "Baba" Martin   b 25 Oct 1914 / d 16 Dec 1986

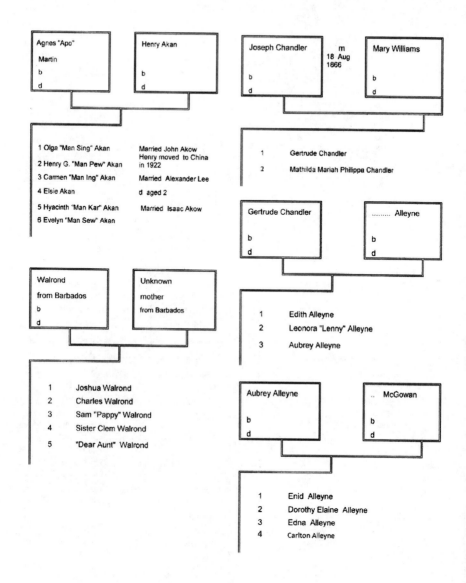

Agnes "Apo"
Martin
b
d

Henry Akan
b
d

1 Olga "Man Sing" Akan
2 Henry G. "Man Pew" Akan
3 Carmen "Man Ing" Akan
4 Elsie Akan
5 Hyacinth "Man Kar" Akan
6 Evelyn "Man Sew" Akan

Married John Akow
Henry moved to China
in 1922
Married Alexander Lee
d aged 2
Married Isaac Akow

Joseph Chandler   m
18 Aug
1866
b
d

Mary Williams
b
d

1   Gertrude Chandler
2   Mathilda Mariah Philippa Chandler

Gertrude Chandler
b
d

.... Alleyne
b
d

1   Edith Alleyne
2   Leonora "Lenny" Alleyne
3   Aubrey Alleyne

Walrond
from Barbados
b
d

Unknown
mother
from Barbados

1   Joshua Walrond
2   Charles Walrond
3   Sam "Pappy" Walrond
4   Sister Clem Walrond
5   "Dear Aunt" Walrond

Aubrey Alleyne
b
d

.. McGowan
b
d

1   Enid Alleyne
2   Dorothy Elaine Alleyne
3   Edna Alleyne
4   Carlton Alleyne

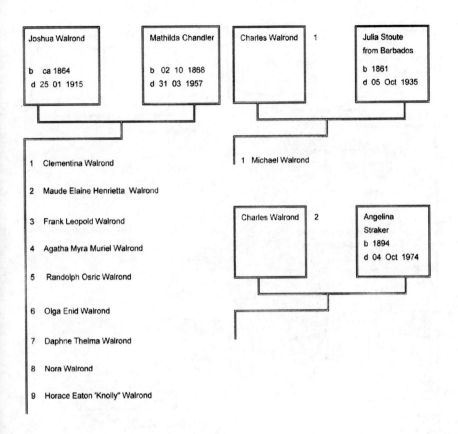

Joshua Walrond	Mathilda Chandler
b ca 1864	b 02 10 1868
d 25 01 1915	d 31 03 1957

Charles Walrond	1	Julia Stoute from Barbados
		b 1861
		d 05 Oct 1935

1   Clementina Walrond

2   Maude Elaine Henrietta Walrond

3   Frank Leopold Walrond

4   Agatha Myra Muriel Walrond

5   Randolph Osric Walrond

6   Olga Enid Walrond

7   Daphne Thelma Walrond

8   Nora Walrond

9   Horace Eaton 'Knolly" Walrond

1   Michael Walrond

Charles Walrond	2	Angelina Straker b 1894 d 04 Oct 1974

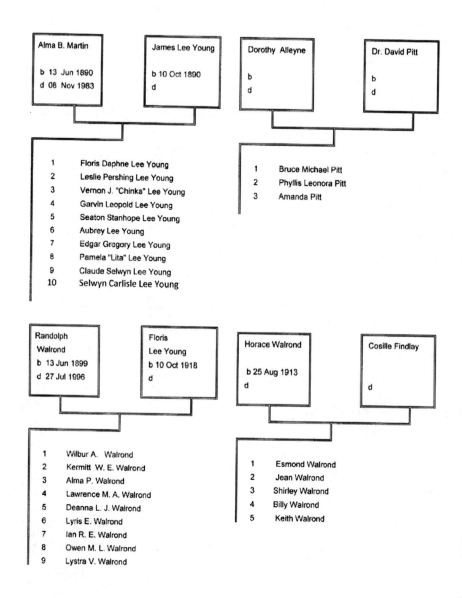

Ratoon

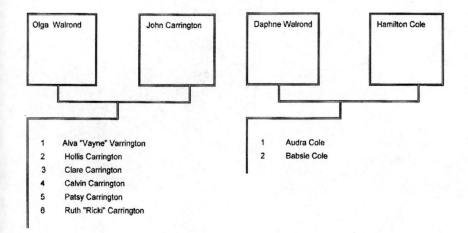

| Olga Walrond | John Carrington |
| Daphne Walrond | Hamilton Cole |

1   Alva "Vayne" Varrington
2   Hollis Carrington
3   Clare Carrington
4   Calvin Carrington
5   Patsy Carrington
6   Ruth "Ricki" Carrington

1   Audra Cole
2   Babsie Cole

Appendix G: Bibliography

Online Sources

"Arthur Hutton McShine." Trinidad and Tobago Icons, Volume 2. Accessed 24 September 2013. http://www.niherst.gov.tt/icons/tt-icons-2/33-arthur-hutton-mcshine.htm

"Atlantic Slave Trade." Updated 23 January 2014. Accessed 4 March 2013. http://en.wikipedia.org/wiki/Atlantic_slave-trade.

"Barbados: Eminent Planters (1673)." Accessed 29 January 2014. http://www.geni.com/projects/Barbados-Eminent-Planters-1673/3290.

"Ben Sealey." Updated 29 April 2013. Accessed 24 September 2013. http://en.wikipedia.org/wiki/Ben_Sealey

Besson, Gerard A. "Education and the First Model Schools." The Caribbean History Archives. Paria Publishing Co Ltd, 12 October 2011. Accessed 17 September 2013. http://caribbeanhistoryarchives.blogspot.ca/2011/10/education-and-the-first-model-schools.htm.

Besson, Gerard A. Lord Harris: Live and Learn. The Caribbean History Archives. Paria Publishing Co Ltd 11, August 2011. Accessed 17 September 2013. http://caribbeanhistoryarchives.blogspot.ca/2011/08/lord-harris-live-and-learn-html.

"Biography of King Charles the First." BCWPROJECT British Civil Wars, Commonwealth & Protectorate 1638–1660. David Plant. Updated 20 January 2013. Accessed 26 February 2013. http://bcw-project.org/biography/charles-the-first.

Bisnath, Deosaran. "Indian Indentured Immigration to Trinidad." 16 May 2008. Accessed 10 March 2013. http://deosaranbisnath.blogspot.ca/2008/05/indian-indentured-immigration-to.html.

Bloy, Marjorie, Ph.D. "The Anti-Slavery Campaign in Britain." The Victorian Web, April 1997. Updated 13 December 2010. Accessed 14 February 2014. http://65.107.211.206/victorian/history/antislavery.html.

Brock, Pope. "Chief Anderson." 28 November 1988, Vol. 30, No. 22. http://www.people.com/people/archive/article/0,,20100610,00.html.

Byrnes, Dan. "Questions on Slavery." The Blackheath Connection. Updated 30 January 2010. Accessed 27 September 2013. Accessed 24 January 2014. http://www.danbyrnes.com.au/blackheath/bcslave.htm.

"Cape Bojador." Accessed 5 March 2013. http://www.britannica.com/EBchecked/topic/71896/Cape-Bojador.

"Caribbean History." Accessed 10 March 2013. ITZCARIBBEAN.COM. http://www.itzcaribbean.com/trinidadhistory.

"Chapter III: Brief History of Early Primary Education." Accessed 17 September 2013. http://www.educoas.org/Portal/bdigital.contenido. interamer/BkIACD/Interamer/Interame.

Note: To access this item, Google "Brief history of early primary education."

"Chief and Forsythe Goodwill Tour." 2012 C. Alfred "Chief" Anderson Legacy Foundation Inc. Accessed 27 September 2013. http://chief-anderson.com/chief-forsythethe-goodwill-tour/.

"Chinese in the English-Speaking Caribbean History and Cultural Relations." Accessed 14 February 2014. http://www.everyculture.com/Middle-America-Caribbean/Chinese-in-sthe-English-Speak.

"Chinese Trinidadian and Tobagonian." Updated 11 January 2014. Accessed 14 February 2014. http://en.wikipedia.org/wiki/Chinese_Trinidadian_and_Tobagonian.

"Christopher Columbus: A Culinary History." 1997. Castello Banfi. Accessed 14 February 2014. http://www.castellobanfi.com/features/story_3.html.

"Christopher Columbus Biography — Facts, Birthday, Life Story." Accessed 7 April 2013. http://www.biography.com/people/christopher-columbus-9254209.

"Christopher Columbus Third Voyage." Updated 25 July 2013. Accessed 6 July 2013. http://columbus-day.z12.net/the-third-voyage.php.

"Christopher Columbus." Updated 7 February 2104. Accessed 24 February 2103. http://en.wikipedia.org/wiki/Christopher_Columbus.

"Codford Parish Council Codford History." Accessed 23 February 2013. http://www.westwilts-communityweb.com/site/Codford-Parish-Council/CodfordHistory.htm.

"Dai Ailian, a Legendary Ballerina." China Internet Information Center. Accessed 25 July 2013. http://www.china.org.cn/english/NM-e/158762.htm.

"Dai Ailian." Updated 28 February 2013. Accessed 25 July 2013. http://en.wikipedia.org/wiki/Dai_Ailian.

"Domesday Book." Updated 13 January 2014. Accessed 15 January 2014 http://en.wikipedia.org/wiki/Domesday_Book.

"The Domesday Book." *History Magazine,* October/November 2001 Issue. Accessed 23 February 2013. http://www.history-magazine.com/domesday.html.

"Dorsetshire Domesday Book." Accessed 21 January 2014. http://www.dorsetshire.com/dday/domesday.html.

"Emancipation of the British West Indies." Updated 26 September 2012. Accessed 9 March 2013. http://en.wikipedia.org/wiki/Emancipation_of_the_British_West_Indies.

"English Civil War." Updated 13 February 2013. Accessed 15 February 2013. http://simple.wikipedia.org/wiki/English_Civil_War.

"European Voyages of Exploration: Christopher Columbus." The Applied History Research Group, 1997. Accessed 14 February 2014. http://www.ucalgary.ca/applied_history/tutor/eurvoya/columbus.html.

"European Voyages of Exploration: The Sugar & Slave Trades." The Applied History Research Group, 1997. Accessed 5 March 2013. http://ucalgary.ca/applied_history/tutor/eurovoya/Trade.html.

"From T&T to Beijing: Dai Ailian." Accessed 01 June 2014. http:/guardian.co.tt/lifestyle/2014-06-01/tt-beijing-dai-ailian.

"The Golden Age: Ferdinand and Isabella." Accessed 2 March 2013. http://countrystudies.us/spain/7.htm.

"Headstones: The Walrond Monument to Humphrey Walrond abt 1580 St.Mary's Church." 2006–2014. Accessed 9 March 2013. http://www.red1st.com/axholme/showmedia.php?mediaID=30417&cemeteryID=156.

"Historical Developments of Education in Barbados, 1686–2000." Prepared by the Planning Research and Development Unit of the Ministry of Education, Youth Affairs and Culture, 2 November 1977. Accessed 17 February 2014. pdf://mes.gov/bb/UserFiles/Historical_ Developments.pdf.

"History of Sugar Cane — Ornamental Heirloom Cane." Accessed 19 February 2013. http://chewingcane.com/sugarcane_history.html.

"History of Sugar." Updated 21 January 2014. Accessed 22 January 2014. http://en.wikipedia.org/wiki/History_of_sugar.

"History." Accessed 22 February 2013. http://suttonwaldron.info/sutton_ waldron_11_003.htm.

Homer, Louis B. "Ste Madeleine makes its mark." *Business Express,* 31 December 2012. Accessed 23 December 2013. http://www.trinida- dexpress.com/news/Ste_Madeleine_makes_its_mark_185246582. html.

"The House of Normandy: William the Conqueror, 1066–1087." 2004– 2005. Accessed 15 January 2014. http://www.englishmonarchs. co.uk/normans.htm.

"How did Britain become involved in the Slave Trade?" Accessed 8 March 2013. http://uk.answers.yahoo.com/questions/index?qid=20080626 101418AAKQt8p.

"Humphrey Walrond (c 1600–c 1670)." Updated 2 February 2013. Accessed 14 February 2013. http://en.wikipedia.org/wiki/ Humphrey_Walrond.

"Huntsman." Accessed 22 February 2013. http://www.domesdaybook.net/ helpfiles/hs2660.htm.

"Invasion of England, 1066." Eyewitness: History through the eyes of those who lived it, 1997. Accessed 22 January 2104. http://www.ibis.com.

"Invasion of Trinidad (1797)." Updated 18 February 2013. Accessed 10 March 2013. http://en.wikipedia.org/wiki/Invasion_of_Trinidad_(1797).

Islamia, Lengua. "TIA Primary School History." 2012. Accessed 12 September 2013. http://lenguaislamiatia.edu.tt?page_id=40.

"Islamic Spain and the Reconquista Historical Atlas of the Mediterranean." Accessed 2 March 2013. http://www.explorethemed.com/ Reconquista.asp?c=1.

Jefferies, Richard. *A memoir of the Goddards of North Wilts.* Accessed 22 February 2013. http://www.ebooksread.com/authors-eng/ richard-jefferies/a-memoir-of-the-goddards.

Kisselgoff, Anna. "Dai Ailian, Vital Figure in Building Ballet in China, Dies at 89." 20 February 2006. Accessed 25 July 2013. http://www.nytimes.com/2006/02/20/arts/dance/20dai.html?_r=0.

"Last Name: Waleran." The Internet Surname Database. Accessed 2 July 2013. http://www.surnamedb.com/Surname/Waleran.

"The Manor." Maiden Newton and Frome Vauchurch, Dorset, England. Accessed 22 February 2013. http://www.maidennewton.info/page/the+manor.

Maraj, D. Parsuram. "The Importance of the Indian to Trinidad." NRI internet.com. Accessed 18 March 2013. http://www.nriinternet.com/Trinidad/History/3_the%20Importance_Indian_Culture.htm.

"Norman conquest of England." Accessed 21 January 2013. http://en/wikipedia.org/wiki/Norman_conquest_of_England.

"The Notable Personalities who have contributed ..." Accessed 17 February 2014. http://belizeinfocenter.org/wp-content/uploads/2013/05/The-Notable-Personalities-who-have-contributed-to-the-Rice-Industry-of-Belize.pdf. *Note:* Can be easily accessed by Googling "Daniel Darius Haynes."

Obadina, Tunde. "Slave Trade: A Root of Contemporary African Crisis." Accessed 4 March 2013. Africa Economic Analysis, 2000. http://www.afbis.com/analysis/slave/htm.

O'Callaghan, Marion. "The McShines and rise of middle class." *Trinidad and Tobago Newsday*, 28 December 2009. Accessed 4 March 2013. http://www.newsday.co.tt/commentary/0,113262.html Accessed 25 September 2013.

"Old Sturminster Newton." Accessed 22 February 2013. http://dorsetshire.com/old/oldstur.html.

Parker, Matthew. "Barbados: Cavaliers of the Caribbean." *History Today*: Volume 61, Issue 7, 2011. Accessed 6 April 2013. http://www.historyatoday.com/matthew-parker/barbados-cavaliers-caribbean.

"The Pragnells of West Tytherley." Dorsetbay History, Genealogy & Travel. Stephen and Helen Jones, 2007. Accessed 22 February 2013. http://www.dorsetbay.plus.com/gen/pragnell/pragnell03.htm.

Quamina-Aiyejina, Lynda, J. Mohammed, B. Rampaul, J George, M. Kallon, and C. Keller, S. Lochan. "A Baseline Study of the Teacher Education System in Trinidad and Tobago." School of Education,

Faculty of Humanities and Education, University of the West Indies, St. Augustine, 2001. Accessed 17 February 2014. http://uwispace.sta. uwi.edu/dspace/handle/2139/.../Monograph1.pdf?.

"Robert de Bradfelle." ADuPree. Accessed 16 May 2013. http://adupree. com/Gen800/getperson.php?personID=1402672&tree=adupree.

"Robert Walerand." Updated 17 May 2013. Accessed 16 June 2013. http:// en.wikipedia.org/wil\ki/Robert_Walerand.

Simkin, John. "William the Conqueror: Biography September." 1997–November 2013. Accessed 18 January 2014. http://spartacus.school-net.co.uk/MEDwilliam1.htm.

"Slave Trade." Kura Hulanda Resorts Curacao. Accessed 5 March 2013. http://www.kurahulanda.com/slavery/slave-trade.

"Slavery." *New World Encyclopedia.* Updated 4 February 2009. Accessed 2 March 2013. http://www.newworldencyclopedia.org/entry/Slavery.

"Slavery." *Wikipedia, the free encyclopedia.* Updated 20 February 2014. Accessed 2 March 2013. http://en.wikipedia.org/wiki/Slavery.

"Slavery Timeline 1400–1500: A Chronology of Slavery, Abolition and Emancipation." Updated 4 November 2009. Accessed 5 March 2013. http://www.brycchancarey.com/slavery/chrono2.htm.

Standfield, Shaun. "John Hawkins and the origins of the English slave trade." 23 March 2012. Accessed 17 February 2014. http://www.docin. com/p-368337441.html.

"Steeple Langford." 20 March 2014. Accessed 23 February 2013. http:// en.wikipedia.org/wiki/Steeple_Langford.

"Sutton Waldron." Parish Records, Dorset Sutton Waldron. Accessed 22 February 2013. http://www.opcdorset.org/SuttonWaldron/ SuttonWaldron.htm.

"Thomas Fairfax, 3rd Lord Fairfax of Cameron." Accessed 27 February 2013. http://en.wikipedia.org/wiki/ Thomas_Fairfax,_3rd_Lord_Fairfax_of_Cameron.

"Tribute to Chief Anderson." Negro Airmen International, Inc. Accessed 27 September 2013. http://www.blackwingsinaviation.org/tribute.html.

"Trinidad Ancestry: Indigenous and Immigrant." Accessed 10 March 2013. http://www.trinidadnandtobagofamilyhistory.org/trinidadancestry. html.

"Voyages of Christopher Columbus." Updated 23 January 2014. Accessed 15 July 2013. http://en.wikipedia.org/wiki/ Voyages_of_Christopher_Columbus.

Watson, Dr. Karl. "The Civil War in Barbados." April 2001. *Wars and Conflict.* Updated 17 February 2011. Accessed 14 February 2014. http://www.bbc.co.uk/history/war/englishcivilwar/barbados_01. shtml.

"William the Conqueror Timeline." HistoryOnTheNet, 2000–2013. Accessed 22 January 2014. http://www.historyonthenet.com/chro-nology/timelinewilliami.htm.

Wiltshire, Ernest M. "Slave naming in Barbados." Caribbean-L Archives, 16 March 2003. Accessed 7 March 2013. http://archiver.rootsweb. ancestry.com/th/read/CARIBBEAN/2003-03/1047845524.

"Writings of Hon. Bismark Ranguy." Exported from *Amandala Newspaper.* Accessed 17 February 2014. http://amandala.com.bz/ news/?p=251783&upm_export=pdf. *Note:* Can be easily accessed by Googling "Daniel Darius Haynes."

Books

Anthony, Michael. *The Making of Port of Spain.* Key Caribbean Publications.

Anthony, Michael. *Towns and Villages of Trinidad and Tobago.* Marabella: Printmaster (W.I.) Limited, 2001.

Beckles, Sir Hilary McD. *A History of Barbados from Amerindian Settlement to Caribbean Single Market.* 2nd ed. Cambridge University Press.

Besson, Gerard & Bridget Brereton. *The Book of Trinidad.* Paria: Paria Publishing Company Limited.

Bridenbaugh, Carl and Roberta. *No Peace Beyond the Line: The English in the Caribbean, 1624–1690.* New York: Oxford University Press, 1972.

Burns, Alan. *History of the British West Indies.* George Allen and Unwin Limited.

Campbell, P.F. *Early Maps of Barbados.*

Carmichael, Gertrude. *The History of the West Indian Islands of Trinidad and Tobago 1498–1900.* London: Alvin Redman.

Carter, E.H., G.W. Digby, & R. N. Murray. *History of the West Indian Peoples: Book Two: The Story of Our Islands.* Nelson Caribbean.

Carter, E.H., G.W. Digby, & R. N. Murray. *History of the West Indian Peoples: Book IV: Eighteenth Century to Modern Times*. Nelson Caribbean.

De Suze, Jos A. *The New Trinidad and Tobago*. London: Collins.

Dunn, Richard S. *Sugar and Slaves: The Rise of the Planter Class in the English West Indies, 1624–1713*. New York: W. W. Norton and Company Inc.

Hinde, Thomas, ed. *The Domesday Book England's Heritage: Then and Now*. New York: Crown Publishers, Inc.

Hoyos, F.A. *Barbados: A History from the Amerindians to Independence*. McMillan Caribbean.

Hunte, George. Barbados. New York: Hastings House Publishers.

Ligon, Richard. *A True and Exact History of the Island of Barbadoes, 1657, Excerpts*.

Lux, William. *Historical Dictionary of the British Caribbean*.

Natkiel, Richard & Antony Preston. *Atlas of Maritime History*. New York: Facts on File, Inc.

Nicole, Christopher. *The West Indies: Their People and History*. London: Hutchison and Co. Ltd., 1965.

Tree, Ronald. *A History of Barbados*. 2nd ed. Toronto.

CPSIA information can be obtained
at www.ICGtesting.com
Printed in the USA
FSOW02n2224290915
11624FS